ABRIENDO PASO

LECTURA

Lesson Plans
Script
Answer Key

José M. Díaz

Mary A. Mosley

María T. Vázquez-Mauricio

PEARSON

Prentice Hall

Boston, Massachusetts
Upper Saddle River, New Jersey

Credits appear on page iv, which constitutes an extension of this copyright page.

Copyright © by Pearson Education, Inc., publishing as Pearson Prentice Hall, Boston, Massachusetts 02116. All rights reserved. Printed in the United States of America. This publication is protected by copyright, and permission should be obtained from the publisher prior to any prohibited reproduction, storage in a retrieval system, or transmission in any form or by any means, electronic, mechanical, photocopying, recording, or likewise. For information regarding permission(s), write to: Rights and Permissions Department, One Lake Street, Upper Saddle River, New Jersey 07458.

Pearson Prentice Hall™ is a trademark of Pearson Education, Inc.
Pearson® is a registered trademark of Pearson plc.
Prentice Hall® is a registered trademark of Pearson Education, Inc.

ISBN 0-13-166099-3

4 5 6 7 8 9 10   10 09 08

Program Components

Abriendo paso: Lectura
A reader that incorporates all four skill areas.

Abriendo paso: Lectura **Testing Program**
Test masters and answer key for *Abriendo paso: Lectura*.

Abriendo paso: Lectura **Lesson Plans • Script • Answer Key**

Lesson Plans
Complete lesson plans cover each *Capítulo* in depth.

Script
Audio script for *Comprensión auditiva* sections in each chapter, Simulated Conversation activities in certain chapters, and Formal Writing and Formal Oral Presentation activities in *Un poco más de práctica*.

Answer Key
Answers to activities in the *Abriendo paso: Lectura* Student Book.

Abriendo paso: Lectura **Audio CDs**
Includes listening activities for *Comprensión auditiva,* Simulated Conversation, and Formal Writing and Formal Oral Presentation activities.

Abriendo paso: Lectura **Web site**
Visit www.PHSchool.com for Internet activities for each *Capítulo*.

Also available: *Abriendo paso: Gramática*

Abriendo paso: Gramática
A complete grammar review.

Abriendo paso: Gramática **Tests • Script • Answer Keys**

Text Answer Key
Complete answers to *Abriendo paso: Gramática* exercises.

Tests
Test masters for *Abriendo paso: Gramática*.

Test Answer Key
Answer key to the test masters.

Scoring Guide
A scoring guide to accompany the test masters.

Script
Audio script of Informal Speaking—Simulated Conversation and Formal Oral Presentation (Integrated Skills) sections included on Audio CD.

Abriendo paso: Gramática **Audio CD**
Includes Informal Speaking—Simulated Conversation and Formal Oral Presentation (Integrated Skills) listening activities.

Credits

page 144: "Me gustas cuando callas" from VEINTE POEMAS DE AMOR Y UNA CANCIÓN DESESPERADA by Pablo Neruda. Sociedad Chilena.

page 145: "Proverbios y cantares: Poema XXIX" by Antonio Machado. Used by permission of Editorial Biblioteca Nueva, S.L. page 145: *Despedida* by Federico García Lorca from *Obras Completas* (Galaxia Gutenberg, 1996 edition) © Herederos de Federico García Lorca. All rights reserved. Inquiries regarding rights and permissions for works by Federico García Lorca should be addressed to **lorca@artslaw.co.uk**. page 146: *Canción de jinete* by Federico García Lorca from *Obras Completas* (Galaxia Gutenberg, 1996 edition) © Herederos de Federico García Lorca. All rights reserved. Inquiries regarding rights and permissions for works by Federico García Lorca should be addressed to **lorca@artslaw.co.uk**. page 148: "Canción de otoño en primavera" by Rubén Darío. Aguilar, S.A. de Ediciones. S.A. page 151: "El uso regular de ordenadores favorece unos mejores resultados escolares" from EL MUNDO 1/2006. page 152: "El altruismo en niños y chimpancés" from BBCMUNDO.COM 3/2006. page 153: "Población gitana: Una campaña para luchar contra los prejuicios" from EL MUNDO 1/18/2006. page 155: "Sólo para mujeres" from BBCMUNDO.COM 9/2005. page 157: "Los Chuchos de Alaska" by Francisco Mauricio Martínez from PRENSA LIBRE 1/15/2006. page 158: "Las posadas en México" by Fernando Briones © ECOS de España y Latinoamérica December 2003, www.ecos-online.de. Used by permission. page 159: "Las barreras a una buena educación universitaria" by Ángeles Vázquez from HOY NUEVA YORK, 3/21/2006. page 160: "Los expertos recomiendan que el volumen de los reproductores digitales no sobrepase los 100 decibeles" from ELTIEMPO.COM 3/18/2006. page 161: "Cuando el miedo no deja vivir" from BBCMUNDO.COM 1/30/2006. page 163: "Se resiste a morir" by Gustavo Adolfo Montenegro from PRENSA LIBRE 1/8/2006. page 164: "Buenas noticias en una vieja ciudad" by Suzanne Murphy-Larronde reprinted from AMERICAS, a bimonthly magazine published by the General Secretariat of the Organization of American States (OAS). Used by permission.

Note: Every effort has been made to locate the copyright owner of material reprinted in this book. Omissions brought to our attention will be corrected in subsequent editions.

Contents

Lesson Plans

Cuentos

Poesía

De la prensa

Teatro

Script for Audio CD

Cuentos

Teatro

Poesía

Un poco más de práctica

Answer Key

Cuentos

Poesía

De la prensa

Teatro

About the *Abriendo paso: Lectura* Lesson Plans

This lesson plan book provides teachers with the information they need to (1) select chapters appropriate for students' interests and developing skills, (2) organize and gather lesson materials prior to class, (3) explore approaches to teaching and working with the material, and (4) provide alternative approaches to suit students' interests, skill levels, and schedules.

The lesson plans should serve as a guide from which you can choose what works best for you and your students. Reading aloud is suggested for some of the prose readings and should be done only when there are exchanges between characters that are appropriate for students to act out. You may also choose to have students read the poems aloud. For activities in which students are asked to present their work to the class, students should be encouraged to prepare notes (key vocabulary, phrases, etc.) and to speak without a written script. This will help them to be more focused and, at the same time, more creative.

Organization of Lesson Plans

- Genre and author of the reading
- Summary of the reading's content with a key illustrative quote from the selection
- Themes and contexts that are explored in the reading
- Difficulty level of the reading activities
- Key grammar with references to specific units of *Abriendo paso: Gramática*
- Key vocabulary
- Estimated time needed to complete the chapter
- Chapter divisions
- Ideas for approaches, alternatives, and expansions to individual activities

Using *Abriendo paso: Lectura*

Abriendo paso: Lectura provides students with the opportunity to experience the true purpose of literature to reflect the nature and the lives of humans. The text invites students to share their personal histories with others. Through carefully crafted pre- and post-reading activities and vocabulary work, students are provided with the motivation and means to express their own thoughts, experiences, and reflections. Since each chapter includes a variety of activities, teachers should carefully choose which activities to cover, keeping in mind the skills and interests of their students.

Pacing and Coverage

From this rich collection, you can most likely use 10–15 chapters effectively. The estimated time given for each chapter in the Lesson Plans is a <u>suggested</u> pace that helps you stay on track and compare that chapter's complexity with that of the others. Please note that it is not necessary to complete the chapters in sequential order.

Coping with Different Levels in the Same Class

Because of the wealth of activities included in *Abriendo paso: Lectura,* the teacher must use his or her judgment in choosing activities that match students' needs and skill levels. While some chapters and activities will deeply engage their imaginations and interest, others may be less compelling or perhaps too difficult to use effectively. Teachers may wish to divide the activities according to the abilities of individual students. For example, the *Al punto* activities may be appropriate for those students whose skills allow them to deal only with the facts of the story. The *Antes de leer, Para conversar,* and *Para escribir* activities are not designed for use by the entire class. You may wish to do all of these activities with your students, but you should assign them according to students' interests and skill levels. Other activities that require a more sophisticated level of language can be assigned to the more advanced students or to the native speakers in the class. Since most activities are to be shared with the class, all students will feel a sense of accomplishment. As the course progresses, each student will gain the confidence and skill needed for the most complex activities.

Using *Abriendo paso: Gramática* with *Abriendo paso: Lectura*

The companion *Abriendo paso: Gramática* provides students with practice in the key grammatical areas found in the readings, occasionally with portions of the reading appearing in the student activities. The sections of *Abriendo paso: Gramática* that address key grammar points from the chapter are noted in the Lesson Plans and in the box on the chapter's opener page.

The Companion Web Site

In each chapter, students will find a *Go Online* icon that gives them a Web Code for direct access to the *Abriendo paso: Lectura* companion Web site at www.PHSchool.com. Have them go to the site and enter the Web Code to be taken to the activities and links for that chapter.

Cuentos
Capítulo 1
El décimo

Selection: short story by Emilia Pardo Bazán (Spain)

A rich man buys a lottery ticket from a poor young woman and on a whim promises to share the money with her if he wins. When he loses the winning ticket, he finds instead the generosity of spirit of the young woman—a prize worth holding on to. *"...en [ella] he hallado más felicidad que la que hubiera podido comprar con los millones del décimo"*.

Themes: personal values and character, especially when placed under stress

Difficulty level: low to moderate. The reading is straightforward and appealing with a clear plot and exploration of aspects of character. Students are required to reflect on their own experiences and fortunes, to evaluate their values, and to talk about character traits.

Key grammar: Preterite, imperfect, and pluperfect indicative: Unidad 1, págs. 1 a 29; Reglas gramaticales (RG) 1, págs. 30 a 48

Key vocabulary: body and face, character traits, weather and environment, rooms and home furnishings, clothing, numbers

Estimated time needed: 550 minutes (11 classes maximum traditional schedule, 6 classes maximum block)

Antes de leer

A. Para discutir en clase
Approach: In small groups or pairs, have students collaborate to describe the picture and tell the story, noting key vocabulary. Then have the class tell the story, adding to the vocabulary list to which they can refer throughout the chapter.

Alternative: Have one group work on the picture while other groups work on Activity B and / or C. The groups then share their work with the class, providing background stories about good fortune and values for discussion in later activities.

Expansion: Students and / or the teacher bring in pictures of objects and settings of poverty and elegance. Students identify, classify, and describe the pictures and then comment on their own reactions to them. What would they do to obtain certain material things? What would they not do? What are their values and how do they influence how they act in certain situations?

B. Nuestra experiencia
Approach: Have students share their experiences with a partner or with the teacher to find common reactions and / or a surprising reaction to winning.

Alternative: Have a group or pair analyze the responses to find common and / or unusual reaction(s) to winning and then report to the class, perhaps as part of background preparation involving Activities A and C.

Expansion: (1) Provide pairs or groups with one or more stories of winning from newspapers, magazines, or movies, having them summarize the story and report on the reactions of winners. It may be helpful if you keep a file of these stories for future use. (2) Have students interview school or community members to discover experiences and reactions that others have had.

C. El día que papá se sacó un premio
Approach: (1) As a pre-reading activity, have students read the questions at the end of the reading selection. Discuss any unfamiliar vocabulary and information acquired before students begin to read the story, so that students have some prior knowledge about the reading selection. Note that this activity introduces some of the vocabulary that students will encounter in the reading. (2) Have students read with a partner or small group to discover how their reactions differ from the father's, the author's, and each other's.

Alternative: Have a group or pair read and then summarize the story and their reactions to it. Share their summary with the class, and then record their classmates' reactions.

Expansion: (1) Have a group of students rework the story in the form of a skit and perform it for the class. Afterwards, the class shares reactions to the father's decision. (2) Have students share a story about a time when they were generous and how they felt about it.

D. La generosidad
Approach: Have students divide into small groups or pairs to share their personal reactions. Select several to present their reactions to the class and receive feedback.

Alternative: Have students respond individually in a brief writing. As each scenario is read aloud, students share their reactions while a recorder notes the number and types of reactions on the board. Hold a class discussion about patterns of behavior.

Expansion: (1) Students provide the class or group with additional situations in written and / or oral form, or in a skit, asking for reactions and responses. (2) Students interview school or community members, comparing their responses with those of the class.

E. Una selección
Approach: After reinforcing the concept of the importance and effectiveness of contextual clues, have students read the opening selection at least twice, silently or with a partner. Afterwards, students work together to determine the meaning of vocabulary identified with a question mark and to find the information and vocabulary indicated in the bulleted list. Finally, students predict the outcomes of the story based on what they have read.

Al leer

Approach: Draw students' attention to these advance organizers, helping them to identify the vocabulary, verb forms, and themes that they are likely to encounter.

Expansion: Refer to vocabulary identified in Activities A–E under *Antes de leer*, creating a vocabulary web that reinforces and connects the themes.

Lectura

Approach: You may have students read the story in a group and then reread it at home.

Comprensión

A. ¿Cierta o falsa?
Expansion: Students support their answers to this true / false activity with direct quotes from the reading, followed by their own interpretations.

B. Comprensión general
Approach: Have students jot down ideas about their understanding of the story and share their ideas with the class.

C. De la misma familia
Expansion: After students identify one word from the same family, ask for additional words. Note which part of speech each word is, and use the categories to help generate additional vocabulary.

D. En contexto
Approach: Have students write their own phrases or word equivalents and then share them with the class as one records them on the board or on a transparency. Train students in alternative ways to talk about the vocabulary. Help them identify which word or phrase best matches the word provided and why.

Expansion: Have students identify the part of speech of each word and note how knowing the part of speech helps in determining the meanings of words. Students may choose additional words from the story and provide their own equivalents to challenge their classmates.

E. Al punto
Expansion: Have students select additional phrases from the story and create their own rephrasing to check their classmates' comprehension.

F. Ahora te toca a ti
Approach: Assign the bulleted list of themes—or themes created by students—to different pairs or groups. Have the groups ask the class or other groups their questions to determine the questions' effectiveness and to reinforce comprehension. This approach shifts the burden of asking questions from you to the students, who often generate challenging questions.

G. Los personajes principales
Expansion: In groups, have students describe personal characteristics of each of the characters. One member of the group reports to the class.

H. El debate sobre el feminismo

Approach: Students work with a more traditional format. Select two pairs or small groups to debate for and against the argument; the rest of the class is the audience. Provide clear guidelines for the number of argument points to be made, examples to back up their opinions, and time limits for each side's members to present their points. The rest of the class should note which side's arguments were best presented and supported. After separating a debate format from the expressions of personal opinion, class discussions can then follow based on students' feelings about the issues presented.

Un paso más

Approach: Remind students to refer to the *Vocabulario útil para conversar y para escribir* list and to the Appendix on pp. 404–406 to help them with the speaking and writing activities.

Para conversar

Approach to this section: Students may express preferences about topics that interest them in this section. Based on their interests and skill levels, <u>you may wish to address only one or several of the activities or you may wish to divide the activities according to interest and have each group present its work to the class,</u> inviting reactions and responses.

A. Una explicación difícil and B. Una reacción inesperada

Alternative: Have students work in teams to develop a skit of this story—or a modern, personalized version—starring themselves and their own personal reactions.

C. Los números de la suerte

Expansion: Provide a number puzzle or any other number game for students to work through.

D. Por casualidad

Expansion: Have students share an incredible coincidence that they have experienced or read about.

E. Algo perdido and F. Una situación parecida

Expansion: Combine both activities. Students put items / situations in order of importance, share information with the group about something they lost, and describe the situation and the final outcome. Students report to the class.

Para escribir

Approach to this section: The activities in this section build students' writing skills incrementally, from summary to personal reaction to creation. Students will need time to express themselves and to share their writing with classmates and with the teacher. Students may express preferences about topics that interest them in this section. Based on their interests and skill levels, <u>you may wish to address only one or several of the activities or you may wish to divide the activities according to interest and have each group present its work to the class,</u> inviting reactions and responses.

A. Un resumen
Approach: Students collaborate on compiling a possible vocabulary list that can be used to summarize the plot, actions, and feelings in the story. Students write a summary essay based on the story, following guided questions. Students share their information with the class.

B. (No) me gusta
Alternative: Students jot down answers to the questions regarding their opinions / feelings about the story. As they express their feelings, students reference specific lines / situations in the story to support their answers. As this is done students focus on the key vocabulary provided as a point of departure for the activity.

C. ¿El amor o el dinero?
Approach: This is appropriate for a class assessment on essay writing. Allow time for reviewing the essential components of essay writing.

D. ¿La historia de mi...?
Alternative: Students read the short selection from the story, paying close attention to the style used. As students prepare to write their own short stories, review with them the different components mentioned: description, action, dialogue, and narration. Students incorporate these components into another example from the class so that they feel more comfortable with the assignment as they begin to write *¿La historia de mi...?*

Comprensión auditiva
Approach: Have students look over the options for each selection carefully before they begin to listen. Check that they are comfortable with both the meaning and pronunciation of the vocabulary. If students do not understand words / phrases, provide Spanish explanations, but avoid English translations. Have students identify key words so that they can predict the topic, vocabulary, and structures that they are likely to hear. Careful preparation, combined with a willingness to use intuition and an understanding of contexts, will ensure that students need to listen only once to understand each passage.

Go Online
Approach: Have students visit the *Abriendo paso: Lectura* Web site at www.PHSchool.com for activities and links related to the content of the chapter.

Capítulo 2
Rosa

Selection: short story by Ángel Balzarino (Argentina)

After being employed for 43 years, Rosa learns that she is going to be moved to a new location. She is very saddened by the news, most of all because she has to leave her close friends. They try to encourage her, but she is truly disheartened by the entire situation. All she ever wanted was to do her job the best that she could, and this is the thanks she gets. At the end of the story Rosa is carried away into a room filled with old computers, where she will be put to rest. Rosa, the computer, has become outdated, but all computers are slowly becoming outdated. *"...ya estaba a punto de finalizar la Era de las Máquinas"*.

Themes: age of technology, feeling awkward, sad, helpless, and out of style

Difficulty level: low to moderate. The plot is easily visualized and flows logically. However the ending is subtle and students need to pay close attention to the part in which the men come to take Rosa, the old computer, away. *"...Se la conoce por el nombre de Rosa... la computadora de mayor tamaño cuyo material se notaba algo deteriorado por el uso y los años"*.

Key grammar: Future and future perfect: Unidad 5, págs. 174 a 202; RG 5, págs. 203 a 206; Conditional and conditional perfect: Unidad 6, págs. 220 a 227; RG 6, págs. 233 a 236

Key vocabulary: technology, feelings, and emotions

Estimated time needed: 500 minutes (10 classes maximum traditional schedule, 5 classes maximum block)

Antes de leer

A. Para discutir en clase

Approach: In small groups or pairs, have students collaborate to describe the picture and tell the story. Have the groups or pairs tell the story to the class, incorporating the vocabulary list into their narration.

Alternative: While some groups work on the picture description, other groups can work on Activity B and / or C. The groups then share their work with the class, providing personal stories related to (1) purchasing technological equipment and realizing how fast it becomes outdated, (2) the rapid growth of technology, and (3) what can be done to keep up with technology.

Expansion: Have students bring in pictures of the latest computer models. Students identify and describe the pictures, making references to changes in technology. Students should incorporate the new vocabulary list into their picture descriptions.

B. Los avances tecnológicos

Approach: Ask students to cut out and bring in pictures of items that are representative of the rapid growth / advancement of technology. Suggest to students that they go to the library or use the Internet to look through old editions of magazines and newspapers to get pictures of older models of computers, cell phones, digital cameras, camcorders, or other objects that show changes over time. Have students compare these pictures with current pictures.

C. La Era de las Máquinas

Approach: Have students prepare notes (key vocabulary, phrases, etc.) and later share with the class different examples of how *las máquinas* are part of our daily lives. Encourage them to think of examples from school, home, and work.

Expansion: Have students bring in topic-related pictures from newspaper circulars and magazines. Use pictures to expand further on the description, always emphasizing the newly acquired vocabulary.

D. Nuestra experiencia

Approach: In small groups, have students share experiences related to situations in which they or someone they know felt inadequate or helpless. Students should incorporate the vocabulary list from the activity into their discussion.

Alternative: Have students relate to the class some personal experience / situation related to feeling inadequate, misinformed, or not keeping up with the latest trends. Vocabulary should be incorporated into the narration. Time should be allowed for possible reactions from other students, perhaps to share experiences related to similar situations.

E. Una selección

Approach: As a pre-reading activity, have students read the questions at the end of the short reading selection. Check for understanding of vocabulary and provide explanations of meanings in Spanish, if necessary. This will help students to focus on key vocabulary and themes. Encourage students to add to the vocabulary list already provided and to use the new words in the class discussion.

Alternative: Students read the short selection and react / answer questions, always supporting their answers with information directly from the reading.

Expansion: Students read the passage in class or at home. Have them write or tell the main ideas about the short passage. The discussion should include possible main characters and possible plot.

F. Expresiones idiomáticas

Approach: Review with students the idiomatic expressions that are listed. Have them complete the activity, using the appropriate expressions. Students should always justify their answers.

Expansion: In small groups, have students prepare a list of questions they can ask each other, following the same format as the activity.

G. Otra selección

Approach: After students read the selection once or twice, they should answer the questions. Each answer should be supported with examples from the reading.

Expansion: Now that students have more information, have them reflect on the first reading selection and encourage them to predict what is going to happen in the story, using the statements they have prepared for question 5.

Al leer

Approach: Draw students' attention to these advance organizers, helping them to identify the vocabulary, verb forms, and themes that they are likely to encounter.

Expansion: Refer to vocabulary identified in Activities A–G under *Antes de leer* and create a vocabulary web that reinforces and connects the themes.

Lectura

Approach: Have students read the story in a group and then reread it at home. The class may also read parts of the story aloud, with students taking turns role-playing the various characters. Since there is significant movement and emotion in the story, encourage students to pantomime the actions of the characters as they read the story aloud.

Comprensión

A. Frases para completar

Approach: Before discussing the reading, students should complete the activity. Encourage them to support their answers with evidence from the reading.

B. Comprensión general

Approach: Have students jot down ideas about their understanding of the story and share their ideas with the class. Allow class time for discussion about the unexpected ending.

C. En contexto

Approach: Have students write their own definitions for the words listed in the activity. Students collaborate in making a master vocabulary list for the class. Encourage students to provide more than one definition for each word.

Expansion: (1) Students choose additional words from the story and provide their own equivalents to challenge their classmates. (2) Jeopardy game format – student gives a definition, and others give the possible word / answer.

D. De la misma familia

Approach: Referring to the reading, students find words associated with the words provided in the activity.

E. Al punto

Approach: Students complete the activity, referring to lines in the reading where they found the answers.

F. Ahora te toca a ti

Approach: Students direct questions to the class or to groups of two or three. Have students ask the class or other groups their questions to determine the questions' effectiveness and to reinforce comprehension. This approach shifts the burden of asking questions from you to the students, who often generate challenging questions.

Expansion: Put all questions in a box and have students pick one / several to ask the class or answer for the class.

Un paso más

Approach: Remind students to refer to the *Vocabulario útil para conversar y para escribir* list and to the Appendix on pp. 404–406 to help them with the speaking and writing activities.

Para conversar

Approach to this section: Students may express preferences about topics that interest them in this section. Based on their interests and skill levels, <u>you may wish to address only one or several of the activities or you may wish to divide the activities according to interest and have each group present its work to the class,</u> inviting reactions and responses.

A. Una entrevista

Approach: Good paired activity. Students can take turns role-playing, using vocabulary from the list.

Expansion: Have students also work on Activities B, C, and D. Students present different sections to the class.

B. ¿Computadoras o seres humanos?

Approach: Students answer questions in groups. Focus class or group discussion on the human aspect of computers, that is, how much computers are part of our lives. Have students work on Activities A, C, and D and report to the class.

C. El destino de las otras computadoras

Approach: Focus the discussion on the fast pace of technology. Discussion should deal not only with the rapid changes in computer technology and how the equipment has changed but also with how much computers are able to do. Good activity for students to personalize. Motivate students to use vocabulary from the list.

Expansion: Compare advancements in computer technology with the aging process in humans. Good activity to connect with Activity D below.

D. Para seguir siendo útil

Approach: Lead students through the process of comparing what happened to Rosa with what happens to human beings when they retire. Encourage students to use higher level thinking skills. Vocabulary related to emotions and feelings is appropriate for use in this section.

Expansion: Talk about the activities, sports, etc., pictured in advertisements for retirement communities. Compare these communities with Rosa's removal. Does the age at which people retire affect what they are able to do? Have students talk about some possible activities, hobbies, etc., for retirees and compare this with what older computers might be able to do for people who have never had one.

E. Un debate

Expansion: As students brainstorm the possible human qualities of computers, point out some things that computers can do that resemble human actions, for example, taking messages, recognizing human voices, or keeping track of important dates.

Para escribir

Approach to this section: The activities in this section build students' writing skills incrementally, from summary to personal reaction to creation. Students will need time to express themselves and to share their writing with classmates and with the teacher. Students may express preferences about topics that interest them in this section. Based on their interests and skill levels, <u>you may wish to address only one or several of the activities or you may wish to divide the activities according to interest and have each group present its work to the class,</u> inviting reactions and responses.

A. Un resumen

Approach: Focus on one activity or all three writing activities in one class period.

Activity one: In pairs / groups, students explain why they would eliminate certain vocabulary words from the list. Each group shares its information with the class.

Activity two: Individual students give examples of the words they added to the list and justify their answers to the class.

Activity three: Good assessment activity on the reading. Encourage students to be precise in their summary of the reading, using the new vocabulary list.

B. Una reacción al cuento

Expansion: Call students' attention to previous class discussions about the ending to the story. This is the time for each student to put his or her reactions and thoughts in writing and share them with the class.

C. Después de la Era de las Máquinas

Expansion: Point out the phrase *Después de la Era de las Máquinas*. In groups of two or three, ask students to brainstorm how different their lives would be without the use of technology. Have groups share their ideas with the class. After group collaboration, have students write their personal thoughts.

D. El valor de la edad

Expansion: Possible class discussion on the knowledge and wisdom of older family members: how older people teach values and traditions; contributions made to the community by senior citizens. Focus on how wisdom is sometimes acquired through age. Touch upon the idea that you shouldn't throw something away just because it's old.

E. El orgullo del trabajo

Expansion: Focus the pre-writing discussion on modesty and pride.

F.   Otro final

Expansion: Individual or group work. Students create other possible endings to the story and then share them with the class.

G.   Si yo fuera Rosa...

Expansion: Pre-writing activity. Call students' attention to the personal characteristics of computers previously discussed. Also refer to the discussion on the role of the elderly in society. Guide students through the suggested writing tips before they begin to write.

Comprensión auditiva

Approach: Have students look over the options for each selection carefully before they begin to listen. Check that they are comfortable with both the meaning and pronunciation of the vocabulary. If students do not understand words / phrases, provide Spanish explanations, but avoid English translations. Have students identify key words so that they can predict the topic, vocabulary, and structures that they are likely to hear. Careful preparation, combined with a willingness to use intuition and an understanding of contexts, will ensure that students need to listen only once to understand each passage.

Go Online

Approach: Have students visit the *Abriendo paso: Lectura* Web site at www.PHSchool.com for activities and links related to the content of the chapter.

Capítulo 3
Un oso y un amor

Selection: short story by Sabine Reyes Ulibarrí (New Mexico)

A young man relates the story of some of his fondest childhood memories, including his memories of his first love, Shirley. His relationship with Shirley began as a friendship between two young people and, over a period of time, the couple realized that they were in love with each other. And even though it was not their destiny to be together as adults, the narrator continues to have fond memories of the time they spent together. *"Shirley Cantel y yo crecimos juntos. Desde niños fuimos a la escuela juntos. Yo cargaba con sus libros. Más tarde íbamos a traer las vacas todas las tardes. Jugábamos en las caballerizas o en las pilas de heno... Nunca se nos ocurrió que estuviéramos enamorados. Este año pasado, por primera vez, lo descubrimos..."*

Themes: adolescent school memories, life in the country

Difficulty level: moderate. The story is a nostalgic look at the author's life as a youth among the *hispanos* of Tierra Amarilla, the small rural village in New Mexico where he was raised. Ulibarrí's style is direct and indicates his skill as a storyteller who borrows heavily from the strong oral tradition associated with this area. Through the author's vivid descriptions of the countryside, students will gain some insight into the daily lives, values, and feelings of the inhabitants of this area. Students will enjoy the author's suspenseful narration of the encounter with the young bear.

Key grammar: Present indicative and adjectives: Unidades 2 y 3, págs. 49 a 72 y 95 a 115; RG 2 y 3, págs. 73 a 94 y 116 a 132; Preterite and imperfect indicative: Unidad 1, págs. 1 a 15; RG 1, págs. 30 a 45; Indefinite and negative words: Paso 7, págs. 298 a 301

Key vocabulary: feelings and emotions, nature, camping

Estimated time needed: 500 minutes (10 classes maximum traditional schedule, 7 classes maximum block)

Antes de leer

A. Para discutir en clase
Approach: In small groups or pairs, have students collaborate to describe the picture, using the vocabulary provided to help them through the narration. Then have the class tell the story and create a vocabulary list to which they can refer throughout the chapter.

B. Nuestra experiencia
Approach: Have students share their experiences with a partner / group about surprising reactions to a dangerous, unexpected situation involving an animal. Students share their stories with the class.

Alternative: Have a group or pair analyze reactions to dangerous situations and report to the class.

C. El amor imposible
Alternative: Have students share with their partner or group their stories of separation from loved ones. If students don't have personal stories to share on this topic, they may

brainstorm the theme of "Impossible Love," using plots from literature, movies, etc. Students then share these stories with the class.

D. Una selección
Approach: After reinforcing the concept of the importance and effectiveness of contextual clues, have students read this opening selection at least twice, silently or with a partner. Afterwards, have students report to the class their assumptions and predictions about the story.

Expansion: Students create word-definition pairs to clarify unfamiliar vocabulary from this selection.

Al leer

Approach: Draw students' attention to these advance organizers, helping them to identify the vocabulary, verb forms, and themes that they are likely to encounter. Have them reflect on their own experiences discussed in Activities B and C under *Antes de leer* before they begin the reading.

Expansion: Draw students' attention to Activity B under *Comprensión*. Review the statements and clarify any unfamiliar vocabulary so that students will have a better understanding of what to expect in the story.

Lectura

Approach: You may have students read the story in a group and then reread it at home.

Comprensión

A. ¿Cierta o falsa?
Expansion: Students support their answers to this true / false activity with direct quotes from the reading, followed by their own interpretations.

B. La sucesión de los eventos
Approach: Have students work in groups to organize the sentences in sequential order. Assign each group to narrate a certain part of the story for the class.

C. Comprensión general
Approach: Have students jot down ideas about their understanding of the story and share their ideas with the class.

D. De la misma familia and **E. En contexto**
Alternative: Students write words that come to mind and share them with the class. As a student notes the possible answer on the board or on a transparency, attention should be focused on the different parts of speech of the words provided.

F. Al punto
Expansion: Have students create multiple-choice items that clarify aspects of the story.

G. Ahora te toca a ti
Alternative: Once students have prepared their questions and directed them to their partners or to small groups, have selected questions directed to the class or to other groups to determine the questions' effectiveness and to reinforce comprehension.

Expansion: Have students do Internet research on different aspects of the culture of New Mexico and then report to the class, making a connection to the story.

Un paso más

Approach: Remind students to refer to the *Vocabulario útil para conversar y para escribir* list and to the Appendix on pp. 404–406 to help them with the speaking and writing activities.

Para conversar

Approach to this section: Students may express preferences about topics that interest them in this section. Based on their interests and skill levels, <u>you may wish to address only one or several of the activities or you may wish to divide the activities according to interest and have each group present its work to the class,</u> inviting reactions and responses.

A. Después de tantos años
Alternative: This section may be completed in conjunction with Activities B and C under *Para escribir.*

B. La sierra
Approach: Focus students' attention on how the passage of time can change one's perspective on how certain things are viewed, that is, how it can help us see things in a different light.

C. Los amigos del narrador
Alternative: *Cobardes, ¿ Sí o no?* Using a graphic organizer, students write down possible reasons why the narrator's friend did not help him when he was confronting the bear. These reasons should be representative of the feelings and emotions discussed throughout the story. Once the chart has been completed, students make references to personal circumstances and explore their own personal feelings and reasons for such behavior. Students share their stories and outcomes with the class.

D. "También ella se acuerda"
Alternative: Students refer to the reading and answer the questions, hypothesizing about possible feelings of jealousy and or nostalgia on the part of the narrator. The class needs to establish the tone at the end of the story, using some of their own personal stories that might have unambiguous endings.

Para escribir

Approach to this section: The activities in this section build students' writing skills incrementally, from summary to personal reaction to creation. Students will need time to express themselves and to share their writing with classmates and with the teacher. Students may express preferences about topics that interest them in this section. Based on their interests and skill levels, <u>you may wish to address only one or several of the activities or you may wish to divide the activities according to interest and have each group present its work to the class,</u> inviting reactions and responses.

A. Un resumen
Expansion: Students draw a storyboard based on the summary they wrote. Students need to pay close attention to the correct use of the preterite and imperfect in their narration.

B. Otro final
Expansion: Students present their story ending to the class in oral or visual mode.

B. Otro final and C. La vida de Shirley
Expansion: After listening to possible story endings and possible descriptions of Shirley's life, groups write a short story based on their classmates' summaries.

D. Una sola sociedad
Alternative: Prior to starting this writing activity, have a class discussion on the topic "The United States is a Melting Pot" or, as some social studies teachers are saying in their classes, "The United States is a Caesar salad." Students might bring in ideas from their social studies classes. Encourage students to write an outline before they start the essay.

E. La separación
Approach: Draw students' attention to these advance organizers, helping them to focus on the sequence of events in the story. Students write a story with a happy ending, using the sequence of events from the story or one of their own.

Comprensión auditiva
Approach: Have students look over the options for each selection carefully before they begin to listen. Check that they are comfortable with both the meaning and pronunciation of the vocabulary. If students do not understand words / phrases, provide Spanish explanations, but avoid English translations. Have students identify key words so that they can predict the topic, vocabulary, and structures that they are likely to hear. Careful preparation, combined with a willingness to use intuition and an understanding of contexts, will ensure that students need to listen only once to understand each passage.

Go Online

Approach: Have students visit the *Abriendo paso: Lectura* Web site at www.PHSchool.com for activities and links related to the content of the chapter.

Capítulo 4
Continuidad de los parques

Selection: short story by Julio Cortázar (Belgium - Argentina)

The author takes us to a quiet reading room where a man sits down to read a book that he had started a few days ago. The detailed description lets us feel as if we are actually part of the scenery and in the room, in the comfort of the velvet chair. The author brings the characters to life, using vivid images of their actions and movements throughout the story. When the murder is about to take place, we have to stop and think: Who is the victim, the man reading the novel or the character in the novel he is reading? Students will enjoy the suspense. *"Gozaba del placer casi perverso de irse desgajando línea a línea de lo que lo rodeaba, y sentir a la vez que su cabeza descansaba cómodamente en el terciopelo del alto respaldo, que los cigarrillos seguían al alcance de la mano, que más allá de los ventanales danzaba el aire del atardecer bajo los robles. Palabra a palabra, absorbido por la sórdida disyuntiva de los héroes, dejándose ir hacia las imágenes que se concertaban y adquirían color y movimiento, fue testigo del último encuentro en la cabaña del monte".*

Themes: fantasy vs. reality, living through reading

Difficulty level: moderate to high. Students will need some background information about the author and his use of the literary technique known as *el realismo mágico*. Students will be able to offer other examples of this genre once they understand the concept.

Key grammar: Preterite and imperfect indicative: Unidad 1, págs. 1 a 15; RG 1, págs. 30 a 45; Adjectives: Unidad 2, págs. 49 a 72; RG 2, págs. 73 a 94; Gerund (present participle): Unidad 3, págs. 102 a 109; RG 3, págs. 128 a 130

Key vocabulary: furniture, homicide-related vocabulary, feelings, emotions

Estimated time needed: 350 minutes (7 classes maximum traditional schedule, 4 classes maximum block)

Antes de leer

A. Para describir en clase
Approach: In small groups or pairs, have students collaborate to describe the picture and tell the story, noting the detail that surrounds the main character in the drawing. Then have one member from each group or pair present their story to the class, creating a vocabulary list to which they can refer throughout the chapter.

B. Nuestra experiencia, C. El abandono total, and D. El título
Approach: It is suggested that you complete Activities B, C, and D in sequential order to guide students through the plot, as they will encounter it in the reading. Students will understand the style and content better by following the activities in this order.

B. Nuestra experiencia
Expansion: Students can work in pairs or in groups to share similar experiences they might have had after reading a book, watching a movie, or listening to a song. Have students share their experiences with the class.

C. El abandono total
Expansion: Students read the paragraph as a group and brainstorm possible answers to the questions. Students can role-play the narrator.

D. El título
Approach: Using a graphic organizer, students discuss possible meanings for the title of the story. Call students' attention to previous class discussions from Activities B and C.

Al leer

Approach: Draw students' attention to these advance organizers, helping them to identify the vocabulary, verb forms, and themes that they are likely to encounter. Have them reflect on their experiences from Activity B under *Antes de leer* before they read the story.

Alternative: Draw students' attention to Activity B under *Comprensión general*. Students should read the questions as a pre-reading activity. This will give students preliminary information about the characters and some insight into the plot.

Lectura

Approach: You may have students read the story in a group and then reread it at home.

Comprensión

A. ¿Cierta o falsa?
Expansion: Students support their answers to this true / false activity with direct quotes from the reading, followed by their own interpretations.

B. Comprensión general
Approach: Have students jot down ideas about their understanding of the story and share their ideas with the class.

Alternative: Have one group prepare and present this activity while other groups work on Activities C and D.

Expansion: Students compare the story with the other books / movies / songs that they mentioned in Activity B under *Antes de leer*.

C. De la misma familia
Expansion: After students identify one word from the same family, ask for additional words. Note which part of speech each word is, and use the categories to help generate additional vocabulary.

D. En contexto
Approach: Have students write their own phrases or word equivalents and then share them with the class as one records them on the board or on a transparency. Train students in alternative ways to talk about the vocabulary. Help them identify which word or phrase best matches the word provided and why.

 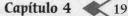

Expansion: Have students identify the part of speech of each word and note how knowing the part of speech helps in determining the meanings of words. Students may choose additional words from the story and provide their own equivalents to challenge their classmates. Students can create a Jeopardy game or any other that will help them remember the meanings of the words from Activities C and D.

E. Al punto
Expansion: Students create multiple-choice items that clarify additional aspects of the story.

F. Ahora te toca a ti
Alternative: Once students have prepared their questions and directed them to their partners or to small groups, have selected questions directed to the class or to other groups to check on the questions' effectiveness and to reinforce comprehension. This approach shifts the burden of asking questions from you to the students, who often generate challenging questions.

Un paso más

Approach: Remind students to refer to the *Vocabulario útil para conversar y para escribir* list and to the Appendix on pp. 404–406 to help them with the speaking and writing activities.

Para conversar

Approach to this section: Students may express preferences about topics that interest them in this section. Based on their interests and skill levels, you may wish to address only one or several of the activities or you may wish to divide the activities according to interest and have each group present its work to the class, inviting reactions and responses.

A. Paso a paso en la casa
Expansion: Guide students through this section by having them create a graphic organizer to show the things that the lover should have found in the house and the things that he didn't find. Students share results with the class using a transparency or the board to illustrate their findings.

B. Una explicación lógica
Expansion: In groups of two or three, students assume the identity of the narrator to describe the untold actions in the story. One student is selected from each group to present their narration to the class. The class then votes for the most convincing narration / presentation.

C. Unas horas después
Alternative: Students explore new situations and present them as skits.

D. Una entrevista

Alternative: Provide students with possible choices for asking questions. Make guidelines very specific and be sure that you are prepared to answer all questions. Complete each activity by simulating a talk show called "Ask the Author," and videotape for future use. Encourage students to use the Internet to get information on Julio Cortázar. Students can expand this activity by role-playing the author.

Para escribir

Approach to this section: The activities in this section build students' writing skills incrementally, from summary to personal reaction to creation. Students will need time to express themselves and to share their writing with classmates and with the teacher. Students may express preferences about topics that interest them in this section. Based on their interests and skill levels, <u>you may wish to address only one or several of the activities or you may wish to divide the activities according to interest and have each group present its work to the class,</u> inviting reactions and responses.

A. Un resumen

Approach: As students prepare to write their reviews, call their attention to the "Book review" section in any magazine or newspaper or on the Internet, which will help them focus on the appropriate format for this activity.

Expansion: Copy all writing samples and distribute them to the class, making sure that the writers' identities remain anonymous.

B. Los días antes del encuentro

Approach: In small groups or pairs, students describe possible scenarios between the two lovers prior to their meeting. Students collaborate in writing a detailed description of the events and location.

Expansion: Students present their scenarios to the class in the form of skits.

C. El encuentro

Approach: In small groups or pairs, students describe possible feelings and emotions associated with the scenario of being taken by surprise in this unfortunate situation. Students share their lists of words with the class before individual writing is done.

Expansion: Students share their descriptions with the class, inviting criticism and reactions.

D. Mi opinión

Approach: Before students start the writing process, recall the discussions from Activity B under *Para conversar* and Activity A under *Para escribir,* where students summarized the story and expressed opinions about it and the characters. In small groups or pairs, have students add more adjectives to the list provided. Adjectives should focus on expressing personal feelings about the story, not only about the characters but also about the author's technique of writing a story within a story. Students share their lists with the class, inviting reactions and comments.

E. Las técnicas de algunos escritores

Approach: The author's style was probably discussed in Activity D, *Mi opinión*, and students also had a chance to experience this technique when they wrote their scenarios in Activity B, *Los días antes del encuentro*. Students share additional stories from books, magazines, etc., that employ the same technique. Students reflect on previous class discussions and write personal reactions to the author's technique of writing a story within a story.

Comprensión auditiva

Approach: Have students look over the options for each selection carefully before they begin to listen. Check that they are comfortable with both the meaning and pronunciation of the vocabulary. If students do not understand words / phrases, provide Spanish explanations, but avoid English translations. Have students identify key words so that they can predict the topic, vocabulary, and structures that they are likely to hear. Careful preparation, combined with a willingness to use intuition and an understanding of contexts, will ensure that students need to listen only once to understand each passage.

Go Online

Approach: Have students visit the *Abriendo paso: Lectura* Web site at www.PHSchool.com for activities and links related to the content of the chapter.

Capítulo 5
Cajas de cartón

Selection: short story by Francisco Jiménez (Mexico)

The narrator, an 11-year-old boy, and his family have to move constantly from county to county during harvest season. They are migrant workers who spend twelve hours a day in the fields picking grapes, strawberries, and other crops in the hot California sun. One day, as the school bus lets the narrator off in front of the old garage where his family has been living, he sees all of their belongings packed in cardboard boxes and ready to be moved again. The narrator had finally found new friends and a teacher who was helping him to learn English and also teaching him how to play the trumpet, and now it was time to move again. *"Un viernes durante la hora del almuerzo, el señor Lema me invitó a que lo acompañara a la sala de música. '¿Te gusta la música?', me preguntó. 'Sí, muchísimo', le contestó entusiasmado, 'me gustan los corridos mexicanos'. Él cogió una trompeta, la tocó un poco y luego me la entregó... '¿Te voy a enseñar a tocar esta trompeta durante las horas de almuerzo...' Ese día casi no podía esperar el momento de llegar a casa y contarle las nuevas a mi familia. Al bajar del camión me encontré con mis hermanitos que gritaban y brincaban de alegría. Pensé que era porque ya había llegado, pero al abrir la puerta de la chocita, vi que toda estaba empacado en cajas de cartón..."*

Themes: family values, life of migrant workers in the United States, appreciating what you have

Difficulty level: moderate. This sad story is rich with emotions and feelings. Students will learn how difficult life is for migrant workers and for their children. It will make the students appreciate what they have.

Key grammar: Preterite and imperfect indicative: Unidad 1, págs. 1 a 15; RG 1, págs. 30 a 45; Reflexive verbs: Unidad 3, págs. 109 a 115; RG 3, págs. 130 a 132; Object pronouns: Paso 3, págs. 263 a 273; *Gustar* and verbs like *gustar*: Paso 8, págs. 302 a 304; Compound prepositions: Appendix C, págs. 375 a 376; Idiomatic expressions: Appendix F, págs. 384 a 388

Key vocabulary: household items, kitchen utensils, farm-related vocabulary, feelings and emotions

Estimated time needed: 500 minutes (10 classes maximum traditional schedule, 6 classes maximum block)

Antes de leer

A. Para discutir en clase
Approach: In small groups or pairs, have students collaborate to describe the pictures and tell the story. Students follow the organizational points suggested to narrate the story, using the vocabulary provided. New words should be added to the list, to which students can refer throughout the chapter.

B. Nuestra experiencia
Approach: Students share their experiences with a partner or with the class, discussing feelings about moving to a new home, school, state, country, etc.

C. El trabajo de los inmigrantes
Approach: After researching life-styles of migrant workers, students report their findings to the class, discussing how they would feel if they had to endure such living conditions or accommodations, and any other findings.

D. Una selección
Approach: Students refer to the questions at the end of the selection. After reinforcing the concept of contextual clues, have students read the selection, silently or with a partner. Students work together to answer questions and compare the information in the passage with the information learned in Activity C about the life of migrant workers. Finally, students report their findings to the class.

E. El título
Approach: Students work in small groups or in pairs to answer questions and then share their answers with the class. Refer to Activities B and C for themes on moving and the life of migrant workers.

Al leer

Approach: Draw students' attention to these advance organizers and to Activity B under *Comprensión general,* helping them to identify the vocabulary, verb forms, and themes that they are likely to encounter in the reading. Help them reflect on the experiences of migrant workers discussed in Activity C under *Antes de leer* and also on prior knowledge of this topic from their social studies classes.

Lectura

Approach: You may have students read the story in a group and then reread it at home.

Comprensión

A. ¿Cierta o falsa?
Expansion: Students support their answers to this true / false activity with direct quotes from the reading, followed by their own interpretations.

B. Comprensión general
Approach: Have students jot down ideas about their understanding of the story and share their ideas with the class.

C. De la misma familia
Expansion: After students identify one word from the same family, ask for additional words. Note which part of speech each word is, and use the categories to help generate additional vocabulary.

D. En contexto
Expansion: Students identify the part of speech of each word and note how knowing the part of speech helps in determining the meanings of words. Students choose words from the story and provide their own equivalents.

E. Al punto
Expansion: Students create multiple-choice items that clarify additional aspects of the story.

F. Ahora te toca a ti
Approach: Have students prepare and direct their questions to their partners or in small groups. This approach shifts the burden of asking questions from you to the students, who often generate challenging questions.

Alternative: Once students have prepared their questions and directed them to their partners or to small groups, have selected questions directed to the class or to other groups to check on the questions' effectiveness and to reinforce comprehension.

G. Otras preguntas
Expansion: Refer to Activity F under *Comprensión* for additional student-generated questions to reinforce comprehension of the story.

Un paso más

Approach: Remind students to refer to the *Vocabulario útil para conversar y para escribir* list and to the Appendix on pp. 404–406 to help them with the speaking and writing activities.

Para conversar

Approach to this section: Students may express preferences about topics that interest them in this section. Based on their interests and skill levels, you may wish to address only one or several of the activities or you may wish to divide the activities according to interest and have each group present its work to the class, inviting reactions and responses.

A. Situaciones difíciles
Approach: In small groups or pairs, students develop and discuss the scenarios, allowing time for creating a new situation related to the story or a situation that students might have dealt with at some point in their lives. Students present their scenarios to the class.

B. Una comparación
Approach: In small groups, students use graphic organizers to compare aspects of the narrator's life with their own. Students share their results with the class.

C. La despedida
Alternative: Students explore the situation and the new ideas as skits. Students present their skits to the class.

D. Mi vida

Expansion: Using a collage, students describe the narrator's life. Students will use the new vocabulary from the chapter to present their collages to the class.

E. La vida circular

Expansion: Allow time for students to do Internet research on the life of migrant workers. Findings will help students focus on the idea of "life being a vicious circle" for migrant workers. Students report their findings to the class.

F. Un debate

Approach: Students work with a more traditional debate format. Select two small groups to debate for and against the argument; the rest of the class is the audience. Provide clear guidelines for the number of argument points to be made by the two sides, examples to back up opinions, and time limits to present points. The rest of the class observes and notes which side's arguments were best presented and supported. After separating a debate format from the expressions of personal opinion, class discussion can then follow about students' feelings about the issues presented.

Para escribir

Approach to this section: The activities in this section build students' writing skills incrementally, from summary to personal reaction to creation. Students will need time to express themselves and to share their writing with classmates and with the teacher. Students may express preferences about topics that interest them in this section. Based on their interests and skill levels, <u>you may wish to address only one or several of the activities or you may wish to divide the activities according to interest and have each group present its work to the class,</u> inviting reactions and responses.

A. Un resumen and B. La ayuda de un maestro

Alternative: Students write a summary essay based on the story, following guided questions.

C. Otro final

Expansion: Students write another possible ending to the story based on the information they learned from their research about the life of migrant workers. One or more students from each group can present their narration to the class.

D. El valor de la vida dura and E. Los inmigrantes

Expansion: Guide students through the formal essay format. (You may want to bring in an English teacher to explain the formal essay format.) Help students through the outline process. Students write their essays in class. Students may get topics for their essays from the research suggested in Activity F below. Students brainstorm about personal values.

F. Cómo adaptarse a una nueva cultura

Expansion: Researching the lives of the people on the list will help students acquire a better understanding about immigrants and their contributions to American culture.

Comprensión auditiva

Approach: Have students look over the options for each selection carefully before they begin to listen. Check that they are comfortable with both the meaning and pronunciation of the vocabulary. If students do not understand words / phrases, provide Spanish explanations, but avoid English translations. Have students identify key words so that they can predict the topic, vocabulary, and structures that they are likely to hear. Careful preparation, combined with a willingness to use intuition and an understanding of contexts, will ensure that students need to listen only once to understand each passage.

Go Online

Approach: Have students visit the *Abriendo paso: Lectura* Web site at www.PHSchool.com for activities and links related to the content of the chapter.

Capítulo 6
Jacinto Contreras recibe su paga extraordinaria

Selection: short story by Camilo José Cela (Spain, Nobel Prize 1989)

A generous, naïve man receives his Christmas bonus and dreams of what even this small amount can do to bring happiness to his family. A theft, however, robs him of his money and his family's modest hopes. *"Hay gentes sin conciencia, capaces de desbaratar los más honestos sueños de la Navidad..."*

Themes: the nature of happiness, honesty and dishonesty, personal and family relationships, trust

Difficulty level: low to moderate. The plot is easily visualized and flows logically. The moment of the robbery is subtle and will challenge students: they will have to recognize the unexpected ending and search for the moment of the robbery in the reading. Student discussion about the nature of injustice will be lively.

Key grammar: Preterite and imperfect indicative: Unidad 1, págs. 1 a 15; RG 1, págs. 30 a 45; Imperative: Unidad 4, págs. 133 a 140; RG 4, págs. 154 a 165; *Ser/Estar*: Unidad 3, págs. 98 a 107; RG 3, págs. 119 a 121; Adjectives: Unidad 2, págs. 49 a 72; RG 2, págs. 73 a 94; *Por/Para*: Paso 10, págs. 309 a 311

Key vocabulary: clothing, city, weather, food and drink, family and relationships

Estimated time needed: 500 minutes (10 classes maximum traditional schedule, $5\frac{1}{2}$ classes maximum block)

Antes de leer

A. Para discutir en clase
Approach: In small groups or pairs, have students collaborate to describe the picture and tell the story, noting key vocabulary. Then have the class tell the story and create a vocabulary list to which they can refer throughout the chapter.

Expansion: Students relate the story in various tenses and / or comment on the importance of generosity and good relationships, using the subjunctive mood.

B. Nuestra experiencia
Alternative: Students prepare a skit that tells the story of giving a gift and the response of the recipient.

C. Una relación especial
Approach: Have students work on the various questions with a partner or in small groups and then share their thoughts with the class.

Expansion: Students share stories of people they know who have good relationships. Using the bulleted points as organizers, students give their specific examples of relationship-supporting behavior. The story may be presented orally, in writing, and / or in a skit.

D. Una selección

Expansion: (1) Students create word-definition pairs to clarify additional unfamiliar vocabulary from this selection. (2) Students identify those elements of the selection that illustrate the relationship between, and economic situation of, Jacinto and Benjamina. Based on what they discover, what can they predict about the importance of the Christmas bonus to Jacinto? (3) Students can illustrate in the form of collages, cut-out pictures, or student-generated samples the items that Jacinto wants to buy for his family. Samples can be placed around the room to help students focus on a visual for their newly acquired vocabulary. Having these around the room will provide good conversation starters or warm-up activities.

Al leer

Approach: Draw students' attention to these advance organizers, helping them to identify the vocabulary, verb forms, and themes that they are likely to encounter. Note the *El autor* information about Cela and his approach to creating characters. Note, too, that one bullet asks students to pay attention to the scene on the metro. Don't give too much away. The effect of the ending depends on the element of surprise. Students will benefit from retracing Jacinto's steps and will take pride in sleuthing out the moment of the robbery.

Lectura

Approach: You may have students read the story in a group and then reread the story at home. The class may also read along as parts of the story are read aloud, with students providing the voices of the narrator and the characters. Since there is significant dialogue, movement, and emotion in the story, several students may pantomime the actions of the characters as the story is read aloud.

Comprensión

A. La sucesión de los eventos
Approach: Have students work in groups to organize the sentences in sequential order. Assign each group to narrate a certain part of the story for the class.

B. Comprensión general
Approach: Students jot down ideas about their understanding of the story and then share their ideas with the class.

C. De la misma familia
Expansion: After students identify one word from the same family, ask for additional words. Note which part of speech each word is, and use the categories to help generate additional vocabulary.

D. En contexto
Approach: Have students write their own phrases or word equivalents and then share them with the class as one records them on the board or on a transparency. Train students in alternative ways to talk about the vocabulary. Help them identify which word or phrase best matches the word provided and why.

Expansion: (1) Have students identify the part of speech of each word and note how knowing the part of speech helps in determining the meanings of words. (2) Have students choose additional words from the story and provide their own equivalents to challenge their classmates.

E. Al punto
Expansion: Have students create multiple-choice items that clarify additional aspects of the story.

F. Ahora te toca a ti
Approach: Assign the bulleted list of themes—or themes created by students—to different pairs or groups. Have the groups ask the class or other groups their questions to determine the questions' effectiveness and to reinforce comprehension. This approach shifts the burden of asking questions from you to the students, who often generate challenging questions.

Un paso más

Approach: Remind students to refer to the *Vocabulario útil para conversar y para escribir* list and to the Appendix on pp. 404–406 to help them with the speaking and writing activities.

Para conversar

Approach to this section: Students may express preferences about topics that interest them in this section. Based on their interests and skill levels, you may wish to address only one or several of the activities or you may wish to divide the activities according to interest and have each group present its work to the class, inviting reactions and responses.

A. Aquí tienes las respuestas
Expansion: Have one group of students prepare a Jeopardy game in which answers with point values are placed in categories and teams of students buzz in to win the points. Examples of categories: *comida y bebida, lugares, compras y regalos, nombres y apodos.*

B. ¿Qué comprar?, C. El consuelo, and D. ¿Qué hacemos?
Expansion: In groups, students prepare notes (key vocabulary, phrases, etc.) based on the situations provided and then present them to the class as skits.

E. Mis sentimientos
Expansion: Students note additional aspects of the story that create a mood or expectations, for example, Jacinto's friendship or the small details about the city. Students focus on the nature and purpose of the nicknames: Why do some people receive nicknames? What are some nicknames they have had, known, or given? What does a nickname say about the person who has it or who gives it? What does a nickname say about relationships with peers? Have students share experiences in which nicknames enhanced or harmed a relationship.

F. El bien y el mal

Expansion: In groups, students brainstorm about good and evil in the media (movies, music, and literature). Students present their findings to the class, inviting reactions and responses.

G. Una comparación

Alternative: In groups, students use graphic organizers (on poster board) to illustrate the similarities and differences between the two stories. Use these visuals in the classroom as conversation starters or warm-up activities.

Para escribir

Approach to this section: The activities in this section build students' writing skills incrementally, from summary to personal reaction to creation. Students will need time to express themselves and to share their writing with classmates and with the teacher. Students may express preferences about topics in this section. Based on their interests and skill levels, you may wish to address only one or several of the activities or you may wish to divide the activities according to interest and have each group present its work to the class, inviting reactions and responses.

A. Un resumen

Approach: Students collaborate on compiling a possible vocabulary list that can be used to summarize the plot, actions, and feelings in the story. Students write a summary essay based on the story, following guided questions. Students share their summaries with the class.

B. El robo

Expansion: Draw students' attention again to the *El autor* section. Cela frequently uses subtlety. How powerful is this technique? Have students share experiences in which a subtle action or word was more powerful than a grand gesture or forceful speech. Students may wish to act out such an experience, perhaps contrasting it with an imagined or real scene in which forcefulness was employed with less effectiveness.

C. Mis esperanzas

Approach: In pairs or groups, students comment on their experiences or those learned secondhand. Students use guided statements as points of departure to reveal their stories. Students share their experiences with the class.

D. La sociedad

Alternative: In groups, students answer questions regarding the good and bad in today's society, the representation of hopes and dreams, whether dreams are sometimes destroyed by people's wrongdoings, and whether good always prevails. Students share their answers with the class, making a connection with Jacinto and his unfortunate incident and also with the personal incidents mentioned in Activity C.

Comprensión auditiva 🎧

Approach: Have students look over the options for each selection carefully before they begin to listen. Check that they are comfortable with both the meaning and pronunciation of the vocabulary. If students do not understand words / phrases, provide Spanish explanations, but avoid English translations. Have students identify key words so that they can predict the topics, vocabulary, and structures that they are likely to hear. Careful preparation, combined with a willingness to use intuition and an understanding of contexts, will ensure that students need to listen only once to understand each passage.

Go Online

Approach: Have students visit the *Abriendo paso: Lectura* Web site at www.PHSchool.com for activities and links related to the content of the chapter.

Capítulo 7
Nosotros, no

Selection: short story by José Bernardo Adolph (Germany - Peru)

With a single injection once a century, immortality is finally granted to human beings, but only to the young. What will life be like for this new type of humankind, and what will happen to those whom immortality has left behind? *"Sólo los jóvenes serían los inmortales... nosotros, no"*.

Themes: the nature of humanity and society, youth versus age, human destiny and value

Difficulty level: moderate. The story is compelling and easy to understand. The themes, concepts, story twist, and surprises engage the students to inspire lively discussions.

Key grammar: Pluperfect indicative: Unidad 1, págs. 19 a 29; RG 1, págs. 47 y 48; Future: Unidad 5, págs. 174 a 181; RG 5, págs. 203 a 205; Conditional: Unidad 6, págs. 220 a 227; RG 6, págs. 233 a 236; Indefinite and negative words: Paso 7, págs. 298 a 301

Key vocabulary: emotions, agreement and disagreement, expressing personal opinion

Estimated time needed: 300 minutes (7 classes maximum traditional schedule, 4 classes maximum block)

Antes de leer

A. Para discutir en clase

Approach: In small groups or pairs, have students collaborate to describe the pictures and tell the story, noting key vocabulary. Then have the class tell the story to create a vocabulary list to which they can refer throughout the chapter.

Alternative: Have one group work on the pictures while other groups work on Activities B and C and / or D. Groups then share their work with the class, providing background about the roles and attitudes of, and stereotypes about, young and old people in society.

Expansion: Students and / or the teacher bring in pictures of old and / or young people in various situations (especially ones that are not usually associated with these groups). Discuss normal expectations for youth and old age and students' attitudes toward the appropriateness of these expectations.

B. Nuestra experiencia

Approach: Have students share their experiences with a partner or with the class to discover attitudes of and interactions between young and old people.

Alternative: A group of students, using questions 1 through 4 as models, prepare a skit showing the interaction between and attitudes expressed by a young and an old person. The group can specify whether the skit is based on a particular student's experience or on a compilation of the members' experiences.

Expansion: A group or the class presents a discussion on society's attitude toward the elderly.

 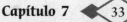

C. Los estereotipos

Approach: Work with the class to get immediate feedback, classify types of responses, and identify additional stereotypes.

Alternative: Have a group consider the questions and their reactions; then share their work as a third approach to looking at youth / age stereotypes along with Activities A and B.

Expansion: (1) Groups and / or pairs of students use the comments provided by the class to prepare skits. What do students discover from seeing stereotypes in action versus seeing them on paper? (2) A group or the class provides stereotypical statements made about young people. Do the students in the class feel more strongly about the stereotypes applied to themselves than about those applied to elderly people?

D. La inmortalidad

Expansion: Students research the topic of overpopulation in some countries and take results into account before completing the activity.

E. Una selección

Approach: Have students do this activity to check their skill in discerning tone, allusions, and the main idea of a short passage. Then have students share with a partner or group and then the class to answer the questions in preparation for the reading.

Alternative: Prepare a copy or transparency of the short selection. As you read the selection aloud, students identify the tone, key words, and the main idea on their own paper or point them out to a student who marks them on the transparency. The class then prepares the statement of the main idea of the selection.

Expansion: Students are directed to prepare alternative titles for the selection after they have finished the reading.

Al leer

Approach: Draw students' attention to these advance organizers, helping them to identify the vocabulary, verb forms, and themes that they are likely to encounter.

Expansion: (1) Students refer to themes, stereotypes, and reactions from Activities A–C under *Antes de leer*. Based only on knowing that the story deals with immortality, what do they think the reaction of young people would be? Of elderly people? Have students note their predictions to compare and contrast later with the reactions found in the story. (2) Students share their predictions about the year 2168. What do they think elderly people will predict about the future? (A group or the class can do a brief interview on this topic with older people they know.) Do the predictions of older people differ from those of younger people? Why or why not?

Lectura

Approach: Have students read the story in a group and then reread it at home.

Comprensión

A. ¿Cierta o falsa?

Expansion: Students support their answers to this true / false activity with direct quotes from the reading, followed by their own interpretations. Students ask questions of the class based on the correct statements that they identified from the activity.

B. Comprensión general

Approach: Have students jot down ideas about their understanding of the story and share their ideas with the class.

Expansion: (1) Students generate new titles for the selection (see Activity E Expansion under *Antes de leer*) and explain why the titles are appropriate. (2) Students choose one or more phrases from the selection that illustrate society's attitude toward the elderly and older people's views toward their own mortality (themes found in Activities A, B, and C under *Antes de leer*). (3) Prepare students for Activity E below by noting questions students ask you about the story. (4) Students prepare for Activity E by preparing additional questions.

C. De la misma familia

Expansion: After students identify one word from the same family, ask for additional words. Note which part of speech each word is, and use the categories to help generate additional vocabulary.

D. En contexto

Approach: Have students write their own phrases or word equivalents and then share them with the class as one records them on the board or on a transparency. Train students in alternative ways to talk about the vocabulary. Help them identify which word or phrase best matches the word provided and why.

Expansion: (1) Have students identify the part of speech of each word and note how knowing the part of speech helps in determining the meanings of words. (2) Have students choose additional words from the story and provide their own equivalents to challenge their classmates.

E. Al punto

Expansion: Point out the comprehension technique used in items 1, 3, 4, 8, 9, 11, 12, and 13 to explore the author's use of metaphor and narrative. Have students select additional phrases from the story and create their own rephrasing to check their classmates' comprehension.

F. Ahora te toca a ti

Approach: Assign the bulleted list of themes—or themes created by students—to different pairs or groups. Have the groups ask the class or other groups their questions to determine the questions' effectiveness and to reinforce comprehension. This approach shifts the burden of asking questions from you to the students, who often generate challenging questions.

Un paso más

Approach: Remind students to refer to the *Vocabulario útil para conversar y para escribir* list and to the Appendix on pp. 404–406 to help them with the speaking and writing activities.

Para conversar

Approach to this section: Students may express preferences about topics in this section. Based on their interests and skill levels, <u>you may wish to address only one or several of the activities or you may wish to divide the activities according to interest and have each group present its work to the class,</u> inviting reactions and responses.

A. La publicidad
Expansion: Students discuss scenarios that show institutionalized disrespect for old people. Students bring in ads from magazines / newspapers that might promote this.

B. Asumiendo otra identidad
Alternative: Students explore the situation and their new identities in the form of skits.

C. ¿Quieres ser inmortal?
Expansion: Students review their predictions from Expansion 1 under *Al leer* about the reactions of young and old people in the story to the promise of immortality. They then compare their predictions, the story, and their own ideas from the previous activities in order to come to some conclusions about the nature of humanity and mortality. Have they changed their opinions at all?

D. Cambios
Expansion: Students make visual presentations such as skits, posters, and collages to show how life might be in the year 2168 and present them to the class. Display the visuals in the classroom and use them to reinforce the chapter vocabulary and theme.

E. Excepciones
Expansion: Each student role-plays a "real person" (someone who is well known or perhaps someone who is not) who is asking for "eternal life." Students should do research using the Internet to find as much information as possible about the characters they are playing. This person should be associated with doing good for humankind. After presentations, students elect the person who most deserves to have eternal life.

Para escribir

Approach to this section: The activities in this section build students' writing skills incrementally, from summary to personal reaction to creation. Students will need time to express themselves and to share their writing with classmates and with the teacher. Students may express preferences about topics in this section. Based on their interests, skill levels, and the expansion activities you may have done so far, <u>you may wish to address only one or two of the activities with the class.</u>

A. La actitud del autor
Expansion: In groups, students take on the identity of the author. One student from each group tells the class his true intention about the theme of immortality.

B. El dilema de muchas familias
Expansion: Students research cultural differences in the Spanish-speaking world regarding living in nursing homes or at home and then present their information to the class for enrichment.

C. Los cumpleaños
Alternative: Have students form pairs and prepare statements about what one of the celebrants would do or be thinking on his / her birthday. Then have the pairs do alternate readings of lines / thoughts, providing point-by-point comparison and contrast.

Expansion: Provide additional birthday ranges (some of which may provide even greater contrasts).

D. Testamentos
Expansion: Students write their own wills, expressing their wishes and opinions on life and mortality. Using the Internet to research this topic might give students some insight about what actually goes into writing a will.

E. Mi propio cuento
Expansion: Students write the story as a group and provide a "screenplay" so that it may be performed.

Comprensión auditiva
Approach: Have students look over the options for each selection carefully before they begin to listen. Check that they are comfortable with both the meaning and pronunciation of the vocabulary. If students do not understand words / phrases, provide Spanish explanations, but avoid English translations. Have students identify key words so that they can predict the topics, vocabulary, and structures that they are likely to hear. Careful preparation, combined with a willingness to use intuition and an understanding of contexts, will ensure that students need to listen only once to understand each passage.

Go Online

Approach: Have students visit the *Abriendo paso: Lectura* Web site at www.PHSchool.com for activities and links related to the content of the chapter.

Capítulo 8
No oyes ladrar los perros

Selection: short story by Juan Rulfo (Mexico)

A father travels a long distance to a town to get medical help for his son. During the journey, we learn that his son, Ignacio, has not been the exemplary son that his father would have wished for but instead has been involved in a life of crime and wrongdoing. Most important, the father blames his son for the death of his wife, Ignacio's mother. *"Me derrengaré, pero llegaré con usted a Tonaya, para que le alivien esas heridas que le han hecho. Y estoy seguro de que, en cuanto se sienta usted bien, volverá a sus malos pasos. Eso ya no me importa... Porque para mí usted ya no es mi hijo. He maldecido la sangre que usted tiene de mí... Lo dije desde que supe que usted andaba trajinando por los caminos, viviendo del robo y matando gente... Y gente buena"*.

Themes: feelings of anger and compassion, family values and ties, irony

Difficulty level: moderate. The movement of the story—the father's journey carrying his son on his shoulders—should help students understand the dilemma of loving his son because of the blood that runs through his veins or hating him because of the life he has chosen.

Key grammar: Gerund (present participle): Unidad 3, págs. 102 a 109; RG 3, págs. 128 a 130; Imperative: Unidad 4, págs. 133 a 140; RG 4, págs. 154 a 165; Imperfect and pluperfect subjunctive: Unidad 6, págs. 207 a 219; RG 6, págs. 228 a 233; Object pronouns: Paso 3, págs. 263 a 273; Indefinite and negative words: Paso 7, págs. 298 a 301

Key vocabulary: feelings, emotions, daily routines, physical and emotional descriptions, personality traits

Estimated time needed: 450 minutes (9 classes maximum traditional schedule, 5 classes maximum block)

Antes de leer

A. Para discutir en clase
Approach: In small groups or pairs, have students collaborate to describe the picture and tell the story, noting key vocabulary. Students should incorporate suggested vocabulary into their narration to the class. Students share picture descriptions with the rest of the class, adding more words to the vocabulary list to which they can refer throughout the chapter.

B. Nuestra experiencia
Approach: Students can work individually, in pairs, or in small groups to explore these topics and then share their results with the class. Keep a tally / record / visual of the range of answers found in the class so that students can refer to it throughout the chapter.

C. Las acciones de los hijos
Alternative: Students discuss different factors that influence the lives of today's youth, not only in school but also in their personal lives. How much time is devoted to family life? What pastimes or hobbies do youngsters have? How do video games / computers / technology affect the short-term and long-term activities of students today? What role does social status play in a child's upbringing? How important are their friends and how do they choose them?

D. Los movimientos físicos

Expansion: (1) Students play "Simon says" to help them remember vocabulary / action words. (2) Students make video presentations resembling exercise videos to demonstrate the verbs. (3) Students act out pictures illustrating the actions presented in the activity to form a collage; post the collage in the room and use it as a visual to reinforce the meanings of the words.

E. Una selección

Expansion: In small groups or pairs, students write lists of adjectives that might describe the father's feelings and then share their lists with the class. Using the board or a transparency, keep a master list of their adjectives to refer to after students have read the story.

Al leer

Approach: Draw students' attention to these advance organizers, helping them to identify the vocabulary, verb forms, and themes that they are likely to encounter. Remind students to keep in mind parental feelings and emotions that are likely to be mentioned as a result of Ignacio's behavior.

Lectura

Approach: Have students read the story in a group and then reread it at home. The class may also read parts of the story aloud, with students taking turns role-playing the various characters. Since there is significant movement and emotion in the story, encourage students to pantomime the actions of the characters as they read the story aloud.

Comprensión

A. ¿Cierta o falsa?

Expansion: Students support their answers to this true / false activity with direct quotes from the reading, followed by their own interpretations.

B. Comprensión general

Approach: Have students jot down ideas about their understanding of the story and share their ideas with the class.

Expansion: In small groups or pairs, students write down the feelings that are evident throughout the story. Students compare the idea of the father carrying the son on his shoulders with the feelings that the father has for his son. Why is the father doing this for his son when Ignacio has turned out to be such a bad person and has led such a bad life?

C. De la misma familia

Alternative: Have one group prepare and present this section to the class while another group does Activity D.

Expansion: After students identify one word from the same family, ask for additional words. Note which part of speech each word is, and use the categories to help generate additional vocabulary.

 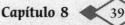

D. En contexto

Approach: Have students write their own phrases or word equivalents and then share them with the class as one records them on the board or on a transparency. Train students in alternative ways to talk about the vocabulary. Help them identify which word or phrase best matches the word provided and why.

Expansion: Have students identify the part of speech of each word and note how knowing the part of speech helps in determining the meanings of words. Students may choose additional words from the story and provide their own equivalents to challenge their classmates.

E. Al punto

Expansion: Students create multiple-choice items that clarify additional aspects of the story.

F. Ahora te toca a ti

Alternative: Once students have prepared their questions and directed them to their partners or to small groups, have selected questions directed to the class or to other groups to determine the questions' effectiveness and to reinforce comprehension. This approach shifts the burden of asking questions from you to the students, who often generate challenging questions.

Alternative: Have students check for comprehension using the Jeopardy game format.

Un paso más

Approach: Remind students to refer to the *Vocabulario útil para conversar y para escribir* list and to the Appendix on pp. 404–406 to help them with the speaking and writing activities.

Para conversar

Approach to this section: Students may express preferences about topics that interest them in this section. Based on their interests and skill levels, <u>you may wish to address only one or several of the activities or you may wish to divide the activities according to interest and have each group present its work to the class,</u> inviting reactions and responses.

A. Si yo hubiera sido...

Approach: As a class, students discuss (1) parents' responsibilities and obligations and (2) limits to parents' responsibilities and obligations. Make a master list on the board or on a transparency, allowing students to contribute their reactions and observations. In small groups or pairs, students praise or criticize the father's behavior. Students then share their comments with the class.

B. La manera de hablar

Expansion: Remind students of the difference between *usted* and *tú,* the formal (distant in this case) vs. the informal (usually friendly, but placid in this case) as part of the culture in Spanish-speaking countries. Although the father is indirectly blaming the son for his mother's death and feels embarrassed to have him for a son, he still helps him. Ask students to think about why the father is doing this. Is it because of love or because of his sense of obligation? Discuss feelings of compassion vs. feelings of anger.

C. La repetición

Approach: As a group, students (1) identify the repetitive phrases that occur throughout the story and (2) justify the author's technique and its effectiveness. In groups, students react to class discussions, form their own opinions, and justify their opinions by citing concrete examples from the story. Groups share their conclusions / answers to the questions with the class.

D. El futuro de Ignacio

Expansion: Students hypothesize about Ignacio's future, create possible scenarios, and share original ideas with the class in the form of skits.

E. Una película

Expansion: Encourage students to cast their movie with English-speaking or preferably Spanish-speaking actors / actresses. Students present their skits to the class based on the story.

F. El final del cuento

Expansion: Students reflect on the father's possible feelings and resentment toward his son. Students should keep in mind the father's previous feelings dealing with his moral obligation and how those feelings influenced him to seek medical attention for his son in the town.

G. El amor de los padres

Expansion: The movie *Mi familia* deals with a father's unconditional love for his sons. This theme might help to generate discussion.

Para escribir

Approach to this section: The activities in this section build students' writing skills incrementally, from summary to personal reaction to creation. Students will need time to express themselves and to share their writing with classmates and with the teacher. Students may express preferences about topics that interest them in this section. Based on their interests and skill levels, <u>you may wish to address only one or several of the activities or you may wish to divide the activities according to interest and have each group present its work to the class,</u> inviting reactions and responses.

A. Un resumen

Alternative: Have the class generate a master vocabulary list that they will incorporate into the summary of the story. The list should complement the other vocabulary lists provided in Activities C and D under *Comprensión*. Students then combine the answers to the guided questions and use suggested vocabulary to create a sequential summary of the story.

B. Otro punto de vista, C. Más información..., and E. Mi opinión sobre Ignacio

Alternative: In small groups or pairs, have students first focus on the adjectives that have been selected for Ignacio in Activity E and then express how the story might have been different, if told by Ignacio. Remind students to take into consideration all of the missing information and that, in spite of everything, a parent's love is always unconditional.

D. El control de los hijos

Expansion: In small groups, have students explore other external factors that help mold a child's character and personality besides the ones in Activity C under *Antes de leer*. Students can interview parents, adults in their families, teachers, community members, etc., for additional input on *el control de los hijos* or *la falta de control* and then show their results before they start writing.

E. Mi opinión sobre Ignacio

Approach: In small groups / pairs or as a class, students should collaborate in making up a list of adjectives that describe Ignacio's personality and life-style. They should include his actions toward his father, the affection or lack of affection between them, and other possible indications of his character.

F. El dilema del padre

Expansion: Students have shared and discussed feelings expressed by the father toward his son and vice versa. Now they can justify whether these feelings are appropriate. How far should a parent go for his / her children? Should children do the same for their parents? Should compassion overrule anger? If a child needs help, should a parent be there no matter what?

G. La reforma de los jóvenes

Alternative: Before students begin to write, discuss with them some alternative measures available for children / adolescents who have been involved in a life of crime and wrongdoing. After the research is done, allow time for students to formulate their own opinions regarding the results. Findings should be incorporated into their essays.

H. Consejos al padre

Approach: As students prepare to write their letters to Ignacio's father, review the subjunctive, affirmative and negative command forms, and appropriate vocabulary. Use this as part of the suggested list for the letter-writing process. Students should be encouraged to write a positive letter.

Comprensión auditiva

Approach: Have students look over the options for each selection carefully before they begin to listen. Check that they are comfortable with both the meaning and pronunciation of the vocabulary. If students do not understand words / phrases, provide Spanish explanations, but avoid English translations. Have students identify key words so that they can predict the topic, vocabulary, and structures that they are likely to hear. Careful preparation, combined with a willingness to use intuition and an understanding of contexts, will ensure that students need to listen only once to understand each passage.

Go Online

Approach: Have students visit the *Abriendo paso: Lectura* Web site at www.PHSchool.com for activities and links related to the content of the chapter.

Capítulo 9
El árbol de oro

Selection: short story by Ana María Matute (Spain)

Young Ivo shares his private vision with a curious schoolmate: a golden tree that he sees through a crack in the old book tower of the school. The schoolmate, unable to see the tree despite a great desire to do so, finally discovers the truth of the vision and its special role in Ivo's life and destiny. *"Entonces Ivo me explicó: Veo un árbol de oro... Las hojas no se caen nunca".*

Themes: childhood, envy and satisfaction, fantasy and reality

Difficulty level: moderate. While challenging in terms of grammar and vocabulary, the images of the fantastic tree and the contrast of the vision with the experiences in the classroom are clear and compelling. Students relate well to the competitiveness within the school setting and are curious about the meaning of the tree and Ivo's destiny.

Key grammar: Preterite and imperfect indicative: Unidad 1, págs. 1 a 15; RG 1, págs. 30 a 45; Present indicative, *ser/estar*, and reflexive verbs: Unidades 2 y 3, págs. 49 a 72 y 95 a 115; RG 2 y 3, págs. 73 a 94 y 116 a 132

Key vocabulary: buildings, personal descriptions, school environment, body, weather, natural environments

Estimated time needed: 500 minutes (10 classes maximum traditional schedule, 5 classes maximum block)

Antes de leer

A. Para discutir en clase
Approach: In small groups or pairs, have students collaborate to describe the picture and answer the questions, noting key vocabulary. Then have the class tell the story and create a vocabulary list to which they can refer throughout the chapter.

Expansion: (1) Students create an illustration of a fairy tale or legend with elements of magic or mystery. If the story is well known, students may collaborate in the retelling of the story based on the illustration. If not, the student artist retells the story. (2) Students create an illustration of a fairy tale and share it with their classmates. (3) Students identify elements frequently found in fairy tales, fables, and fantasy. Which do they find unappealing? Unsettling?

B. Fascinación
Expansion: Students identify and share a specific event or situation that especially illustrates the charisma or mystery of the fascinating person.

C. Una selección
Approach: This individual activity requires each student to select which vocabulary in the selection creates the atmosphere and sensation. Students then share with a partner, small group, and the class to answer the question in preparation for reading.

Alternative: Prepare a copy or transparency of the short selection. As you read the selection aloud, students identify words and phrases that create atmosphere by writing them on their own paper or by pointing them out to a student who writes them on the transparency. The class then prepares a statement about the mood of the selection.

Expansion: Students create word-definition pairs to clarify unfamiliar vocabulary from this selection.

D. Una conversación
Expansion: Without looking ahead to the story, in groups, students brainstorm what might be the plot of the story. Students share with the class and at the end of the story go back and compare their anticipated ending with the actual ending. Students defend their stories / endings.

Al leer

Approach: Draw students' attention to these advance organizers, helping them to identify the vocabulary, verb forms, and themes that they are likely to encounter. Review the concept of the blending of reality with fantasy in the lives of children.

Lectura

Approach: You may have students read the story in a group and then reread the story at home. The class may also read along as parts of the story are read aloud, with students providing the voices of the narrator and characters.

Comprensión

A. La sucesión de los eventos
Approach: Have students work in groups to organize the sentences in sequential order. Assign each group to narrate a certain part of the story for the class.

B. Comprensión general
Approach: Have students jot down ideas about their understanding of the story and then share their ideas with the class.

Alternative: In small groups or pairs, students make a list of adjectives that describe the children and their surroundings. Have students defend their opinions about the relationship between the children in the story with the direct information from the reading.

Expansion: Students prepare for Activity G by writing down questions as they read.

C. Definiciones
Alternative: Have one group of students do this activity and then provide it as a "quiz" for the rest of the class. The group then teaches or clarifies for classmates any vocabulary with which they had difficulty. (Note that other groups should be formed to provide similar challenge and training for Activities D and E.)

Expansion: Students create additional definitions based on the vocabulary questions they wrote as they were reading. (If you approach this activity in the Alternative mode, students could also share these new definitions with their classmates.)

D. Antónimos

Alternative: Have one group of students do this activity and then provide it as a "quiz" for the rest of the class. The group then teaches or clarifies for classmates any vocabulary with which they had difficulty. (Note that other groups should be formed to provide similar challenge and training for Activity E.)

Expansion: (1) Have students identify the part of speech of each word and note how knowing the part of speech helps in determining the meanings of words. (2) Have students choose additional words from the story and provide their own equivalents to challenge their classmates. (If you approach this activity in the Alternative mode, students could also share these two Expansions with their classmates.)

E. Sinónimos

Alternative: Have one group of students do this activity and then, after having classmates review the context of each word, provide their synonyms as a matching "quiz" for the rest of the class. How well were classmates able to find synonyms? After the "quiz," the class should collaborate to come up with the most accurate synonym for each word. (Note that other groups should be formed to provide similar challenge and training for Activities B, C, and D.)

F. Expresiones

Expansion: Using the same format, students write original sentences and / or matching activities to be used as student-generated practice / assessment.

G. Al punto

Expansion: Students create multiple-choice items that clarify additional aspects of the story.

H. Ahora te toca a ti

Approach: Assign the bulleted list of themes—or themes created by students—to different pairs or groups. Have the groups ask the class or other groups their questions to determine the questions' effectiveness and to reinforce comprehension. This approach shifts the burden of asking questions from you to the students, who often generate challenging questions.

Un paso más

Approach: Remind students to refer to the *Vocabulario útil para conversar y para escribir* list and to the Appendix on pp. 404–406 to help them with the speaking and writing activities.

Para conversar

Approach to this section: Students may express preferences about topics that interest them in this section. Based on their interests and skill levels, <u>you may wish to address only one or several of the activities or you may wish to divide the activities according to interest and have each group present its work to the class,</u> inviting reactions and responses.

A. El (La) favorito(a)
Alternative: Students demonstrate the situation and their reactions in skits.

B. La niñez
Approach: (1) As a point of departure, use the suggested vocabulary list to generate class discussion related to ideal childhood experiences. (2) In small groups or pairs, students continue their discussion on childhood experiences and relate their personal experiences. Students share these experiences with the class, adding vocabulary to the existing list.

C. Una persona especial
Approach: In small groups or pairs, students write a vocabulary list representative of Ivo's personality. This list will help in answering the questions. Students share their answers to the questions and justify them using examples from the reading.

D. ¡No veo nada!
Expansion: In pairs, students write possible dialogs and present them to the class as skits or in a video format.

E. Mi secreto and F. Mi fantasía
Expansion: If students have created an illustration for Activity A Expansion 2 under *Antes de leer,* it may be revisited at this point and / or embellished or extended. If they have not yet done so, students can create a drawn or painted object or place (for *Mi secreto*) or an illustrated plot or puppet show (for *Mi fantasía*). The product or performance leads to a conversation enriched by shared images.

Para escribir

Approach to this section: The activities in this section build students' writing skills incrementally, from summary to personal reaction to creation. Students will need time to express themselves and to share their writing with classmates and with the teacher. Students may express preferences about topics that interest them in this section. Based on their interests and skill levels, <u>you may wish to address only one or several of the activities or you may wish to divide the activities according to interest and have each group present its work to the class,</u> inviting reactions and responses.

A. Un resumen
Approach: Before writing a summary of the story, students write a list of adjectives, nouns, and verbs that are representative of the actions and events in the story. Groups share their lists with the class. Create a master list using the board or a transparency.

B. El mundo que crea Ana María Matute and **C. El final**

Expansion: Students research the life, themes, and influences of Ana María Matute. Encourage students to find other similar themes by the author and to share their findings with the class. Students incorporate this information into their writing.

D. Otro punto de vista

Alternative: In small groups, students write paragraphs explaining the plot of the story from three different perspectives. Students share their paragraphs with the class, inviting reactions before individual assignments are done.

E. Otro final

Expansion: Using the different perspectives discussed in *Otro punto de vista,* students write and illustrate other possible endings to the story. Students share their endings with the class; visuals can be placed around the room for students' reactions.

F. La reseña

Expansion: Make copies of the diagram for students. In groups, students prepare their diagrams, and then share them with the class. Guide students in their writing by using concrete examples from the diagrams.

G. Las fantasías

Approach: Call students' attention to previous class discussions regarding positive and negative aspects of "fantasy" as part of growing up (Activities E and F under *Para conversar*). Students express personal opinions regarding "fantasy" following the suggested outline format.

Comprensión auditiva

Approach: Have students look over the options for each selection carefully before they begin to listen. Check that they are comfortable with both the meaning and pronunciation of the vocabulary. If students do not understand words / phrases, provide Spanish explanations, but avoid English translations. Have students identify key words so that they can predict the topic, vocabulary, and structures that they are likely to hear. Careful preparation, combined with a willingness to use intuition and an understanding of contexts, will ensure that students need to listen only once to understand each passage.

Go Online

Approach: Have students visit the *Abriendo paso: Lectura* Web site at www.PHSchool.com for activities and links related to the content of the chapter.

Capítulo 10
Jaque mate en dos jugadas

Selection: short story by Isaac Aisemberg (Argentina)

In this quintessential murder mystery, the chess game not only rests on the table of the authoritarian uncle's library but also reflects the deadly plots of the dangerously frustrated nephews. The nephew who narrates this story believes that he has committed the perfect murder, triumphing over his uncle and inheriting his wealth. Instead, he finds that he has maneuvered himself into a checkmate. *"Yo lo envenené. En dos horas quedaría liberado. Dejé a mi tío Néstor a las veintidós. Lo hice con alegría. Me ardían las mejillas. Me quemaban los labios".*

Themes: murder, treachery, family violence, desire, detective work, guilt

Difficulty level: moderate to high. The plot is exciting. Sentence structure details add complexity and depth to the plot and give the selection a richness of psychological detail that both challenges and stimulates students. Students are asked to reflect on writing techniques and on violence in society.

Key grammar: Preterite and imperfect indicative: Unidad 1, págs. 1 a 15; RG 1, págs. 30 a 45; Future: Unidad 5, págs. 174 a 181; RG 5, págs. 203 a 205; Conditional: Unidad 6, págs. 220 a 227; RG 6, págs. 233 a 236; Reflexive verbs: Unidad 3, págs. 109 a 115; RG 3, págs. 130 a 132; Interrogatives and exclamations: Paso 5, págs. 285 a 290

Key vocabulary: body, daily routine, health, home, city, time, weapons, chess

Estimated time needed: 400 minutes (8 classes maximum traditional schedule, 4 classes maximum block)

Antes de leer

A. Para discutir en clase
Approach: In small groups or pairs, have students collaborate to describe the pictures and answer the questions, noting key vocabulary. Students can then share their stories and responses with the class. Next, the class can re-create the story as students present various aspects of the pictures and create a vocabulary list to which they can refer throughout the chapter.

Expansion: (1) Identify students who know about or play chess. How is it played? Why would this game of strategy play such a prominent role in a murder mystery? (2) Students create pictures based on crime stories they have read in novels or heard about in real life. Note that the emphasis of the chapter and its activities is not the details of the crime per se but its setting, solution, and the destiny of the criminal.

Note about chess: "Checkmate" *(Jaque mate)* refers to the triumphant declaration of the imminent winner of a match that the opponent's most important playing piece, the king, is irretrievably captured. The term comes from the Arabic *shah mat* (the king is dead), making the title of this piece suggestive of both strategy and murder.

B. Los problemas de la familia de hoy

Expansion: Students share stories of family reconciliation and the techniques that led to the reconciliation, either from the news or from their friends' experiences. (Discussions about domestic violence should be avoided as they do not serve the purpose of the activity and may be distressing to students.)

C. Cognados

Expansion: For the underlined words in the story, students note synonyms or equivalent phrases in Spanish instead of using English translations.

D. En contexto

Expansion: Instruct students to look for cognates in the underlined words or simply to try to guess within the context of the story what the words mean.

E. El comportamiento de un criminal

Alternative: Before attempting to do the activity, have students recall characters from literary works or movies that they might be familiar with. They can identify some of their characteristics before and after the crime(s).

F. Unas citas

Expansion: Students reflect on a tense or uncomfortable situation at home, school, work, etc. What images does this situation evoke? What adjectives describe the scene or the people involved? What similes or metaphors could help an outsider understand what the situation feels like?

Al leer

Approach: Draw students' attention to these advance organizers, helping them to identify some of the vocabulary and themes that they are likely to encounter. Remind them, too, of a murder mystery's reliance on details, hints, and psychological insights to tell a believable and compelling story.

Lectura

Approach: You may wish to poll students before deciding on the first reading of the story. Do they enjoy murder mysteries? If they have read some, do they enjoy curling up with the story and letting the images run around in their heads? Conversely, do they enjoy telling each exciting detail to friends as the plot unfolds? Students' reactions may help you decide whether to start with a whole class or an individual reading. Either way, however, students enjoy hearing parts of the story read aloud, with the characters coming alive through the dialogue and Claudio's provocative reflections on his deadly deed.

Comprensión

A. ¿Cierta o falsa?

Expansion: Students support their answers to this true / false activity with direct quotes from the reading, followed by their own interpretations.

B. Comprensión general

Approach: Have students jot down ideas about their understanding of the story and share their ideas with the class.

Expansion: Students prepare for Activity F by writing down questions as they read. Especially effective are questions dealing with identifying and describing people, discerning murderer's motives and methods, and noting the psychological and physiological effects of guilt. Challenge students to read with the eye and heart of a police detective.

C. En contexto, D. De la misma familia, and E. Prefijos

Approach: For each, have students write their own equivalents and meanings as individuals or in pairs and then share as a class as one student records them on the board or on a transparency. Train the students in alternative ways to talk about the vocabulary. Help them identify which word or phrase best matches the word provided and why.

Alternative: Assign these word-study activities to different groups and have each group instruct the rest of the class on its particular word study.

F. Al punto

Expansion: Students create multiple-choice items that clarify additional aspects of the story.

G. Ahora te toca a ti

Alternative: Once students have prepared their questions and directed them to their partners or to small groups, have selected questions directed to the class or to other groups to determine the questions' effectiveness and to reinforce comprehension.

Expansion: (1) Students pair up as detectives reviewing the details of this murder and check each other's observations and conclusions by referring to their questions and notes from Activity A Expansion under *Antes de leer*. (2) Students create the first part of a police report by writing out the details of the people, motives, methods, and brilliant police work that quickly cracked this major murder case.

Un paso más

Approach: Remind students to refer to the *Vocabulario útil para conversar y para escribir* list and to the Appendix on pp. 404–406 to help them with the speaking and writing activities.

Para conversar

Approach to this section: Students may express preferences about topics that interest them in this section. Based on their interests and skill levels, <u>you may wish to address only one or several of the activities or you may wish to divide the activities according to interest and have each group present its work to the class,</u> inviting reactions and responses.

A. Dilemas

Alternative: Students address these points in a skit, taking the role of a counselor to the nephew.

B. El ultimátum

Alternative: In groups of two, students prepare a possible dialogue between Guillermo and Matilde. Students present their dialogues to the class in the form of skits.

C. Reportaje sobre un crimen

Alternative: The student reporter works with the local TV station. The reporter is "on the spot" with interview questions and a summary of the breaking story.

Expansion: The evening news program on the local TV station presents the story of the murder. Some parts of the program may include (1) the news anchor's summary, (2) the on-the-scene reporter, (3) the interview in the studio with the chief of police, and (4) the station manager's or a concerned citizen's editorial on what kind of statement this murder makes about society.

D. Una conversación interesante

Expansion: Assuming that the uncle did not die from poisoning, students write a scenario that includes the uncle, Guillermo, and Claudio. Ask students to reflect on how this situation will change the ending of the story. Students present their scenarios to the class.

E. "Estos jóvenes de hoy..."

Expansion: Students reflect and comment on the following: Why do some adults think that young people don't read enough or get pleasure and satisfaction from reading? Which changes in our society / culture have affected the amount of time available for young people to read for enjoyment?

F. El juicio

Approach: In preparation for the trial, students write sketches of the assigned characters, incorporating the characteristics presented in the story. Students will have to use their imagination to fill any gaps relevant to the sequence of events in the story. You might want to videotape the activity so that students can later critique their ability to capture the true authenticity of each character.

G. Un debate

Alternative: Students work with a more traditional debate format. Select two pairs or small groups to debate for and against the argument; the rest of the class is the audience. Provide clear guidelines for number of argument points to be made by the two sides, examples to back up opinions, and time limits to present points. The rest of the class observes and notes which side's arguments were best presented and supported. After separating a debate format from the expression of personal opinion, class discussion can then follow on students' feelings about the issues presented.

Para escribir

Approach to this section: The activities in this section build students' writing skills incrementally, from summary to personal reaction to creation. Students will need time to express themselves and to share their writing with classmates and with the teacher. Students may express preferences about topics that interest them in this section. Based on their interests and skill levels, <u>you may wish to address only one or several of the</u> <u>activities or you may wish to divide the activities according to interest and have each</u> <u>group present its work to the class,</u> inviting reactions and responses.

A. Un resumen

Expansion: Encourage students to write a summary of the story using all of the elements of suspense without revealing the ending. If students are not familiar with this technique, this might be a good time to introduce it.

B. Mi opinión

Approach: Students use answers to the questions provided to express their personal opinions about the story and to react to each character's actions / behavior throughout the story.

C. Otro punto de vista

Alternative: Students react to the strategy used in chess. Refer to Activity A Expansion 1 under *Antes de leer* and comment on the effectiveness of the character who narrates the story. Students also reflect on how appropriate the title would be, if the narrator had been the uncle or Guillermo.

D. El futuro de los sobrinos

Expansion: Allow students to show their creativity by presenting the activity in the form of a skit.

E. Opinión

Expansion: (1) Students identify additional themes of importance to society about which to write a letter to the editor. (2) Students present in written form the editorial that they had presented on the news program in Activity C Expansion 4 under *Para conversar*.

F. Composición

Alternative: Allow students to do Internet research on the death penalty in your state so that they can form educated opinions on the topic before they start writing. Students should refer to these findings as they write their essays.

Comprensión auditiva

Approach: Have students look over the options for each selection carefully before they begin to listen. Check that they are comfortable with both the meaning and pronunciation of the vocabulary. If students do not understand words / phrases, provide Spanish explanations, but avoid English translations. Have students identify key words so that they can predict the topic, vocabulary, and structures that they are likely to hear. Careful preparation, combined with a willingness to use intuition and an understanding of contexts, will ensure that students need to listen only once to understand each passage.

Go Online

Approach: Have students visit the *Abriendo paso: Lectura* Web site at www.PHSchool.com for activities and links related to the content of the chapter.

Capítulo 11
La viuda de Montiel

Selection: short story by Gabriel García Márquez (Colombia)

A tyrannical, unscrupulous, and violent man dies. His widow, cut off by her husband from the world and from knowledge of his work and deeds, is the only person who mourns him. From the perspective of this isolated woman, readers learn the history of Montiel, observe the reactions of people he mistreated, and accompany the widow down the path of loneliness and loss. *"Cuando murió don José Montiel, todo el mundo se sintió vengado, menos su viuda; pero se necesitaron varias horas para que todo el mundo creyera que en verdad había muerto".*

Themes: death, ambition, political and economic power, leadership, dictatorship, political violence, irony, superstition

Difficulty level: moderate to high. The surrealism of Márquez's writing is evident in the interaction of the widow with her surroundings and the passages that reflect, seemingly from very far away, the lives and sufferings of countless other people whom we never meet. Students will be challenged, if not intrigued, by Márquez's style as well as the activities that ask them to reflect on his weighty themes, such as politics, irony, and violence.

Key grammar: Preterite, imperfect, and pluperfect indicative: Unidad 1, págs. 1 a 29; RG 1, págs. 30 a 48; Imperfect and pluperfect subjunctive: Unidad 6, págs. 207 a 219; RG 6, págs. 228 a 233; Imperative: Unidad 4, págs. 133 a 140; RG 4, págs. 154 a 165; Adjectives: Unidad 2, págs. 49 a 72; RG 2, págs. 73 a 94; *Por/Para*: Paso 10, págs. 309 a 311; Idiomatic expressions: Apendix F, págs. 384 a 388

Key vocabulary: city, home, politics, body, household objects, emotions, character, personal description

Estimated time needed: 450 minutes (9 classes maximum traditional schedule, 5 classes maximum block)

Antes de leer

A. Para discutir en clase
Approach: In small groups or pairs, have students collaborate to describe the picture and answer the questions, noting key vocabulary. Students can then share their responses to the questions with the rest of the class. Next, the class can narrate the story and create a vocabulary list to which they can refer throughout the chapter.

Expansion: Students can create illustrations of mourning, which they narrate. The student artists may also show their pictures to the class and ask other students to reconstruct the story as accurately as possible.

B. Nuestra experiencia
Alternative: Students address items one, two, and three as one general concept with three focal points for expressing a clear, fact-supported position.

Expansion: (1) Students address the first three items in the form of a debate about the role of money and success in our society. Questions to consider may include the following: How much striving for success and gain is too much? How can we tell? Which behaviors merit praise and which ones merit punishment? What type of punishment is most beneficial to society? Divide the class into a pair or small group with one opinion about those who strive for riches and success, a second group with a divergent view, and the rest of the class as the audience. Provide clear guidelines for number of argument points to be made by the two sides, examples to back up their opinions, and time limits to present points. The rest of the class observes and notes which side's arguments were best presented and supported. After separating a debate format from the expression of personal opinion, class discussion can then follow on students' feelings about the issues presented. (2) Students share stories of ironic experiences in their lives in the form of skits.

C. Situaciones irónicas
Expansion: Students prepare skits in which the opening scenario leads to an ironic conclusion.

D. Mi experiencia
Expansion: Make different categories so that students can focus on remembering ironic situations related to family, friends, sports, vacations, school, etc. Students share these situations with the class, inviting comments and reactions.

E. Líderes corruptos
Approach: Students benefit from preparing together beforehand a chart-like summary of the characteristics of dictators and military rulers. Questions that can help students generate categories include the following: What types of actions do such leaders commonly take? How do they treat the common people, and how do they treat their favorites or loyalists? What life-style do they tend to have? What types of situations bring such rulers into power, and what types keep them from power? Students can begin with dictators and military leaders from any country or culture and then turn the focus to Latin American figures. Having such a chart will allow students to do focused, rapid research on as many people and / or countries as your time allows.

F. Una selección
Expansion: Students create a class picture of Montiel based on the description in this paragraph. Students may wish to illustrate Montiel as he was in life, as he appeared in his casket, or both, in order to compare the images as Márquez does in his writing. Students can refer to this illustration after they have read the story, commenting when they do so on the relative accuracy of their portrayal based on this single paragraph. What does the accuracy of their illustration say about the descriptive skill of the author?

Al leer

Approach: Draw students' attention to these advance organizers, helping them to identify some of the vocabulary that they are likely to encounter in a story involving political upheaval and violence. Direct students, too, to jot down questions for Márquez as they read. The questions can be for students to understand the plot and its references better or to follow a new thought based on what has been read. In doing so, students will be prepared for Activity G under *Comprensión*.

Lectura

Approach: Students may find that reading this selection in small groups with pauses to ask questions of each other in Spanish and clarify points will help them to understand both the words and the intimate feel of this piece. After reading it with classmates, students should reread the piece individually.

Comprensión

A. ¿Cierta o falsa?

Expansion: Students support their answers to this true / false activity with direct quotes from the reading, followed by their own interpretations.

B. Comprensión general

Approach: Have students jot down ideas about their understanding of the story and share their ideas with the class.

C. Antónimos, D. Sinónimos, E. Definiciones, and F. En contexto

Alternative: Divide these word-study activities among groups, who then instruct the rest of the class and lead a discussion about the words and their meanings.

F. En contexto

Approach: Have students write their own phrases or word equivalents and then share them with the class as one records them on the board or on a transparency. Train students in alternative ways to talk about the vocabulary. Help them identify which word or phrase best matches the word provided and why.

Expansion: Have students identify the part of speech of each word and note how knowing the part of speech helps in determining the meanings of words. Students may choose additional words from the story and provide their own equivalents to challenge their classmates.

G. Al punto

Expansion: Students create multiple-choice items that clarify additional aspects of the story.

H. Ahora te toca a ti

Approach: Once students have prepared their questions and directed them to their partners or to small groups, have selected questions directed to the class or to other groups to determine the questions' effectiveness and to reinforce comprehension.

Alternative: Use questions generated for the activities under *Al leer.*

Un paso más

Approach: Remind students to refer to the *Vocabulario útil para conversar y para escribir* list and to the Appendix on pp. 404–406 to help them with the speaking and writing activities.

Para conversar

Approach to this section: Students may express preferences about topics that interest them in this section. Based on their interests and skill levels, <u>you may wish to address only one or several of the activities or you may wish to divide the activities according to interest and have each group present its work to the class,</u> inviting reactions and responses.

A. Reflexiones

Expansion: Students bring the widow out of her anonymity. They create a portrait of the widow or a montage of scenes of her life and thoughts. One or more students tell her story, referring to the illustration(s) as they present her to the class.

B. Consejos and C. Los hijos

Expansion: In groups, students role-play the situations and present them to the class in the form of skits.

D. Una entrevista

Expansion: Students do Internet research on the socioeconomic situation in Colombia during the time of the story. Using information obtained from their research, students role-play the parts of the children in the story.

E. La superstición

Expansion: Students talk to friends and family members about superstitions they or others may have. They present a skit demonstrating the superstition and the results of acting on the superstition.

F. En acción

Approach: Taking into account Montiel's character, power, and violence, students discuss possible strategies that the townspeople might have taken to overcome this man's unscrupulous actions. Students present strategies in the form of skits, taking into account Montiel's reaction to the townspeople's actions.

G. Tu opinión

Expansion: Students refer to the results of their Internet research about the socioeconomic situation in Colombia to address the issues covered in the story. Students compare Colombia's situation with that in the United States and hypothesize about how likely / unlikely it might be for this situation to exist in the United States.

H. La civilización

Expansion: Students discuss those aspects of people's character and actions that create, support, or destroy civilization. Montiel's adult offspring are living in what they describe as civilization: Are they people who support or undermine civilization as they or the students have defined it? What responsibilities do individuals have toward civilized society?

Para escribir

Approach to this section: The activities in this section build students' writing skills incrementally, from summary to personal reaction to creation. Students will need time to express themselves and to share their writing with classmates and with the teacher. Students may express preferences about topics that interest them in this section. Based on their interests and skill levels, <u>you may wish to address only one or several of the activities or you may wish to divide the activities according to interest and have each group present its work to the class,</u> inviting reactions and responses.

A. Un resumen
Approach: In small groups or pairs, students prepare a list of words that are representative of all of the actions that transpired in the story. Students can refer to previous vocabulary lists used in the chapter (Activities C, D, E, and F under *Comprensión*). Students share their lists with the class. A master list should be compiled using the board or a transparency so that students have a common starting point for their summaries of the story.

B. Un párrafo
Expansion: The class creates (or chooses) a paragraph describing Montiel or the widow and attaches it to the appropriate illustration developed in Activity F under *Antes de leer*.

C. Opinión
Expansion: Students write a paragraph or more on the isolation of someone they know personally or whose story of isolation they have heard from other sources. Afterwards, they may wish to share the story with the class and / or compare the person's experience with that of the widow.

D. Una carta
Approach: Students write a letter to the widow from the point of view of one of the sons. Remind students of the feelings expressed throughout the story. This is a good time to assess not only the vocabulary related to feelings and emotions but also the present and pluperfect subjunctive tenses.

E. El poder corrompe
Alternative: Students make a list of historical figures whose values, morals, philosophy, etc., changed once they became public figures. Students might want to ask their history teachers to help them compile the list. Students do Internet research on a given public figure. Students then report their findings to the class using pictures and a brief summary, which will be posted in the classroom for enrichment.

 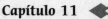

Comprensión auditiva

Approach: Have students look over the options for each selection carefully before they begin to listen. Check that they are comfortable with both the meaning and pronunciation of the vocabulary. If students do not understand words / phrases, provide Spanish explanations, but avoid English translations. Have students identify key words so that they can predict the topic, vocabulary, and structures that they are likely to hear. Careful preparation, combined with a willingness to use intuition and an understanding of contexts, will ensure that students need to listen only once to understand each passage.

Go Online

Approach: Have students visit the *Abriendo paso: Lectura* Web site at www.PHSchool.com for activities and links related to the content of the chapter.

Capítulo 12
Cartas de amor traicionado

Selection: short story by Isabel Allende (Peru - Chile)

Analía, the protagonist, is a young woman whose mother died during childbirth and whose father took his own life shortly after his wife's death. At a very young age, her uncle, who is in charge of her estate and her education, sends her away to a boarding school at a convent. During the 12 years that Analía lived at the convent, her uncle only visited her once, on her sixteenth birthday. On that day, he suggested that she honor the memory of her deceased parents by becoming a nun. Because of her negative reaction to this suggestion, her uncle decides to arrange a marriage between Analía and his son Luis to keep her money in the family. After two years of corresponding through letters, Analía and Luis finally get married. Analía immediately regrets marrying Luis, and even the birth of their son does not improve their loveless marriage, which ends abruptly with Luis's accidental death after being thrown from a horse. The surprise ending, in which it is revealed that Luis's best friend was the author of the love letters Analía received for so many years, will capture students' attention. *"El mismo día de mi matrimonio descubrí que mi marido no podía haberlas escrito y cuando mi hijo trajo a la casa sus primeras notas, reconocí la caligrafía. Y ahora que estoy mirando no me cabe ni la menor duda, porque yo a usted lo he visto en sueños desde que tengo dieciséis años…"*

Themes: feelings of betrayal, life at a boarding school, traditional roles of women

Difficulty level: moderate. The story is compelling and easy to understand. The themes, concepts, story twists, and surprises engage students and inspire lively discussions.

Key grammar: Preterite and imperfect indicative: Unidad 1, págs. 1 a 15; RG 1, págs. 30 a 45; Future: Unidad 5, págs. 174 a 181; RG 5, págs. 203 a 205; Imperfect subjunctive: Unidad 6, págs. 211 a 214; RG 6, págs. 228 a 231; Adjectives: Unidad 2, págs. 49 a 72; RG 2, págs. 73 a 94

Key vocabulary: emotions, feelings, expressing personal opinions

Estimated time needed: 450 minutes (9 classes maximum traditional schedule, 5 classes maximum block)

Antes de leer

A. Para discutir en clase
Approach: In small groups or pairs, have students collaborate to describe the picture and tell the story, noting key vocabulary. Students can share their stories with the class, adding more vocabulary words to the list already provided. Students can refer to this list throughout the chapter.

B. Nuestra experiencia
Expansion: Students share experiences or ideas about boarding schools. Explore positive and negative aspects of boarding schools, socially and academically. Also, bring in the short story series *Madeline,* which deals with the adventures and misadventures of a girl in a boarding school in France. Students will enjoy it.

 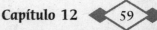

C. La correspondencia

Expansion: Students share experiences related to having a pen pal. If the majority of the class has never had one, it may be the perfect opportunity to start a pen-pal project. It could be with another Spanish class within the school, another local school, or even a school in another state. Try keypals.com as well.

D. Una selección and E. Otra selección

Approach: The emphasis at this point is on students becoming familiar with the author's thesis and the ways in which the author explores her ideas. Help students prepare to read the selection with an open mind and an acceptance of different reasons for courtship. Have students share their answers to the questions with the class.

Alternative: Have students read the questions at the end of the selection as a pre-reading activity to help them continue to focus on Analía's feelings toward Luis and the uncle's true motives for wanting the relationship to continue.

Expansion: In small groups or pairs, have students write a paragraph anticipating why Analía was so disappointed when she first saw Luis. Students share their paragraphs with the class. Revisit this activity at the end of the selection and compare students' responses with what actually happens in the story.

F. Predicciones

Alternative: In small groups or pairs, students anticipate actions / feelings that they expect to encounter in the story and share their predictions with the class. Question 4 is very important. Have students focus on the title "Cartas de amor traicionado" as foreshadowing Analía and Luis's relationship.

Al leer

Approach: Draw students' attention to these advance organizers, helping them to identify more of the vocabulary related to feelings of betrayal, loneliness, and determination that they are likely to encounter in the story.

Lectura

Approach: You may have students read the story in a group and then reread it at home.

Comprensión

A. ¿Cierta o falsa?

Expansion: Students support their answers to this true / false activity with direct quotes from the reading, followed by their own interpretations.

B. Comprensión general

Approach: Have students jot down ideas about their understanding of the story and then share their ideas with the class.

Expansion: Students prepare for Activity G by writing down questions as they read.

C. De la misma familia

Expansion: After students identify one word from the same family, ask for additional words. Note which part of speech each word is, and use the categories to help generate additional vocabulary.

D. Antónimos

Expansion: Students identify additional words from the story and provide their own equivalents. Students then prepare a matching activity as an additional challenge for their classmates.

E. En contexto

Approach: Have students write their own phrases or word equivalents and then share them with the class as one records them on the board or on a transparency. Train students in alternative ways to talk about the vocabulary. Help them identify which word or phrase best matches the word provided and why.

Expansion: Have students identify the part of speech of each word and note how knowing the part of speech helps in determining the meanings of words. Students may choose additional words from the story and provide their own equivalents to challenge their classmates.

F. Al punto

Expansion: (1) Students work in small groups or pairs to help each other identify key words and phrases from the story that point to the correct choice for each item. (2) Students create multiple-choice items that clarify additional aspects of the story.

G. Ahora te toca a ti

Alternative: Once students have prepared their questions and directed them to their partners or to small groups, have selected questions directed to the class or to other groups to determine the questions' effectiveness and to reinforce comprehension. Students may have additional questions from Activity B Expansion.

Un paso más

Approach: Remind students to refer to the *Vocabulario útil para conversar y para escribir* list and to the Appendix on pp. 404–406 to help them with the speaking and writing activities.

Para conversar

Approach to this section: Students may express preferences about topics that interest them in this section. Based on their interests and skill levels, <u>you may wish to address only one or several of the activities or you may wish to divide the activities according to interest and have each group present its work to the class,</u> inviting reactions and responses.

A. Las apariencias

Expansion: Students create their own opinions about whether Analía's views of Luis were accurate or not. Which examples from literature, films, and personal experiences do they have to support their answers? A class discussion should follow about students' opinions on this subject.

B. El papel de la mujer

Expansion: Students express opinions about the role of women in today's society and how their role has changed throughout history. Students can cite examples from history, the media, or other sources. Students can also do Internet research on different stereotypes associated with women or provide some that they have heard.

C. El brillo del espíritu

Expansion: Students write a list of words representative of the idea that "external beauty fades and internal beauty is everlasting." Students then compare their lists. Does the external beauty of objects also fade? Students can also reflect on personal experiences. Have they had boyfriends or girlfriends in the past? Did other people think they were beautiful or handsome? Why or why not?

D. Una conversación

Expansion: Students act out a positive skit between Luis and Analía before Luis's death, in which she tells him that she knows his best friend has written the letters. Students can incorporate *el maestro* as a third person in the skit. Students should present their skits to the class.

E. ¿Cómo piensa Analía?

Approach: Students explore the role that good friends have in one's life: how this role changes as people grow and mature and the importance of having friends. Students should then compare this experience with Analía's, taking into consideration how living in a convent for 12 years without any close friends changed her life and made her who she is.

Para escribir

Approach to this section: The activities in this section build students' writing skills incrementally, from summary to personal reaction to creation. Students will need time to express themselves and to share their writing with classmates and with the teacher. Students may express preferences about topics that interest them in this section. Based on their interests and skill levels, <u>you may wish to address only one or several of the activities or you may wish to divide the activities according to interest and have each group present its work to the class,</u> inviting reactions and responses.

A. Lo que yo cambiaría

Alternative: Students are asked to reflect on the sequence of events in the story. They then change one of the major events and write about how the change would have affected the story.

B. Las opciones de Analía

Approach: In groups, students reflect on the importance of honesty in everyday life. Students share their ideas, opinions, and examples with the class, inviting reactions and responses before starting to write about how Analía and Luis might have benefited from honesty and communication.

C. La puesta del sol

Expansion: Explore the use of metaphors in literature and the use of one in the phrase *la puesta del sol*. Ask students to refer to the ending of the story and how it really is not an ending, since "there will always be a tomorrow." Students reflect and write about what the future might hold for Analía.

D. ¿Mujer fuerte o no?

Alternative: Before identifying whether Analía has a strong or weak character, have students compose a list of adjectives typical of each personal characteristic. You might prepare a transparency for this activity and then copy it for students to use as a reference. Students share their personal opinions about Analía's character with the class.

E. Una carta de amor

Approach: Students develop a slight twist in the sequence of events in the story. Some students role-play Luis and become authors of the love letters in which he confesses his true love to Analía. Other students role-play Analía and answer the letters. Students collaborate in writing a vocabulary list to be used for both letters. (If there are multiple sections of this class, letters could be exchanged between classes.)

Expansion: Students comment on possible changes to the story, if Luis had written the letters himself.

Comprensión auditiva

Approach: Have students look over the options for each selection carefully before they begin to listen. Check that they are comfortable with both the meaning and pronunciation of the vocabulary. If students do not understand words / phrases, provide Spanish explanations, but avoid English translations. Have students identify key words so that they can predict the topic, vocabulary, and structures that they are likely to hear. Careful preparation, combined with a willingness to use intuition and an understanding of contexts, will ensure that students need to listen only once to understand each passage.

Go Online

Approach: Have students visit the *Abriendo paso: Lectura* Web site at www.PHSchool.com for activities and links related to the content of the chapter.

Capítulo 13
Emma Zunz

Selection: short story by Jorge Luis Borges (Argentina)

When Emma Zunz learns of the death of her father, she plans and carries out swift vengeance on the man who ruined his life and career years before. Her revenge involves a shocking personal sacrifice that leads to the death and disgrace of her nemesis. *"Ante Aarón Loewenthal, más que la urgencia de vengar a su padre, Emma sintió la de castigar el ultraje padecido por ello. No podía no matarlo, después de esa minuciosa deshonra"*.

Themes: injustice, revenge, honor and dishonor, murder, reality and unreality, time, working conditions, good and bad reputations, personal dignity

Difficulty level: high. A series of fleeting, harsh images heightens the brutality and desperation in this masterfully crafted story. Swirling around these images are emotions and descriptions that both intensify and obscure the sense of time and the actions of people in the story. Students are challenged by the density and advanced vocabulary of this piece. They need time to decode the story and to appreciate the power of the author's artistry.

Key grammar: Preterite, imperfect, and pluperfect indicative: Unidad 1, págs. 1 a 29; RG 1, págs. 30 a 48; Imperfect subjunctive: Unidad 6, págs. 211 a 214; RG 6, págs. 228 a 231; Reflexive verbs: Unidad 3, págs. 109 a 115; RG 3, págs. 130 a 132; Relative pronouns: Paso 4, págs. 274 a 284; Object pronouns: Paso 3, págs. 263 a 273; Subject and prepositional pronouns: Paso 2, págs. 258 a 262

Key vocabulary: daily routine, emotions, business, adjectives of physical description and personality

Estimated time needed: 500 minutes (10 classes maximum traditional schedule, $5\frac{1}{2}$ classes maximum block)

Antes de leer

A. Para discutir en clase
Approach: In small groups or pairs, have students describe the picture and answer the questions, noting key vocabulary. Then students can share their descriptions and answers with the class and create a vocabulary list to which they can refer throughout the chapter.

Expansion: Students create pictures of their own that show one or more of the following themes: injustice, dishonor, revenge, slander, struggles for respect or proper treatment. A discussion should follow on the need of all people for justice and dignity and what happens to people emotionally and physically when they lose or give up those important aspects of their lives.

B. Nuestra experiencia
Approach: Begin with pair or small-group discussions of these themes; the class can then discuss and note common experiences and / or reactions with regard to threats to one's reputation.

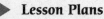

Expansion: The class develops a scenario in which a person is slandered or finds his or her reputation under attack. Individual students or groups then pick up at the point in the skit where the victim can choose how to react, each demonstrating a different approach to overcoming the insult to one's reputation.

C. La venganza y el perdón
Approach: The class discussion on this theme may well be blended with the discussion and / or skits from the preceding activity. Students may also discuss whether or not the revenge actually accomplishes the goal listed in the dictionary definition: Does revenge really repair the injury or harm one has suffered?

D. Una selección
Approach: Take time with this section. Students are asked questions that help to clarify the plot, and they will need the information to understand Emma's actions throughout the story. In addition, students are put on notice that they will encounter much new vocabulary and that Borges packs many emotion-laden images in a few sparse sentences. The factual nature of the questions will help students realize that they should feel comfortable asking straightforward questions that zero in on the hard reality underlying the intensely introspective narration. Follow up with the reading about the author so that students recognize that Borges's style is justifiably famous and admired worldwide.

Al leer

Approach: Draw students' attention to these advance organizers, helping them to identify more of the vocabulary that they are likely to encounter in a story involving a ruined reputation, vengeance, and a search to restore honor to one family while dishonoring another.

Lectura

Approach: Even if this selection is begun as at-home reading and then continued in class in small groups, students will benefit from multiple readings, each to uncover an aspect of the story and of the characters within.

Comprensión

A. ¿Cierta o falsa?
Expansion: Students support their answers to this true / false activity with direct quotes from the reading, followed by their own interpretations.

B. La sucesión de los eventos
Approach: Have students work in groups to organize the sentences in sequential order. Assign each group to narrate a certain part of the story for the class.

C. Comprensión general
Approach: Have students jot down ideas about their understanding of the story and share their ideas with the class.

 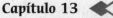

Expansion: As students answer these questions, additional ones of their own may surface. Have them jot these down for use in Activity I.

D. De la misma familia

Expansion: After students identify one word from the same family, ask for additional words. Note which part of speech each word is, and use the categories to help generate additional vocabulary.

E. Sinónimos and F. Antónimos

Expansion: Students identify additional words from the story and provide their own equivalents. Students then prepare a matching activity as an additional challenge for their classmates.

G. En contexto

Approach: Have students write their own phrases or word equivalents and then share them with the class as one records them on the board or on a transparency. Train students in alternative ways to talk about the vocabulary. Help them identify which word or phrase best matches the word provided and why.

Expansion: Have students identify the part of speech of each word and note how knowing the part of speech helps in determining the meanings of words. Students may choose additional words from the story and provide their own equivalents to challenge their classmates.

H. Al punto

Expansion: (1) Students work in small groups or pairs to help each other identify key words and phrases from the story that point to the correct choice for each item. (2) Students create multiple-choice items that clarify additional aspects of the story.

I. Ahora te toca a ti

Alternative: Once students have prepared their questions and directed them to their partners or to small groups, have selected questions directed to the class or to other groups to determine the questions' effectiveness and to reinforce comprehension. Students may have additional questions from Activity C Expansion.

Un paso más

Approach: Remind students to refer to the *Vocabulario útil para conversar y para escribir* list and to the Appendix on pp. 404–406 to help them with the speaking and writing activities.

Para conversar

Approach to this section: Students may express preferences about topics that interest them in this section. Based on their interests and skill levels, <u>you may wish to address only one or several of the activities or you may wish to divide the activities according to interest and have each group present its work to the class,</u> inviting reactions and responses.

Alternative and Expansion for these activities: Assign Activities C, D, E, and G to separate pairs or small groups. Have each accomplish the activity as presented but additionally use the information or product to prepare for a trial. First, the police question Emma at the scene *(La investigación)*. The police, unsure whether to believe her story or not, arrest Emma on suspicion of murder. Next, the tabloids latch on to the story and / or Elsa ends up on a talk show *(Los chismes)*, where the audience liberally expresses opinions about whether Emma murdered Loewenthal or not and, if she did, whether her actions were justified. In the meantime, lawyers for the defense and the prosecution prepare their cases *(¿Debe castigarse?)*. Finally, the trial is held, with the lawyers cross-examining the various characters to uncover all of the actions of the story *(Un programa de entrevistas)*. Does the jury (the observing classmates) convict or acquit Emma? Was this the perfect crime?

A. Una descripción
Alternative: Students illustrate the adjectives that describe Emma by sketching her in a scene or idea from the story. The illustration may be in single-panel or picture-sequence form.

B. ¿La única opción?
Alternative: Students demonstrate the options in the form of skits.

Expansion: Students refer to the discussion from Activity C under *Antes de leer:* Did Emma "solve" her problem through her pursuit of revenge? Why or why not?

C. ¿Debe castigarse? and D. Investigación
Alternative: Students express their feelings toward Emma in the form of skits or perhaps a trial where students decide whether "the end justifies the means." Students incorporate as many characters as possible into this activity, always keeping the plot in mind.

E. Los chismes
Alternative: Students describe the relationship between Elsa Urstein and Emma, hypothesizing about possible reasons why Emma did not confide totally in Elsa. Students generate possible descriptors for both characters, justifying circumstances that evolved throughout the story. Students role-play Emma and the reporter, keeping in mind the possible turn of events if Elsa had any information to reveal.

F. ¿Qué harías?
Expansion: Students refer to the personal scenarios in Activity B Expansion under *Antes de leer.* Do their proposed reactions to Emma's situation ring true to what they had said about their own actions in real, personal situations?

G. Un programa de entrevistas
Approach: In preparation for this activity, call students' attention to Activities A and B under *Comprensión.* The information learned can be incorporated into the questions asked for this activity. Students can work in small groups as an outside project and videotape this activity, later presenting it to the class as a review of the story.

Para escribir

Approach to this section: The activities in this section build students' writing skills incrementally, from summary to personal reaction to creation. Students will need time to express themselves and to share their writing with classmates and with the teacher. Students may express preferences about topics that interest them in this section. Based on their interests and skill levels, <u>you may wish to address only one or several of the activities or you may wish to divide the activities according to interest and have each group present its work to the class,</u> inviting reactions and responses.

A. Un reportaje
Alternative: If assigned to a pair or small group, this article could appear as part of the pre- or post-trial activities from the *Para conversar* section.

B. ¿Cómplice o no?
Alternative: One or more student pairs prepare a short skit in which Emma reveals her plan to Elsa, demonstrating her friend's possible reactions.

C. En defensa del honor
Alternative: A good time to discuss family values and loyalty. You might initiate the discussion before students begin to write with the phrase "an eye for an eye, a tooth for a tooth." Does the end justify the means? Would our society be different if every one took matters into their own hands when they related to family matters? Based on the class discussion, students reflect on the key question: Did Emma have the right to commit such a crime?

D. El crimen perfecto
Alternative: Students brainstorm titles of movies, books, TV programs, etc., that deal with the "perfect crime." What are the characteristics of the perfect crime? How are these characteristics applicable to the events in the story?

E. El perdón
Alternative: Student groups prepare twin skits on a situation, one with an ending in which a person exacted revenge for a wrong and the other with an ending in which the person forgave his / her wrongdoer. Which one did students feel was best for "solving" the victim's problem? Since revenge affects more people than just the victim and the perpetrator, which approach provides a resolution that is best for society as well as for the individuals involved?

F. La opinión del padre
Approach: Prior to writing the letter, students might discuss the following: (1) family honor, (2) her father's possible explanation of the series of events that led to the crime, (3) Emma's honor, and (4) Emma's future. After the discussion, students role-play the father in order to write a letter to Emma expressing his views about what she is about to do. Students share their letters with the class.

Comprensión auditiva

Approach: Have students look over the options for each selection carefully before
they begin to listen. Check that they are comfortable with both the meaning and
pronunciation of the vocabulary. If students do not understand words / phrases, provide
Spanish explanations, but avoid English translations. Have students identify key words
so that they can predict the topic, vocabulary, and structures that they are likely to hear.
Careful preparation, combined with a willingness to use intuition and an understanding
of contexts, will ensure that students need to listen only once to understand each
passage.

Go Online

Approach: Have students visit the *Abriendo paso: Lectura* Web site at
www.PHSchool.com for activities and links related to the content of the chapter.

Poesía
Capítulo 14
Rima LIII

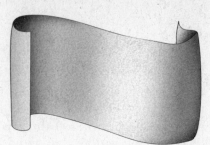

Selection: poem by Gustavo Adolfo Bécquer (Spain)

In this short *rima*, Bécquer uses numerous metaphors to express his feelings of despair. He laments the life that he once shared with his loved one: "*...aquéllas que aprendieron nuestros nombres ésas... ¡no volverán!*"

Difficulty level: low to moderate. The metaphors are easy to visualize. Students will have to be coached in reading / understanding poetry, with some discussion about feelings that are no longer reciprocated.

Key grammar: Future: Unidad 5, págs. 174 a 181; RG 5, págs. 203 a 205; Preterite and imperfect indicative: Unidad 1, págs. 1 a 15; RG 1, págs. 30 a 45

Key vocabulary: nature, feelings, and emotions

Estimated time needed: 200 minutes (4 classes maximum traditional schedule, 2 classes maximum block)

El autor

Approach: Have students read the short introduction about the author and themes that appear in his works. Then have students visit the *Abriendo paso: Lectura* Web site for additional information about the author and his works.

Antes de leer

Activity A.
Approach: In small groups or pairs, have students put the vocabulary in logical categories and create a visual (a drawing or a picture description). Students then share their categories and visuals with the class.

Activity B.
Approach: Students discuss feelings conveyed by the words in the poem and use the list from Activity A to help them create the feelings that they think were intended by the author.

Expansion: Students bring in pictures / paintings or create their own to share with the class as they defend their points.

Activity C.
Expansion: Once students are comfortable with reading the verses from the poem and using hyperbaton *(hipérbaton),* the technique of rearranging word order, have students write their own examples using hyperbaton and share them with the class.

Activity D.
Expansion: Have students illustrate the images presented in two columns: one that illustrates "what will return" and the other that illustrates "what will not return."

Lectura 🎧

Approach: Have students read the poem as they listen to the recorded version on the *Abriendo paso: Lectura* Teacher Audio CDs. Students will benefit from listening to the selection as they read silently. Ask students to read aloud after they have listened to the selection.

Comprensión

Approach: As students prepare to discuss the images and feelings in the poem, revisit Activities A and B under *Antes de leer,* where students have used visuals to illustrate what the author was trying to convey.

Alternative: In small groups or pairs, students discuss the tone and images used in the poem, referring to vocabulary that might help to identify whether it is positive or negative.

Expansion: Students look for other *Rimas* and compare their themes with this one.

Un paso más

Activity A.
Approach: As students prepare to write about the tone and the poet's attitude, have them revisit *Antes de leer* and *Comprensión*. Refer to the last verse of the poem, where the poet alludes to the kind of love that he had for his beloved and how no one will ever love her as he did. Students form their own opinions, supporting the theme with images from the *rima*.

Activity B.
Alternative: In small groups or pairs, students hypothesize about possible events that might have taken place before the author wrote these *rimas*. Students act out the scene using appropriate vocabulary. In small groups or pairs, students collaborate to prepare a vocabulary list.

Expansion: Students illustrate or bring in illustrations showing the meeting place and possible situations or events that led to the author's feeling of *desilusión* or *desesperanza*. Have students compile a vocabulary list that will be used to describe past and future feelings / events.

Go Online

Approach: If students have not already done so, have them visit the *Abriendo paso: Lectura* Web site at www.PHSchool.com for activities and links related to the content of the chapter.

Capítulo 15
Me gustas cuando callas

Selection: poem by Pablo Neruda (Chile, Nobel Prize 1971)

The poet's intense communication with his loved one is expressed even through silence: *"Me gustas cuando callas y estás como distante"*. No verbal communication is needed when two people are in love. Through silence the two souls communicate.

Difficulty level: low to moderate

Key grammar: Imperfect subjunctive: Unidad 6, págs. 211 a 214; RG 6, págs. 228 a 231; Adjectives: Unidad 2, págs. 49 a 72; RG 2, págs. 73 a 94; *Ser/Estar*: Unidad 3, págs. 98 a 107; RG 3, págs. 119 a 121

Key vocabulary: parts of the face, feelings, and emotions

Estimated time needed: 200 minutes (4 classes maximum traditional schedule, 2 classes maximum block)

El autor

Approach: Have students read the short introduction about the author and themes that appear in his works. Then have students visit the *Abriendo paso: Lectura* Web site for additional information about the author and his works.

Antes de leer

Activity A.
Approach: In small groups or pairs, students collaborate to make a list of reasons why Neruda chose this title for his poem. Students reflect on the themes presented under *El autor*. Students also reflect on how silence can sometimes convey many messages that do not need to be expressed with words. Students share with the class their lists of possible reasons why the author chose this title for the poem. Creating a master list will provide students with additional vocabulary to use throughout the chapter.

Activity B.
Approach: In groups, students share personal reactions to and feelings and emotions about silence in situations related to school and / or to other aspects of their daily lives. Students share their feedback with the class.

Activity C.
Expansion: In small groups, students share personal experiences related to communicating without direct dialogue. The use of body language, facial expressions, or silence can be interpreted in many different ways. Students share personal experiences with other groups and / or the class.

Lectura

Approach: Have students read the poem as they listen to the recorded version on the *Abriendo paso: Lectura* Teacher Audio CDs. Students will benefit from listening to the selection as they read silently. Ask students to read aloud after they have listened to the selection.

Expansion: As students listen to the poem, they should summarize the meaning of each stanza. At the end of the poem, students compare their personal interpretations and share them with the class.

Comprensión

Alternative: In small groups or pairs, students collaborate to answer questions addressing the poet's feelings and emotions toward his loved one. Refer to images described in the post-reading activity for Activity A Approach under *Un paso más*, images that show a gradual progression of the feelings as they evolve.

Un paso más

Activity A.
Approach: Using all of the images from the poem and the personal experiences shared in class, students write on the effectiveness of silence for conveying certain feelings and emotions.

Expansion: Students bring in pictures, paintings, etc., representative of two people communicating without words. One painting that comes to mind is the Norman Rockwell painting of two children looking at the sunset while sitting on a log. Students discuss feelings and emotions conveyed in each of the works and share their visuals with the class.

Activity B.
Approach: Students write poems and share them with the class, noting their classmates' comments and reactions.

Go Online

Approach: If students have not already done so, have them visit the *Abriendo paso: Lectura* Web site at www.PHSchool.com for activities and links related to the content of the chapter.

 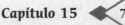

Capítulo 16
Adolescencia

Selection: poem by Vicente Aleixandre (Spain, Nobel Prize 1977)

The poet uses a series of metaphors to express his views of adolescence as a bridge between stages in one's life and to show how subconsciously he wishes to remain in this stage of his life: *"...y en el espejo de tu pasaje fluir, desvanecer"*.

Difficulty level: low to moderate

Key grammar: Imperfect subjunctive and conditional: Unidad 6, págs. 211 a 227; RG 6, págs. 228 a 236

Key vocabulary: feelings, emotions

Estimated time needed: 200 minutes (4 classes maximum traditional schedule, 2 classes maximum block)

El autor

Approach: Have students read the short introduction about the author and themes that appear in his works. Then have students visit the *Abriendo paso: Lectura* Web site for additional information about the author and his works.

Antes de leer

Activity A.
Approach: Using graphic organizers, students write down positive and negative images that are representative of adolescence *(adolescencia)*, noting (1) how this stage in one's life compares with past and future stages, and (2) whether *adolescencia* can be considered the bridge between *la niñez* and *la vejez*. Students answer the questions and explain their graphic illustrations of their views about adolescence to the class.

Activity B.
Approach: Students skim the poem and select nouns and adjectives that will help them set the tone and the mood as they read "Adolescencia." Students share their lists with the class.

Activity C.
Approach: Before students begin to read the poem, they should keep in mind the author's style and themes that might have been important to him during this time in his life. Students answer the questions and share their responses with the class.

Lectura

Approach: Have students read the poem as they listen to you read it aloud. Students will benefit from listening to the selection as they read silently. Ask students to read aloud after they have listened to the selection.

Comprensión

Approach: Students answer the questions, jot down their ideas about the poem, and then share their responses and ideas with the class.

Expansion: As students learn about the life of the author, point out to them that Vicente Aleixandre had several stages in his writing. His early poems represented a Surrealist-influenced phase characterized by poetry that was considered very complex. In his later poems, he shifted to a phase in which he focused more on the human condition and wrote poetry that was considered much more accessible.

Un paso más

Activity A.
Approach: In small groups or pairs, students reflect on the message the poem is trying to convey. Referring to the poem, students select words or phrases that support their views regarding "Adolescencia." Students may reflect on their personal views, but they should address the poem as a statement from the author. Students share their responses with the class, inviting reactions and comments from their classmates.

Activity B.
Approach: (1) Students write their poems about either stage of life, *la niñez* or *la vejez*, and share them with the class. (2) In small groups or pairs, students visualize their poems, showing images that are representative of childhood or old age and illustrating how each stage might be perceived by their classmates. Visuals may be placed around the room for students to compare their views or interpretations with those of their classmates.

Go Online

Approach: If students have not already done so, have them visit the *Abriendo paso: Lectura* Web site at www.PHSchool.com for activities and links related to the content of the chapter.

Capítulo 17
Proverbios y cantares, XXIX

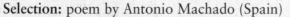

Selection: poem by Antonio Machado (Spain)

The poet sees life as a path that each of us paves every day with our actions. Once steps have been taken down this path in life, there is no turning back: *"...caminante, no hay camino: se hace camino al andar"*.

Difficulty level: low to moderate

Key grammar: Present indicative and impersonal *se*: Unidad 3, págs. 109 a 115

Key vocabulary: everyday life situations

Estimated time needed: 200 minutes (4 classes maximum traditional schedule, 2 classes maximum block)

El autor

Approach: Have students read the short introduction about the author and themes that appear in his works. Then have students visit the *Abriendo paso: Lectura* Web site for additional information about the author and his works.

Antes de leer

Activity A.
Expansion: Bring in pictures or slides of footprints in the sand or snow, the wake of a ship, or anything else that shows how images can be erased with the passing of time. Also bring in other poems or songs that illustrate this theme. Focus on how the images can be related to one's life, that is, how we pave our own road. Students should reflect on how our daily lives will impact our future and how everyday discussions, actions, and behavior will leave *una huella en nuestro camino*.

Activity B.
Approach: Skim the poem. Before reading and listening to the poem, students make a list of unfamiliar vocabulary and phrases from the poem. Students then share their lists with the class, reflecting on previously discussed themes such as life as a journey or passing of time.

Expansion: Show visuals from Activity A Expansion, which show the paths and footprints that leave their mark on someone's else's life or on one's own life. Have students hypothesize and make their own connections.

Lectura

Approach: Have students read the poem as they listen to the recorded version on the *Abriendo paso: Lectura* Teacher Audio CDs. Students will benefit from listening to the selection as they read silently. Ask students to read aloud after they have listened to the selection.

Comprensión

Approach: After reading the poem, students reflect on the themes discussed in *Antes de leer* and then answer the questions. Students share their responses and ideas with the class, inviting reactions and comments.

Un paso más

Approach: In small groups or pairs, students reflect on the themes studied in class. They share personal experiences about actions, events, etc., that have impacted their lives and how they can be related to the message that Machado was trying to convey. After students have written about their personal experiences and reactions, they share them with the class.

Go Online

Approach: If students have not already done so, have them visit the *Abriendo paso: Lectura* Web site at www.PHSchool.com for activities and links related to the content of the chapter.

Capítulo 18
Despedida

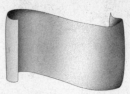

Selection: poem by Federico García Lorca (Spain)

The poet's love for his countryside is expressed in his description of the view that he has from his balcony, a view that he wants to capture and take with him even after he has died: *"¡Si muero, dejad el balcón abierto!"*

Difficulty level: low to moderate

Key grammar: Present indicative: Unidad 3, págs. 95 a 98; RG 3, págs. 116 a 127; Affirmative *vosotros* command: RG 4, págs. 159 a 164

Key vocabulary: everyday life situations

Estimated time needed: 200 minutes (4 classes maximum traditional schedule, 2 classes maximum block)

El autor

Approach: Have students read the short introduction about the author and themes that appear in his works. Then have students visit the *Abriendo paso: Lectura* Web site for additional information about the author and his works.

Antes de leer

Activity A.
Approach: In small groups or pairs, students compile a list of words, phrases, or images associated with farewells *(despedidas)*. Students share their information with the class, generating a master list that contains key descriptions and visual / written images of how they perceive the *despedidas*. This activity should set the tone for the poem.

Activity B.
Approach: Students skim the poem to identify unfamiliar vocabulary. Students learn the meanings of the unknown vocabulary and associate them with the theme established by Lorca.

Expansion: After students have read the poem and learned more about the culture of Andalucía, point out to them how typical these images are of the region: the wheat fields in the northern part of Andalucía, the orange groves that inundate the air with their magnificent scents, and above all, the white houses with open balconies filled with geraniums that adorn the streets.

Lectura

Approach: Have students read the poem as they listen to the recorded version on the *Abriendo paso: Lectura* Teacher Audio CDs. Students will benefit from listening to the selection as they read silently. As students listen to the poem, they should be focusing on the images that Lorca was painting as he spoke of his wish after his death. Ask students to read aloud after they have listened to the selection.

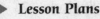

Comprensión

Approach: After reading the poem, students reflect on the themes discussed under *Antes de leer* and then answer the questions. Students share their ideas with the class, inviting reactions and comments.

Expansion: Call students' attention to the information about the author at the beginning of the chapter, noting the poet's ability to capture the beauty of the countryside and how this has served as inspiration for many of his works. Students should also do library or Internet research and comment on the geography of Andalucía, mentioning the orange groves, the wheat fields, etc., and their importance to the region.

Un paso más

Activity A.
Approach: (1) Create the scene for the students by showing pictures of Andalucía. (2) In small groups or pairs, students describe the most beautiful place that they have ever visited, commenting on feelings and emotions inspired by this place. (3) Students relate their feelings to those expressed by Lorca in the poem. He describes the daily scene that he so often saw from his balcony, a typical Andalusian scene, and how even after his death, he wants the balcony to remain open so that his soul can continue to see the same beautiful images.

Activity B.
Approach: If students have not read "El árbol de oro," this might be a good time for them to do so. In small groups or pairs, students read / or review "El árbol de oro" before attempting to do the activity. Remind them about how anxious Ivo was to go to that special room and look through the crack in the tower to see the gold tree that only he was able to see. Students then reread "Despedida" and compare the story with the poem, in which the poet also wants to see his favorite scenery. Students then write poems based on how they think Ivo would respond and share their poems with the class. You might post the poems for the class to enjoy.

Go Online

Approach: If students have not already done so, have them visit the *Abriendo paso: Lectura* Web site at www.PHSchool.com for activities and links related to the content of the chapter.

Capítulo 19
Canción de jinete

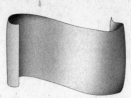

Selection: poem by Federico García Lorca (Spain)

Using his desire to reach Córdoba before he dies as a metaphor for the journey through life, the poet says that he is prepared for this journey with *"aceitunas en mi alforja"*. As he travels a long road, *"¡Ay qué camino tan largo!"*, he fears that he will never reach the beautiful city of Córdoba: *"¡Ay que la muerte me espera, antes de llegar a Córdoba!"*.

Difficulty level: low to moderate

Key grammar: Present indicative and progressive: Unidad 3, págs. 95 a 98 y 101 a 106; RG 3, págs. 116 a 129; Future: Unidad 5, págs. 174 a 181; RG 5, págs. 203 a 205; Imperfect subjunctive: Unidad 6, págs. 211 a 214; RG 6, págs. 228 a 231; Adjectives: Unidad 2, págs. 49 a 72; RG 2, págs. 73 a 94

Key vocabulary: horse-related vocabulary

Estimated time needed: 200 minutes (4 classes maximum traditional schedule, 2 classes maximum block)

El autor

Approach: Have students read the short introduction about the author and themes that appear in his works. Then have students visit the *Abriendo paso: Lectura* Web site for additional information about the author and themes that appear in his works.

Antes de leer

Activity A.
Approach: In small groups or pairs, students do library or Internet research to investigate aspects of the history and culture of Córdoba. Encourage students to look for information in the target language so that they can generate a vocabulary list for their presentation to the class. Students share their reports with the class, including visuals of different aspects of Andalusian culture and history.

Activity B.
Approach: (1) Call students' attention to the information provided about the poem. Students identify and learn unfamiliar words and relate them to the culture of Córdoba and Andalucía. (2) Students skim the poem before reading and listening to it and make a list of unfamiliar vocabulary and phrases reflecting the cultural information learned from their Córdoba presentations from Activity A.

Lectura

Approach: Have students read the poem as they listen to the recorded version on the *Abriendo paso: Lectura* Teacher Audio CDs. Students will benefit from listening to the selection as they read silently. Ask students to read aloud after they have listened to the selection.

Comprensión

Approach: After reading and listening to the poem, in small groups or pairs, students reflect on the theme and answer the questions, sharing their information with the class. Students discuss the tone and the technique used in the poem. Draw students' attention to the images created by the author that lead us to believe that Córdoba was indeed at a far distance.

Un paso más

Activity A.
Approach: Students summarize the poem using a short-story format. Encourage them to use the student-generated vocabulary list from Activity B Approach 2 under *Antes de leer*. Students then share their paragraphs with the class.

Activity B.
Approach: In small groups or pairs, students discuss various scenarios that explain why the horseman *(el jinete)* never makes it to Córdoba. Students then share their information with the class.

Expansion: Students write a letter or a postcard to a friend in Córdoba, explaining why they will not be able to see him / her.

Go Online

Approach: If students have not already done so, have them visit the *Abriendo paso: Lectura* Web site at www.PHSchool.com for activities and links related to the content of the chapter.

Capítulo 20
Selecciones de *Versos sencillos*

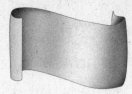

Selections: poems by José Martí (Cuba)

In "Selección de *Versos sencillos,* XXXIX," the poet expresses the importance of true friendship and peace. He uses a white rose as a symbol for peace: "*Cultivo una rosa blanca,... Para el amigo sincero... Y para el cruel que me arranca el corazón... Cultivo la rosa blanca*".

In "Selección de *Versos sencillos,* XLIV," through the use of metaphors, the poet expresses the importance of true friendship: "*...No hay cojín como un amigo... Y un tesoro en oro y trigo: Tengo más, tengo un amigo*".

Difficulty level: low to moderate

Key grammar: Present indicative: Unidad 3, págs. 95 a 98; RG 3, págs. 116 a 127; Adjectives: Unidad 2, págs. 49 a 72; RG 2, págs. 73 a 94; Relative pronouns: Paso 4, págs. 274 a 284

Key vocabulary: feelings, emotions, royalty, animals, months, and seasons

Estimated time needed: 450 minutes (9 classes maximum traditional schedule, $4\frac{1}{2}$ classes maximum block)

El autor

Approach: Have students read the short introduction about the author and themes that appear in his works. Then have students visit the *Abriendo paso: Lectura* Web site for additional information about the author and his works.

Antes de leer

Activity A.
Approach: (1) In small groups or pairs, students define *pureza, inocencia,* and *paz,* creating a vocabulary list of phrases and images associated with the words and with the symbolism of a white rose. Based on these definitions, ask students to reflect on the kinds of persons to whom white roses should be or are given. (2) Students discuss the proverb *ojo por ojo, diente por diente* and focus their discussion on the idea that "two wrongs do not make a right." Students then share their views with the class.

Activity B.
Approach: Students skim the poem before reading and listening to it, identifying and defining unfamiliar words or phrases.

Lectura

Selección de *Versos sencillos*, XXXIX

Approach: Have students read the poem as they listen to the recorded version on the *Abriendo paso: Lectura* Teacher Audio CDs. Students will benefit from listening to the selection as they read silently. While reading and listening to the poem, students should keep in mind the symbolism of a white rose and also recall previous discussions on peace, innocence, and purity. Ask students to read aloud after they have listened to the selection.

Comprensión

Approach: In small groups or pairs, students reflect on Martí's theme and message in this poem based on his life and beliefs. Students discuss the meaning of true friendship and honesty. Students answer questions and share views / responses with the class.

Expansion: Students relate this poem to Martí's life, based on the information obtained from *El autor* and the information obtained from the *Abriendo paso: Lectura* Web site.

Otra selección de *Versos sencillos*

Approach: Students skim the poem before reading and listening to it, identifying and defining unfamiliar words or phrases. Students read and listen to the poem, keeping in mind the themes discussed regarding *Versos sencillos* XXXIX.

Lectura

Selección de *Versos sencillos*, XLIV

Approach: Have students read the poem as they listen to the recorded version on the *Abriendo paso: Lectura* Teacher Audio CDs. Students will benefit from listening to the selection as they read silently. Ask students to read aloud after they have listened to the selection.

Comprensión

Approach: Before students read and / or listen to the poem again, they should read the questions so that their reading becomes more focused the second time around. After they read and / or listen to the poem, in small groups or pairs, students complete the questions, reflecting on the theme of the poem and comparing it with Martí's values and beliefs discussed in connection with *Versos sencillos* XXXIX. They might also revisit the information under *El autor* and the information obtained from the *Abriendo paso: Lectura* Web site. Students share their answers and opinions with the class.

Un paso más

Activity A.

Approach: Students reflect on the life and values that Martí expressed in his poems. In small groups or pairs, students write lists of words that are representative of Martí. Students share their lists with the class and make a master list on the board or on a transparency to be incorporated into their written paragraphs describing the author. Students write about the author and then share their views with the class.

Activity B.

Approach: Students reread and / or listen again to *Versos sencillos* XXXIX and reflect on the importance of friendship and how it was described by Martí. Students brainstorm possible items / themes that are appropriate to incorporate into / imitate in their own original versions of the poem. Before attempting to complete the assignment, in small groups or pairs, or individually, students complete their own poems and share them with the class.

Activity C.

Approach: Students reread and / or listen again to *Versos sencillos* XLIV and observe the author's technique / style as well as the use of imagery to get his point across. By now students are familiar with some themes and styles used by Martí in his poetry. This might be a good time to introduce other selections from *Versos sencillos*. Students write their own poems resembling *Versos sencillos* XLIV and share them with the class.

Alternative / Expansion: The writing / editing process for the poem could be done in various stages or class periods. During one part of the class, students write their drafts and share them with the class or in small groups. During the second part of the class, students listen to and / or read other selections from *Versos sencillos*. They might also listen to the song "Guantanamera." Listening to the lyrics of this song can serve as part of a listening activity. Students reflect / comment on the theme and share their views with the class.

Go Online

Approach: If students have not already done so, have them visit the *Abriendo paso: Lectura* Web site at www.PHSchool.com for activities and links related to the content of the chapter.

Capítulo 21

Canción de otoño en primavera

Selection: poem by Rubén Darío (Nicaragua)

The poet tells of his adventures during his youth and how the passage of time, together with the women in his life, has left him alone. The longing to return to his younger years is expressed in the repetition of the lines *"Juventud, divino tesoro, ¡ya te vas para no volver!"*.

Difficulty level: moderate

Key grammar: Present indicative: Unidad 3, págs. 95 a 98; RG 3, págs. 116 a 127; Preterite, imperfect, and present perfect indicative: Unidad 1, págs. 1 a 19; RG 1, págs. 30 a 47; Adjectives: Unidad 2, págs. 49 a 72; RG 2, págs. 73 a 94

Vocabulary: feelings, emotions, seasons

Estimated time needed: 300 minutes (6 classes maximum traditional schedule, 3 classes maximum block)

El autor

Approach: Have students read the short introduction about the author and themes that appear in his works. Then have students visit the *Abriendo paso: Lectura* Web site for additional information about the author and his works.

Antes de leer

Activity A.
Approach: In this activity, students will be reviewing vocabulary related to feelings, emotions, and seasons, particularly fall and spring. In small groups or pairs, students write a list of words / phrases describing weather, feelings, and emotions during fall and spring. Students share their lists with the class and create a master list on the board or on a transparency to which they can refer throughout the chapter.

Alternative: Students bring in pictures that are representative of fall and spring. Students use the pictures to generate vocabulary related to feelings and emotions associated with fall and spring.

Activity B.
Approach: Students read the verses and answer the questions. Students then share their responses and personal opinions with the class.

Activity C.
Approach: In small groups or pairs, students identify the meanings of the words provided and determine which six they associate with love. Students add two more words to the list that have special significance for them. Students then share their responses and justify them to the class.

Activity D.

Approach: Before students begin to read the poem, make sure that they understand the vocabulary related to possible themes in the poem. In small groups or pairs, students skim the poem to identify and learn unfamiliar vocabulary / phrases related to possible themes. Students then share their responses with the class and create a master list on the board or on a transparency that incorporates comments from the class discussion.

Lectura

Approach: If possible, provide photocopies of the poem for students; they will benefit from being able to make notations as they read and listen to the poem. Have students read the poem as they listen to the recorded version on the *Abriendo paso: Lectura* Teacher Audio CDs. Students will benefit from listening to the selection as they read silently. Ask students to read aloud after they have listened to the selection.

Comprensión

Approach: Students read the questions before they read and / or listen to the poem for the second time. This will help them to identify themes and also the progression of time in the poet's life. After students read and / or listen to the poem, they respond to the questions. They then share their responses with the class, justifying them with direct quotations and examples from the poem.

Expansion: Students will benefit from reading additional works by Darío. These can be obtained by doing library or Internet research on the author and the themes in his works. Students read selected poems / prose, compare these works with "Canción de otoño en primavera," and explain how these works are representative of the poet's life.

Un paso más

Activity A.

Approach: Students determine the tone of the poem, referring to specific verses or stanzas that justify their choice. Students refer to the list of themes for the poem that they generated for Activity D under *Antes de leer* as they prepare to write their personal opinions about "Canción de otoño en primavera." Students share their writing with the class.

Activity B.

Approach: Students write an outline of possible topics to include in the letter. Preview with students the letter-writing format and also the subjunctive, since students are asked to write direct / indirect commands and also to give advice. Students write the letter incorporating vocabulary from the master list compiled for Activity D under *Antes de leer* and share their letters with the class.

Go Online

Approach: If students have not already done so, have them visit the *Abriendo paso: Lectura* Web site at www.PHSchool.com for activities and links related to the chapter.

Capítulo 22
Oda al tomate

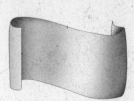

Selection: poem by Pablo Neruda (Chile, Nobel Prize 1971)

Through the use of personification, Neruda gives life / human qualities to a tomato, making the description appeal to all five senses: *"...se hunde el cuchillo en su pulpa viviente, es una roja víscera,..."* / *"...llena las ensaladas de Chile, se casa alegremente con la clara cebolla, y para celebrarlo se deja caer aceite, hijo esencial del olivo,..."* / *"agrega la pimienta su fragancia,..."* / *"el asado golpea con su aroma en la puerta,..."* .

Difficulty level: moderate

Key grammar: Present indicative and reflexive verbs: Unidad 3, págs. 109 a 115; RG 3, págs. 129 a 132

Key vocabulary: food-related items, table settings, the five senses

Estimated time needed: 300 minutes (6 classes maximum traditional schedule, 3 classes maximum block)

El autor

Approach: Have students read the short introduction about the author and themes that appear in his works. Then have students visit the *Abriendo paso: Lectura* Web site for additional information about the author and his works.

Antes de leer

Activity A.
Approach: In small groups or pairs, students define an ode and its characteristics, drawing from prior knowledge acquired in their English classes. Students share their responses to the questions with the class, citing examples of odes and reinforcing their characteristics.

Activity B.
Approach: In small groups, pairs, or as a whole class, students identify and learn the vocabulary provided. Students then place the vocabulary in appropriate categories.

Activity C.
Approach: Students review the definition and examples of an ode and answer the questions. Students share their responses with the class, noting reactions and comments. Students will need this information for *Un paso más*.

Activity D.
Approach: Before reading the poem, in small groups or pairs, students should collaborate to identify unfamiliar words. Students then read the poem, noting images that are characteristic of a tomato.

Lectura

Approach: If possible, provide photocopies of the poem for students; they will benefit from being able to make notations as they read and listen to the poem. Have students read the poem as they listen to you read it aloud. Students will benefit from listening to the selection as they read silently. Ask students to read aloud after they have listened to the selection.

Comprensión

Approach: Students read and listen to the poem once again, noting examples of personification in the ode. In small groups or pairs, students share their responses to the questions with the class.

Alternative: Students illustrate the images in the ode with their own drawings or cutouts from magazines, catalogs, etc. Students present their visual odes to the class. The visuals can be placed on a bulletin board and used for review of vocabulary and content.

Un paso más

Activity A.
Approach: In small groups or pairs, students refer to their definitions of an ode from Activity A under *Antes de leer* and make any changes necessary to establish a new definition of an ode according to "Oda al tomate." Students exchange questions and answers with partners in class.

Expansion: (1) Students will benefit from reading additional odes by Neruda such as "Oda a la alcachofa" and "Oda a los calcetines," both of which include elements of personification. Students read and compare odes and illustrate images from the odes. (2) Students select additional odes by doing library or Internet research and present their odes to the class.

Activity B.
Expansion: Students express their personal views, likes, and dislikes about "Oda al tomate" (or any other ode the class might have read) in a well-written essay. Students refer to question 5 under *Comprensión* for ode descriptors that can be incorporated into their essay writing.

Activity C.
Approach: Remind students of all of the elements of personification and images illustrated in the ode. Students comment on and express personal views about this technique in their writing assignment.

Activity D.
Approach: Through the use of personification, students have been exposed to a new way of describing an object that before had no significant form or importance. Present other odes to the class for students' enrichment. Discuss these odes and compare them, allowing students to give examples of personification in the selections presented. In small groups or pairs, students answer questions and share responses with the class, inviting reactions and comments.

Activity E.
Alternative: Students do library or Internet research on additional works by Neruda and present their findings to the class.

Activity F.
Alternative: Students will find writing an ode much easier if they write about something that is meaningful to them (stuffed animal, childhood toy, musical instrument, etc.). Students brainstorm a list of adjectives / phrases to be used in writing their odes. Students also include examples of personification in their odes. Students write their odes and share them with the class.

Expansion: Collect odes from students, make photocopies, and distribute all copies in booklet form to students for their enjoyment.

Go Online

Approach: If students have not already done so, have them visit the *Abriendo paso: Lectura* Web site at www.PHSchool.com for activities and links related to the content of the chapter.

De la prensa
Capítulo 23
La fiesta de San Fermín

Selection: magazine article by Carmen Roman

The article deals with the origins of and the events associated with the popular *fiesta de San Fermín,* an annual festival that takes place in Pamplona, Spain. It focuses on the main activities connected with the celebration, starting with *el txupinazo,* which takes place on July 6, and ending with *el pobre de mí,* which takes place on July 14. Students will enjoy reading about the daily festivities, but most of all, they will enjoy reading about the daring act of releasing the bulls into the streets of the city to chase the large crowds dressed in red and white.

Theme: customs, traditions, festival-related activities

Difficulty level: moderate. Students are given many opportunities to communicate about their own experiences involving different and unique celebrations.

Key grammar: Present and past indicative tenses and impersonal *se*: Unidades 1 y 3, págs. 1 a 29 y 109 a 115; RG 1 y 3, págs. 30 a 48; Relative pronouns: Paso 4, págs. 274 a 284; *Por/Para*: Paso 10, págs. 309 a 311

Key vocabulary: feelings, emotions, geography, geographic features, festival-related vocabulary

Estimated time needed: 360 minutes (6 classes maximum traditional schedule, 4 classes maximum block)

Antes de leer

A. Para discutir en clase
Approach: In small groups or pairs, students collaborate to compile a vocabulary list that will be used to describe the photos of *la fiesta de San Fermín* in Pamplona. Students describe the photos and share their narrations with the class, noting key vocabulary. The class can create a master vocabulary and phrase list to which they can refer throughout the chapter.

Expansion: (1) Students do library or Internet research on holidays and traditions in Spain and report their findings to the class, indicating their personal preferences. (2) Students share pictures and stories about actual historical events.

B. Nuestra experiencia
Approach: In small groups or pairs, students discuss characteristics of a feat *(una hazaña),* commenting on personal experiences related to a celebration, a trip to an amusement park, etc. Students share, describe, and explain their personal *hazañas* to their group or partner, also commenting on whether or not each one was worth the risk. Students should also share visuals if possible.

C. Los riesgos de la juventud

Approach: In small groups or pairs, students answer questions related to risk-taking behavior. Students discuss factors involved in young people taking risks such as a lack of maturity or looking for a thrill. Stuntman Evel Knievel, magician The Great Houdini, and illusionist David Blaine are some examples of famous risk-takers. Students comment on and discuss the acts for which these people are famous.

Expansion: Students bring in other examples of famous risk-takers or examples of risks taken by ordinary people. Students can do library or Internet research or consult the *Guinness Book of World Records* to locate this information.

D. Pamplona y sus alrededores and E. La corrida de toros

Approach and Expansion: In small groups or pairs, have students research the region of Navarra, focusing on Pamplona and its tradition of bullfighting. Before the individual groups share their information with the class, have them prepare an outline of their presentations and some questions for the class regarding the information that they will present. Distribute photocopies of the outlines and questions to students so that they can follow along during the presentations. After each presentation, the class answers questions from the presenters. When all of the presentations have been completed, prepare an overview of questions asked as a review of the cultural component of this chapter.

Al leer

Approach: Draw students' attention to these advance organizers, helping them to identify the vocabulary and themes that they are likely to encounter. Remind them to keep in mind the cultural information that they obtained from their research and from the presentations.

Lectura

Approach: Have small groups read the article together. As students read, have them stop on a regular basis to identify words and passages that address the information obtained from the cultural presentations in Activities D and E under *Antes de leer*.

Comprensión

A. ¿Cierta o falsa?

Expansion: Students support their answers to this true / false activity with direct quotes from the reading, followed by their own interpretations.

B. Comprensión general

Approach: Have students jot down ideas about their understanding of the article and share their ideas with the class.

Expansion: Students refer to the information obtained from their previous research on this celebration and compare it with the information in the article.

C. De la misma familia

Expansion: After students identify one word from the same family, ask for additional words. Note which part of speech each word is, and use the categories to help generate additional vocabulary.

D. En contexto

Approach: Have students write their own phrases or word equivalents and then share them with the class as one records them on the board or on a transparency. Train students in alternative ways to talk about the vocabulary. Help them identify which word or phrase best matches the word provided and why.

Expansion: Have students identify the part of speech of each of the words and note how knowing the part of speech helps in determining the meanings of words. Students may choose additional words from the article and provide their own equivalents to challenge their classmates.

Un paso más

Approach: Remind students to refer to the *Vocabulario útil para conversar y para escribir* list and to the Appendix on pp. 404–406 to help them with the speaking and writing activities.

Para conversar

Approach to this section: Students may express preferences about topics that interest them in this section. Based on their interests and skill levels, you may wish to address only one or several of the activities or you may wish to divide the activities according to interest and have each group present its work to the class, inviting reactions and responses.

A. ¿Participas o no?

Approach: Students use a graphic or an illustration to list positive and negative consequences of participating in *el encierro*. In small groups or pairs, students share their thoughts, taking into consideration the suggested words and ideas associated with *el encierro*. Students compare their group's or pair's results with their individual views and share them with the class.

Expansion: Students compare and contrast the running of the bulls during *la fiesta de San Fermín* with a bull fight.

B. Una celebración estadounidense

Approach: Students brainstorm information about celebrations in the United States that might be considered extravagant or rare to people from other cultures. In small groups or pairs, students describe these events or celebrations in detail and share their information with the class.

Expansion: Students do library or Internet research about customs, traditions, and festivals in the United States and then share their information with the class.

C. ¿Al encierro?

Approach: In small groups or pairs, students brainstorm questions to ask their friend about his / her participation in *el encierro,* with one student in each group role-playing the friend. Based on the friend's responses, students try to persuade him / her to participate or not to participate in this event.

Para escribir

Approach to this section: The activities in this section build students' writing skills incrementally, from summary to personal reaction to creation. Students will need time to express themselves and to share their writing with classmates and with the teacher. Students may express preferences about topics that interest them in this section. Based on their interests and skill levels, <u>you may wish to address only one or several of the activities or you may wish to divide the activities according to interest and have each group present its work to the class,</u> inviting reactions and responses.

A. Un resumen

Approach: Students select ten words that they consider to be most important for summarizing the article and then use them in their paragraph summaries.

B. Un evento emocionante

Approach: Students write about a memorable event using vocabulary from the article that emphasizes feelings and emotions.

C. Una carta a mis padres

Approach: Students write a letter to their parents explaining their desire to participate in *el encierro* and / or to visit Pamplona. Students revisit the information that they obtained about the city, its customs, and its traditions. Review with students the letter-writing format and key vocabulary for use in the salutation and the closing.

D. El trato de los animales

Approach: In small groups or pairs, students discuss events in which animals are used for entertainment (circuses, dog shows, horse races, etc.). Using library or Internet resources, students find information related to the illegal or unethical use of animals for entertainment. Students share their information with the class. Based on what they have learned, students write an essay expressing their views on this matter, using the suggested ideas as a guide.

Expansion: Students work with a more traditional debate format. Select two small groups to debate for and against; the rest of the class is the audience. Provide clear guidelines for the number of argument points to be made by the two sides, examples to back up opinions, and time limits to present points. The rest of the class observes and notes which side's arguments were best presented and supported. After separating a debate format from the expressions of personal opinion, class discussion can then follow about students' feelings about the issues presented.

Go Online

Approach: Have students visit the *Abriendo paso: Lectura* Web site at www.PHSchool.com for additional activities and links related to the content of the chapter.

Capítulo 24

Fernando Botero, El espejo convexo

Selection: magazine article by Patricia Venti

The article deals with Fernando Botero, a Colombian painter whose unique style is influenced by that of Mexican muralist José Clemente Orozco and the Florentine painters of the quattrocento, or fifteenth-century, period. Although the figures in Botero's paintings are voluminous, he treats them with dignity and respect. Students will be exposed not only to Botero's painting styles and themes but also to the culture of and socioeconomic situation in South America. The culture will serve as a backdrop for the students to learn about and enjoy Botero's work.

Themes: art, culture

Difficulty level: moderate. Students are given many opportunities to express their own art preferences.

Key grammar: Preterite and present perfect indicative: Unidad 1, págs. 1 a 7 y 16 a 19; RG 1, págs. 30 a 44 y 46 y 47; Present indicative and *ser/estar*: Unidad 3, págs. 95 a 107; RG 3, págs. 116 a 127; Adjectives: Unidad 2, págs. 49 a 72; RG 2, págs. 73 a 94

Key vocabulary: emotions, geography, geographical features, art (styles and characteristics)

Estimated time needed: 300 minutes (6 classes maximum traditional schedule, 4 classes maximum block)

Antes de leer

A. Los cuadros de Botero
Approach: In small groups or pairs, students identify and define the words provided, which are appropriate for describing Botero's works. Students select the best descriptors from the list to describe the photos of Botero's work used in the article. Students write four additional words to describe the photos. Students share their comments and reactions with the class, using both the words provided and their new words to describe Botero's style and works.

Expansion: Students do library or Internet research on Botero's life, works, style, etc. Students bring in additional examples of his paintings and / or sculptures and share them with the class, commenting on style, influences, or any other important information.

B. La dignidad de los cuadros
Approach: After researching Botero's life, works, and style, students work in groups and comment on the significance of size in his works and how representative it is of his childhood years in Colombia. Students answer questions and share ideas and comments with the class, inviting reactions and responses.

C. Nuestra experiencia

Approach: In small groups or pairs, students research the style of other artists and present this information to the class. Students provide examples of the artists' works, explaining the style, influences, time period, etc. Provide very specific guidelines regarding the amount of information to be presented, since students may try to provide too much information for the class. Small groups or pairs present their information to the class, inviting reactions and responses.

Alternative: Students research the lives of Latin American painters and muralists such as José Clemente Orozco and report on their lives, style, influences, etc., and bring examples of their works to share with the class.

Al leer

Approach: Draw students' attention to these advance organizers, helping them to identify the vocabulary and themes that they are likely to encounter. Remind them to keep in mind the cultural information that they obtained from their research.

Lectura

Approach: Have small groups read the article together. As students read, have them stop on a regular basis to identify words and passages that address the information obtained from their research in Activity A Expansion and Activity B under *Antes de leer.*

Comprensión

A. ¿Cierta o falsa?

Expansion: Students support their answers to this true / false activity with direct quotes from the article, followed by their own interpretations.

B. Comprensión general

Approach: Have students jot down ideas about their understanding of the article and share their ideas with the class.

Expansion: Students refer to the information obtained from their previous research on Botero and compare it with the information in the article.

C. De la misma familia

Expansion: After students identify one word from the same family, ask for additional words. Note which part of speech each word is, and use the categories to help generate additional vocabulary.

D. En contexto

Approach: Have students write their own phrases or word equivalents and then share them with the class as one records them on the board or on a transparency. Train students in alternative ways to talk about the vocabulary. Help them identify which word or phrase best matches the word provided and why.

Expansion: Have students identify the part of speech of each word and note how knowing the part of speech helps in determining the meanings of words. Students may choose additional words from the story and provide their own equivalents to challenge their classmates.

Un paso más

Approach: Remind students to refer to the *Vocabulario útil para conversar y para escribir* list and to the Appendix on pp. 404–406 to help them with the speaking and writing activities.

Para conversar

Approach to this section: Students may express preferences about topics that interest them in this section. Based on their interests and skill levels, <u>you may wish to address only one or several of the activities or you may wish to divide the activities according to interest and have each group present its work to the class,</u> inviting reactions and responses.

A. Una entrevista

Approach: In pairs, students prepare an interview with Botero, with one of the students role-playing Botero and the other role-playing the interviewer. As students brainstorm questions and answers, they should keep in mind the information obtained from the reading and from their research. Students prepare questions and answers and present them in the form of skits.

B. El sello personal

Approach: Students prepare oral presentations on "their personal touch." Students bring in visuals that will help the class to focus on and remember the topic and the information presented.

C. Orozco

Approach: In small groups, students research different aspects of Orozco's life, works, style, and themes. Students then share their information with the class. Research on this may have already been done for Activity C Alternative under *Antes de leer*.

Para escribir

Approach to this section: The activities in this section build students' writing skills incrementally, from summary to personal reaction to creation. Students will need time to express themselves and to share their writing with classmates and with the teacher. Students may express preferences about topics in this section. Based on their interests and skill levels, <u>you may wish to address only one or several of the activities or you may wish to divide the activities according to interest and have each group present its work to the class,</u> inviting reactions and responses.

A. Un resumen
Approach: In small groups, students select words that are most appropriate for summarizing the story. Students incorporate these words and others from the master list from Activity A under *Antes de leer* in their essays, together with the suggested information regarding influences in Botero's works, descriptions of his works, and the artist's views about his own work.

B. Una reseña
Alternative: Students view several examples of Botero's works, making comparisons and connections among them. After viewing examples of Botero's works, students prepare a visual presentation (videotape or role-play) representative of an art critic's review. Students share their presentations with the class.

C. Naturalezas muertas
Approach: Students select one of Botero's still lifes from the research that they did for Activity A Expansion and Activity B under *Antes de leer* and compare it with one from their favorite artist or from an artist with whom they are familiar. Students compare form, style, and color in both paintings, noting the artist's life and style.

D. Una exposición
Approach: Before students start to write the letter, they should decide on the overall tone that they are going to use in the letter. Students incorporate the vocabulary from *Vocabulario útil para conversar y para escribir* in their letter to Botero, expressing their approval or disapproval of the figure that they believe resembles them.

Go Online

Approach: Have students visit the *Abriendo paso: Lectura* Web site at www.PHSchool.com for additional activities and links related to the content of the chapter.

Capítulo 25
La Tomatina

Selection: magazine article by Alberto Ibáñez

The article focuses on the unique and somewhat messy tomato-throwing festival, La Tomatina, which takes place annually on the last Wednesday in August and which put the small town of Buñol, near Valencia, on the map of Spain. The town council provides truckloads of ripe tomatoes and, after the participants shout *"tomate, tomate, queremos tomate,"* the tomatoes are distributed from the trucks and the food fight officially begins. Everyone wears their worst clothes, since no one is spared, especially the most passive and neutral witnesses to the event. Because of the increasing national and international attention that the festival has received, more people are attending and more tomatoes are thrown every year.

Themes: customs, traditions, festival-related activities

Difficulty level: moderate. Students are given many opportunities to comment on their own experiences involving appropriate and inappropriate behavior.

Key grammar: Present indicative: Unidad 3, págs. 95 a 98; RG 3, págs. 116 a 127; Preterite and imperfect indicative: Unidad 1, págs. 1 a 15; RG 1, págs. 30 a 45; Demonstratives: Unidad 2, págs. 56 a 60; RG 2, págs. 80 a 84; *Por/Para*: Paso 10, págs. 309 a 311; Numbers: Paso 6, págs. 291 a 297

Key vocabulary: feelings, emotions, food items, celebrations, geography, geographic features, festival-related vocabulary

Estimated time needed: 400 minutes (8 classes maximum traditional schedule, 4 classes maximum block)

Antes de leer

A. Para discutir en clase
Approach: In small groups or pairs, students collaborate to define the most appropriate vocabulary words to be used in describing the photos of *La Tomatina* in Buñol. Students describe the photos and share their descriptions with the class, noting key vocabulary. The class creates a master vocabulary list to which they can refer throughout the chapter.

B. Nuestra experiencia
Approach: In small groups or pairs, students discuss and share past experiences related to food fights. Students describe incidents that they might have participated in or witnessed in a school cafeteria or seen in movies or on TV. Students share one of the experiences from the group with the class, using the master vocabulary list. Students may also introduce new vocabulary from their presentations to the class.

C. Las guerras de comida
Alternative: As a group, students discuss one of the incidents described in Activity B. In the class discussion, students should include consequences of the food fight, risk factors involved, and reasons for such an act. In small groups, students discuss other incidents, commenting on consequences, risk factors, and reasons. Students share the most interesting story from their groups with the class.

Al leer

Approach: Draw students' attention to these advance organizers, helping them to identify the vocabulary and themes that they are likely to encounter. Remind them to keep in mind the topic discussed in the previous activities (food fights).

Lectura

Approach: Have small groups read the article together. As students read, have them stop on a regular basis to identify words and phrases that are related to the topic addressed in Activities B and C under *Antes de leer*. Ask students to keep track of any historical information that they might come across as they read the article.

Comprensión

A. ¿Cierta o falsa?
Expansion: Students support their answers to this true / false activity with direct quotes from the reading, followed by their own interpretations.

B. Comprensión general
Approach: Have students jot down ideas about their understanding of the article and share their ideas with the class.

Expansion: Assign a group of students to do brief research on the life of dictator Francisco Franco. Students then share their information with the class.

C. Definiciones
Alternative: Have one group of students do this activity and then provide it as a "quiz" for the rest of the class. The group then teaches or clarifies for classmates any vocabulary with which they had difficulty.

D. De la misma familia
Expansion: After students identify one word from the same family, ask for additional words. Note which part of speech each word is, and use the categories to help generate additional vocabulary.

E. Sinónimos
Alternative: Have one group of students do this activity and then provide it as a "quiz" for the rest of the class. The group then teaches or clarifies for classmates any vocabulary with which they had difficulty.

Expansion: (1) Have students identify the part of speech of each word and note how knowing the part of speech helps in determining the meanings of words. (2) Have students choose additional words from the article and provide their own equivalents to challenge their classmates.

Un paso más

Approach: Remind students to refer to the *Vocabulario útil para conversar y para escribir* list and to the Appendix on pp. 404–406 to help them with the speaking and writing activities.

Para conversar

Approach to this section: Students may express preferences about topics that interest them in this section. Based on their interests and skill levels, <u>you may wish to address only one or several of the activities or you may wish to divide the activities according to interest and have each group present its work to the class,</u> inviting reactions and responses.

A. ¿Diversión o tontería?
Approach: Students discuss personal feelings and views about the celebration, commenting on risks one may have to take and consequences of the risks taken.

B. Nos hacen falta...
Approach: Students read the headlines and discuss possible alternative headings for each celebration.

Alternative: Put all of the headlines in a box and have students select one to present to the class. In groups, students prepare plans to present to the community. Their plans should include a press release as a follow-up to the headlines and a proposal with positive alternative ways to celebrate the specified events. Students then present their information to the class.

C. Valencia
Approach: In groups, students do library or Internet research to find information about Valencia's history, customs, traditions, places of interest, etc. Each group then shares its information with the class.

D. Prohibido bailar
Approach: In groups, students express their opinions about the town banning dancing. Students discuss possible measures, including the use of persuasion, to convince town officials to change the law.

Para escribir

Approach to this section: The activities in this section build students' writing skills incrementally, from summary to personal reaction to creation. Students will need time to express themselves and to share their writing with classmates and with the teacher. Students may express preferences about topics that interest them in this section. Based on their interests and skill levels, <u>you may wish to address only one or several of the activities or you may wish to divide the activities according to interest and have each group present its work to the class,</u> inviting reactions and responses.

A. Un resumen
Approach: Students select ten words that they consider to be most important for summarizing the article and use them in their summary essays.

B. ¿Cínico o no?
Alternative: Students refer to the last part of the reading, lines 94–100, and express personal feelings and emotions regarding the townspeople's attitude about this massive waste of nutrients. Students express their views about the following quote: *"Además la Tomatina ha traído fama internacional y una derrama económica importante al minúsculo Buñol"*. Does this statement make the event seem justifiable? Students share their views with the class.

C. Una propuesta
Alternative: In small groups or pairs, students write letters regarding the proposal of a new town or event. Students outline the proposal, taking into consideration positive / negative and short-term / long-term benefits to the community.

D. Una respuesta a la propuesta
Alternative: One half of the class writes a proposal to be presented to town officials outlining the events, the kinds of activities planned, and the positive outcomes of the event for the community. The other half of the class evaluates and gives feedback on all topics / points presented. Both groups then present their information to the class.

Lectura adicional

Approach: In small groups or pairs, students read "Oda al tomate," pp. 311–313, and discuss the images created through personification and how they might change the mental image of the tomato.

Go Online

Approach: Have students visit the *Abriendo paso: Lectura* Web site at www.PHSchool.com for activities and links related to the content of the chapter.

Capítulo 26
Los indios kunas

Selection: magazine article by César A. Yunsán M.

The article focuses on the history, occupations, customs, and traditions of the Kuna Indians. It pinpoints the geographic location of this group and introduces us to some of the fears that haunt them today. Students will learn about their means of survival, artistic talents, and the close family ties that have kept this civilization alive and vibrant for many years.

Themes: customs, traditions, means of survival

Difficulty level: moderate. Students are given many opportunities to discuss their feelings about the customs and traditions associated with the Kuna Indians and with other indigenous groups.

Key grammar: Present indicative and reflexive constructions: Unidad 3, págs. 109 a 115; RG 3, págs. 129 a 132; Preterite, imperfect, and present perfect indicative: Unidad 1, págs. 1 a 19; RG 1, págs. 30 a 47; Adjectives: Unidad 2, págs. 49 a 72; RG 2, págs. 73 a 94; Numbers: Paso 6, págs. 291 a 297

Key vocabulary: feelings, emotions, crops, seafood, indigenous civilizations, geography, geographic features

Estimated time needed: 400 minutes (8 classes maximum traditional schedule, 4 classes maximum block)

Antes de leer

A. La geografía de Panamá
Approach: Have students draw their maps and indicate the sites listed. Students then share their maps with the class, and the class chooses the best map, based on the presentation and the quality of information.

Alternative: Give students a map showing Central and South America. Students do library or Internet research to help them label the map.

Expansion: Students share with the class the information that they have found about Panama, Colombia, and Costa Rica.

B. Grupos de palabras
Approach: In small groups or pairs, students identify and define the vocabulary words and then group the words according to geography, traditions, and occupations. Students then compare their lists with those of the rest of the class and agree upon the correct groupings. Students justify their answers with definitions of the words.

C. Nuestra experiencia
Approach: In small groups, students share information regarding buying and / or collecting objects, artifacts, etc., from other cultures and then share it with the class. If students have not bought or collected such objects, they can comment on objects that they would like to collect from other countries and cultures. Students then share this information with the class.

D. El regateo

Approach: In small groups or pairs, students share personal opinions regarding the practice of haggling to lower the price of a product. Students comment on this practice and on how it is used today, not only among indigenous peoples, but also in outdoor markets. Students share opinions on this subject with the class.

Al leer

Approach: Draw students' attention to these advance organizers, helping them to identify the vocabulary and themes that they are likely to encounter. Remind them to keep in mind the topics discussed in the activities under *Antes de leer*.

Lectura

Approach: Have small groups read the article together. As students read, have them stop on a regular basis to identify words and phrases that address the cultural topics addressed in Activities B and C under *Antes de leer*. Ask students to keep track of any historical information that they might come across as they read the article.

Comprensión

A. ¿Cierta o falsa?

Expansion: Students support their answers to this true / false activity with direct quotes from the reading, followed by their own interpretations.

B. Comprensión general

Approach: Have students jot down ideas about their understanding of the article and share their ideas with the class.

Expansion: In small groups or pairs, students answer the questions and respond with direct quotes from the reading. Students share their information with the class.

C. Un resumen gráfico

Approach: In small groups or pairs, students identify the topics as they reread the article. They should also note different aspects of Kuna culture, focusing on geography, traditions, food, occupations, problems, and physical appearance. Students write information about each of the categories on their graphic organizers. These will serve as good tools for summarizing the article.

D. Un resumen oral

Approach: Using their graphic organizers from Activity C, students summarize different aspects of Kuna culture. Students then share their summaries with the class.

E. De la misma familia

Expansion: After students identify one word from the same family, ask for additional words. Note which part of speech each word is, and use the categories to help generate additional vocabulary.

F.   En contexto

Approach: Have students write their own phrases or word equivalents and then share them with the class as one records them on the board or on a transparency. Train students in alternative ways to talk about the vocabulary. Help them identify which word or phrase best matches the word provided and why.

Expansion: Have students identify the part of speech of each word and note how knowing the part of speech helps in determining the meanings of words. Students may choose additional words from the article and provide their own equivalents to challenge their classmates.

Un paso más

Approach: Remind students to refer to the *Vocabulario útil para conversar y para escribir* list and to the Appendix on pp. 404–406 to help them with the speaking and writing activities.

Para conversar

Approach to this section: Students may express preferences about topics that interest them in this section. Based on their interests and skill levels, <u>you may wish to address only one or several of the activities or you may wish to divide the activities according to interest and have each group present its work to the class,</u> inviting reactions and responses.

A.   Un pedido

Approach: Students do library or Internet research on the art of making *molas* and on the importance of this activity to the Kunas. After their research is done, students should be able to identify and purchase a *mola* of the highest quality.

Expansion: Students bring in pictures and / or actual *molas* to describe to the class. As students prepare to complete the activity, they should jot down possible information to share with their friend who is planning to buy a *mola* of high quality for them while on vacation in Panama. In pairs, students act out the activity, with one role-playing the friend who will be buying the *molas* and the other role-playing the friend who will be receiving them.

B.   Debate

Expansion: Students work with a more traditional debate format. Select two small groups to debate for and against; the rest of the class is the audience. Provide clear guidelines for the number of argument points to be made by the two sides, examples to back up opinions, and time limits to present points. The rest of the class observes and notes which side's arguments were best presented and supported. After separating a debate format from the expressions of personal opinion, class discussion can then follow about students' feelings about the issues presented.

C. Las injusticias

Alternative: In small groups or pairs, have students do library or Internet research to find the following information: (1) Which explorers are credited with discovering parts of the Americas? (2) How did these explorers treat the indigenous populations that they encountered when they first arrived at this destination? (3) How fair or unfair do they think this treatment was? Students might also do research on Native Americans. Based on their research, students answer the questions provided and then share their responses with the class.

Expansion: Show the film *The Mission,* which is an excellent example of what happened to *los guaraníes* in South America.

Para escribir

Approach to this section: The activities in this section build students' writing skills incrementally, from summary to personal reaction to creation. Students will need time to express themselves and to share their writing with classmates and with the teacher. Students may express preferences about topics that interest them in this section. Based on their interests and skill levels, <u>you may wish to address only one or several of the activities or you may wish to divide the activities according to interest and have each group present its work to the class,</u> inviting reactions and responses.

A. Un tema de interés

Approach: Using the information that they learned from the article and from their research, students write an essay about one of the topics related to the life, culture, and physical characteristics of the Kuna Indians.

B. Los matrimonios planeados

Approach: (1) Students discuss cultures that have prearranged marriages and report to the class on their customs and traditions related to this practice. (2) Based on the information learned, students write well-constructed paragraphs expressing their personal opinions about prearranged marriages.

C. Otro grupo indígena

Approach: Based on prior knowledge and / or information obtained from their research on indigenous groups, students write at least three paragraphs commenting on the history, customs, traditions, etc., that are relevant to the indigenous group about whom they have chosen to write. Students can also include information about other aspects of their culture that they find admirable.

Go Online

Approach: Have students visit the *Abriendo paso: Lectura* Web site at www.PHSchool.com for additional activities and links related to the content of the chapter.

Teatro
Capítulo 27
El delantal blanco

Selection: one-act play by Sergio Vodanović (Chile)

La señora criticizes her *empleada* for wasting time reading the ever-popular paperback novels, which *la señora* thinks are nothing more than nonsense. In these novels, the characters are often social climbers trying to gain access to the upper echelons of society but whose demeanor reflects their true social status. Using her characteristic sarcastic tone, *la señora* points out that class is something that you are born with and uses the contrast between her own social status and that of her husband, Álvaro, as an example: *"Álvaro no tiene clase. Yo sí la tengo. Y podría vivir en una pocilga y todos se darían cuenta de que soy alguien..."*

She reminds her *empleada* to live in the real world because dressing up and pretending to be someone else only happens in paperback novels: *"Los príncipes azules ya no existen. No es el color lo que importa, sino el bolsillo"*.

The plot has a clever twist about halfway through the play when the two main characters switch clothes to see how it would feel to walk in the other's shoes. The author does an excellent job of using literature as a forum for criticizing the corruption that is so prevalent in contemporary Chilean society.

Themes: role reversal, hypocrisy, fantasy, reality, corruption in society

Difficulty level: moderate. The author uses the play as a vehicle to critique different aspects of society. Students will have many opportunities to express their opinions about the two main characters, especially about the changes in their behavior after their role reversal.

Key grammar: Present indicative, *ser/estar*, and gerund (present participle): Unidad 3, págs. 95 a 109; RG 3, págs. 116 a 130; Preterite and imperfect indicative: Unidad 1, págs. 1 a 15; RG 1, págs. 30 a 45; Future: Unidad 5, págs. 174 a 181; RG 5, págs. 203 a 205; Imperfect subjunctive and conditional: Unidad 6, págs. 211 a 227; RG 6, págs. 228 a 236; Imperative: Unidad 4, págs. 133 a 140; RG 4, págs. 154 a 165

Key vocabulary: beach scenes, beach attire, feelings, emotions, personal characteristics

Estimated time needed: 450 minutes (9 classes maximum traditional schedule, 5 classes maximum block)

Antes de leer

A. Para discutir en clase
Approach: In small groups or pairs, have students collaborate to describe the picture and tell the story, noting key vocabulary. Students should incorporate the suggested vocabulary into their narration to the class. Students share picture descriptions with the rest of the class, adding words to the vocabulary list to which they can refer throughout the chapter.

B. Otra personalidad

Approach: In small groups or pairs, have students discuss possible situations in which they might adopt a new identity or role-play someone else. Students describe possible changes (behavior, personality, voice, etc.) that might occur with the new identity or role-playing situation. Students share their ideas with the class.

Expansion: Students act out their new identities or role-playing situations for the class.

C. Reflexión

Alternative: In small groups or pairs, students select a particular new identity or role-playing situation and demonstrate to the class how the new personality would change their normal behavior. Students present their ideas to the class in the form of skits.

D. Una selección and E. Otra selección

Alternative: In small groups or pairs, students read the short selections, answer the questions, share their answers with the class, and reflect on the consequences of role reversals.

Al leer

Approach: Draw students' attention to these advance organizers, helping them to identify some of the vocabulary and themes that they are likely to encounter. Remind them of the information in the *El autor* section about themes that appear in many of Vodanović's works.

Lectura

Approach: You may wish to poll students before they read the play. Do they enjoy one-act plays? If they have read some, do they enjoy role-playing the characters or do they prefer to read the play and imagine the setting? Students' reactions may help you to decide whether to start with role-playing or individual reading.

Comprensión

A. ¿Cierta o falsa?

Alternative: Students support their answers to this true / false activity with direct quotes from the play, followed by their own interpretations.

B. Comprensión general

Approach: Have students jot down ideas about their understanding of the play and share their ideas with the class.

C. De la misma familia

Expansion: After students identify one word from the same family, ask for additional words. Note which part of speech each word is, and use the categories to help generate additional vocabulary.

 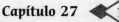

D. En contexto

Approach: Have students write their own phrases or word equivalents and then share them with the class as one records them on the board or on a transparency. Train students in alternative ways to talk about the vocabulary. Help them identify which word or phrase best matches the word provided and why.

Expansion: Students identify the part of speech of each of the words and note how knowing the part of speech helps in determining the meanings of words. Students choose additional words from the play and provide their own equivalents.

E. Al punto

Expansion: Students create multiple-choice items that clarify additional aspects of the play.

F. Ahora te toca a ti

Approach: Assign the bulleted list of themes—or themes created by students—to different pairs or groups. Have the groups ask the class or other groups their questions to determine the questions' effectiveness and to reinforce comprehension. This approach shifts the burden of asking questions from you to the students, who often generate challenging questions.

Un paso más

Approach: Remind students to refer to the *Vocabulario útil para conversar y para escribir* list and to the Appendix on pp. 404–406 to help them with the speaking and writing activities.

Para conversar

Approach to this section: Students may express preferences about topics that interest them in this section. Based on their interests and skill levels, <u>you may wish to address only one or several of the activities or you may wish to divide the activities according to interest and have each group present its work to the class,</u> inviting reactions and responses.

A. El regreso de Álvaro

Approach: In groups of three, students discuss possible scenarios for Álvaro's return and for his finding out about the incident at the beach from *la señora* and *la empleada*. Students write a script and present it to the class.

Expansion: Students prepare storyboards for the scenarios and videotape them. Students view all possible scenarios and select the one that best fits the plot.

B. Una conversación con el caballero distinguido

Approach: In pairs, students refer to lines 289–314 in the play where *el caballero distinguido* comments on social status and probable causes for the behavior of *la señora*. Students create possible dialogues and present them to the class.

C. Diez años más tarde

Approach: In pairs, students set the stage, taking into account that ten years have passed during which the two women have not seen each other. Students should note any possible changes in the social status of either woman. Students create dialogues referring to the incident on the beach and reflecting the status attributed to *la señora* and *la empleada*. Students present their dialogues to the class.

Expansion: Students present their dialogues to the class in the form of videos.

D. El reparto

Alternative: In groups, students identify some contemporary English-speaking or preferably Spanish-speaking actors / actresses that they think would be ideal to play the individual roles and then justify their choices. Students can do library or Internet research to find additional information about these or other Spanish-speaking actors / actresses. Groups share their ideas and suggestions with the class. The class then selects the final cast for the play.

Expansion: In groups, students present the play to the class.

E. Otros personajes

Approach: Students express their views / opinions to the class about whether the existing number of characters is sufficient or whether there should be an additional character, justifying their comments / opinions with information from the play. If students decide that another character is needed, they should offer suggestions about who that character should be and why he / she should be added to the play.

F. La vida de la empleada

Alternative: Refer students to lines 134–161, the dialogue between *la señora* and *la empleada* about renting a bathing suit. In groups, students discuss the author's effectiveness in criticizing different aspects of society. Students share their views and opinions with the class.

G. El esposo

Alternative: In groups of three, students discuss the effectiveness of the two women having the major roles and possible changes if the husband had appeared in the play. Students share their views with the class.

Para escribir

Approach to this section: The activities in this section build students' writing skills incrementally, from summary to personal reaction to creation. Students will need time to express themselves and to share their writing with classmates and with the teacher. Students may express preferences about topics in this section. Based on their interests and skill levels, <u>you may wish to address only one or several of the activities or you may wish to divide the activities according to interest and have each group present its work to the class,</u> inviting reactions and responses.

A. Un resumen

Alternative: In groups, students collaborate to compile a possible vocabulary list to be used in summarizing the play. Students then write short summaries of the play and present them to the class.

B. Los personajes principales and C. Mi solidaridad

Alternative: Using graphic organizers, students group the adjectives according to the character that they best describe. Have students reflect on the roles of *la señora* and *la empleada* and the author's message in the play. Students select additional adjectives and write descriptive paragraphs about *la señora* and *la empleada,* expressing their personal preferences and feelings about each of the characters.

D. Una reseña

Expansion: In groups, students write and rate the reviews of the play, expressing personal views about each of the characters and the situations provided. Collect students' reviews, photocopy them, and distribute them in the form of play / movie reviews.

E. Las novelas fotografiadas

Expansion: In groups, students create their own versions of *una novela fotografiada,* based on the personality / character selected in Activity B under *Antes de leer.* Students may cut out pictures from magazines or newspapers or use original creations to illustrate their *novelas.* They also write captions for the illustrations in their novels. Students then share their novels with the class.

F. Otros personajes

Expansion: In groups, students select other possible pairs that might have served as the main characters for the play and write scripts criticizing an aspect of society / daily life. Students then present their scripts to the class in the form of skits.

G. ¿Un comentario social?

Expansion: In groups, students comment on the effectiveness of *El delantal blanco* as social criticism or commentary on how people's actions are determined by their social class and / or the possibility of attaining / changing one's social status by role reversal.

Expansion: Students identify additional themes of importance to society about which they might write a letter to the editor of a newspaper or magazine.

H. ¿Ser o no ser?

Alternative: Students share stories about wanting to be someone else such as wanting to be older when they were younger or wanting to be the oldest if they were the youngest. In groups, students write their opinions about wanting to be someone else and present them to the class.

I. Un refrán

Expansion: Students reflect on and state personal opinions about the meaning of the proverb *El hábito no hace al monje.* Students choose specific situations or examples that reflect their point of view and explain them in the form of essays.

Comprensión auditiva

Approach: Have students look over the options for each selection carefully before they begin to listen. Check that they are comfortable with both the meaning and pronunciation of the vocabulary. If students do not understand words / phrases, provide Spanish explanations, but avoid English translations. Have students identify key words so that they can predict the topic, vocabulary, and structures that they are likely to hear. Careful preparation, combined with a willingness to use intuition and an understanding of contexts, will ensure that students need to listen only once to understand each passage.

Go Online

Approach: Have students visit the *Abriendo paso: Lectura* Web site at www.PHSchool.com for activities and links related to the content of the chapter.

Script for
Abriendo paso: Lectura
Audio CD

José M. Díaz

Cuentos
Capítulo 1
El décimo

Comprensión auditiva

Escucha las siguientes selecciones. Después de cada selección vas a escuchar varias preguntas. Escoge la mejor respuesta para cada pregunta entre las opciones impresas en tu libro.

Selección número 1
La selección que vas a escuchar trata de algo que pasó con la lotería en los estados de Nueva York y Connecticut.

Hace unos meses los oficiales del Departamento de Transporte notaron un inexplicable aumento en el tráfico en varias de las ciudades cerca de la línea divisoria entre los estados de Nueva York y Connecticut. Generalmente el tráfico entre los dos estados aumenta durante los fines de semana, pero ese día era un miércoles, y esto intrigaba mucho a los policías que patrullaban las carreteras. No fue hasta que uno de ellos compró un periódico local que se enteró de que el premio gordo de la lotería de Nueva York había aumentado a un récord de casi cien millones de dólares. Era por esta razón que la gente del estado de Connecticut iba a las tiendas de Nueva York a comprar billetes de lotería. Aunque la popularidad del juego les agrada a los oficiales de la lotería, al mismo tiempo les preocupa. Esta preocupación se debe a que muchas personas, generalmente las que no tienen suficientes medios económicos, gastan demasiado dinero en billetes de lotería para aumentar sus posibilidades de ganar. Una vez que los números ganadores son seleccionados, muchas de estas personas caen en un agudo estado de depresión, ya que sus esperanzas han sido defraudadas, y de repente se dan cuenta de que han gastado sus ahorros en un juego que en general no ofrece ninguna garantía y muy pocas posibilidades de ganar.

Número 1 ¿Qué vieron aumentar los oficiales del Departamento de Transporte?

Número 2 ¿Cuándo se enteró un policía de lo que pasaba?

Número 3 ¿Qué les preocupa a los oficiales de la lotería?

Número 4 ¿Cómo se sienten muchas personas después de que los números son seleccionados?

Selección número 2
Escucha la siguiente conversación sobre lo que le pasó a Genaro el día que recibió el primer cheque de su nuevo trabajo.

—Por allí va Genaro. El pobre, ¡está tan triste…!

—¿Qué le pasó?

—Después de no haber trabajado por más de tres meses, consiguió un puesto muy bueno. La semana pasada recibió su primer cheque. Ya había hecho planes para comprarle a su familia muchas cosas que necesitaba. Fue al banco, puso el dinero en el bolsillo y cuando llegó a su casa se dio cuenta de que tenía el bolsillo roto y que el dinero probablemente se le había caído en la calle.

—¡Qué pena! ¿Y cómo no se había dado cuenta de que el bolsillo estaba roto?

—Aparentemente no había usado los pantalones desde el año pasado y se había olvidado de que estaban rotos. Pero gracias a su amigo Clemente pudo recuperar algo del dinero. Clemente decidió pedirle contribuciones a sus colegas y pudieron darle más de la mitad de lo que había perdido.

—¡Qué suerte! Por lo menos debe estar contento. No sólo por el dinero, sino también por el buen amigo que tiene.

—Creo que lo reconoce, aunque se siente un poco incómodo por haber tenido que aceptar dinero de otros.

—Pero, ¿sabes qué fue irónico? Su amigo Clemente se enojó con sus colegas porque algunos no contribuyeron mucho y él pensó que no tenían compasión.

—¡Ay, qué desagradecido! Hoy día todo el mundo tiene muchas presiones económicas y aunque la contribución haya sido pequeña, es una muestra de generosidad.

—Estoy de acuerdo. Espero que Clemente eventualmente comprenda su error.

—Oh, ya lo comprendió y decidió pedirles perdón a todos. Quería ayudar a su amigo con la mayor cantidad de dinero posible. Luego, el mismo admitió que le daba pena no haber podido darle tanto como él quería.

Número 1 ¿Qué le pasó a Genaro?

Número 2 ¿Qué hizo Clemente cuando supo la noticia?

Número 3 ¿Qué pensó Clemente de sus colegas?

Número 4 Al final del diálogo, ¿qué hizo Clemente?

Número 5 ¿Cómo podemos describir a Clemente?

Capítulo 2
Rosa

Comprensión auditiva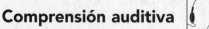

Escucha las siguientes selecciones. Después de cada selección vas a escuchar varias preguntas. Escoge la mejor respuesta para cada pregunta entre las opciones impresas en tu libro.

Selección número 1

La selección que vas a escuchar es un comentario de la radio acerca de la tecnología.

Queridos oyentes… amigos míos. Uds. ya saben muy bien que los adelantos tecnológicos siguen inundándonos. Cada semana hay algo nuevo en el mercado que va a revolucionar nuestra vida. El modelo de computadora que salió hace dos años ya está pasado de moda. No sirve para nada… si Ud. le cree a la publicidad. Y cada invención es el milagro que nos librará de nuestras labores cotidianas. ¡Basta! ¿Cuándo vamos a darnos cuenta de que esta tecnología—estas respuestas a nuestros problemas—no nos facilitan el modo de vivir? Sí, hacen la vida más rápida, pero… ¿es eso un adelanto? ¿un beneficio? La verdad es que a mí me gusta más el paso lento. Tener tiempo para reflexionar. Claro, no queremos volver a los tiempos prehistóricos, pero es preciso, a mi parecer, que observemos, que estudiemos la ruta que tomamos. Realmente hay dos preguntas: primero, ¿adónde vamos? y segundo, ¿cómo llegaremos allí?

Número 1 ¿Qué le molesta a la comentadora?

Número 2 ¿Qué piensa la comentadora acerca de las computadoras?

Número 3 ¿Qué quisiera la comentadora?

Selección número 2

Escucha la siguiente conversación entre Paula y Sergio. Paula está de visita en el apartamento de Sergio. Sergio parece muy preocupado. Mientras los dos hablan, Sergio continúa buscando algo que ha perdido.

—Sergio, ¿qué haces?

—Estoy buscando unos papeles que necesito para el lunes próximo.

—Aquí no hay suficiente luz, nunca los vas a encontrar. Yo no puedo ver nada.

—Sí, tengo que reemplazar las bombillas. Todo está muy desorganizado. No he tenido tiempo de sacar todos estos periódicos.

—Parece que los vienes amontonando desde hace más de un mes.

—En las últimas semanas he estado trabajando en un proyecto para mi jefe y nunca llego a casa antes de las ocho. No tengo tiempo libre para nada.

—¿Qué clase de proyecto?

—Queremos reemplazar varias de las computadoras que compramos hace unos años porque con los nuevos programas, ahora son inútiles.

—Me sorprende que una compañía tan pequeña tenga tanto dinero para reemplazar todas las computadoras.

—Tienes razón, no tenemos mucho dinero. Pero, para poder comunicarnos con las otras oficinas, necesitamos nuevos programas y las máquinas que tenemos ahora no tienen suficiente memoria. Por eso, tengo que buscar una manera eficiente de resolver el problema.

—Ahora comprendo por qué estás trabajando tanto... ¿Te ayudo a mover esas cajas?

—No, gracias. Son muy pesadas y es inútil que siga buscando esta noche. Estoy cansadísimo.

—Continúa tu búsqueda mañana. Si quieres puedo pasar por aquí y ayudarte un poco.

—Gracias, Paula. Acepto tu oferta. Te llamaré mañana desde la oficina y después de que me ayudes, podemos ir a cenar.

—De acuerdo. La ventaja es que tu apartamento es pequeño. Estoy segura de que no tendremos muchos problemas en encontrar los papeles.

Número 1 ¿Por qué piensa Paula que Sergio nunca va a encontrar los papeles que busca?

Número 2 ¿Por qué no tiene mucho tiempo libre Sergio?

Número 3 ¿Qué problemas hay en la oficina de Sergio?

Número 4 ¿Qué le ofrece Paula a Sergio?

Número 5 Según Paula, ¿por qué será fácil encontrar los papeles en el apartamento de Sergio?

Simulated Conversation

(a) El mensaje

Hola. Es Rosa. ¿Estás ahí? Necesito hablar contigo. Llámame en cuanto puedas.

(b) La conversación

Rosa: [El teléfono suena.] Aló.

[student response]

Rosa: Hola, te llamé porque estoy muy triste y preocupada. Acabo de perder mi trabajo a tiempo parcial y no sé qué hacer. Necesito el dinero.

[student response]

Rosa: Es que además de necesitar el dinero, me gustaba mucho el trabajo y tenía muy buenos compañeros.

[student response]

Rosa: Me encantaría conversar en persona. Necesito que me ayudes a aclarar mis pensamientos y a hacer planes.

[student response]

Rosa: Bueno, hasta entonces. Y gracias por comprenderme. [Cuelga el teléfono.]

Capítulo 3
Un oso y un amor

Comprensión auditiva

Escucha las siguientes selecciones. Después de cada selección vas a escuchar varias preguntas. Escoge la mejor respuesta para cada pregunta entre las opciones impresas en tu libro.

Selección número 1

La selección que vas a escuchar es una conversación entre Ana y Pablo. Los amigos no se veían desde hacía mucho tiempo y finalmente Pablo decidió llamar a Ana por teléfono.

—Hola, Ana. Hace varios años que estaba por llamarte pero nunca me atreví.

—Yo también, Pablo. Siempre te recuerdo y he pensado mucho en ti principalmente en los últimos meses. Tú siempre fuiste tan buen amigo y siempre me dabas tan buenos consejos. ¿Cómo has pasado los últimos años?

—Bueno, después de la universidad, conseguí un puesto muy bueno en Arizona, me casé y ahora tengo dos hijos.

—¡Qué casualidad, Pablo! Yo tengo dos niños también, pero mi esposo murió hace unos meses y todos le echamos mucho de menos. Ahora la compañía para la cual trabajo se va a mudar a otro estado y voy a necesitar un puesto nuevo.

—¡Ay Ana, cuánto lo siento! Pero no te preocupes. Estoy seguro de que poco a poco la situación mejorará.

—Así lo espero. ¿Y tú? ¿Qué has estado haciendo todos estos años?

—Bueno, empecé mi propia compañía. Sabes que siempre me ha gustado la agricultura. Administro una compañía que ayuda a los campesinos para que sus tierras les rindan más. Y, ¿sabes qué?

—Dime.

—Vamos a abrir una oficina en Arizona y pienso irme a vivir allí. Por eso te llamaba. Un viejo amigo me dio tu número.

—Ésas sí son buenas noticias, Pablo. Me encantaría verte de nuevo.

—A mí también, Ana. Te llamaré cuando finalice los planes y así podremos encontrarnos y recordar aquellos días fantásticos que pasábamos en la sierra cuando estábamos en la universidad.

—Los recuerdo muy bien, Pablo. Llámame pronto.

—Así lo haré. Hasta pronto, Ana, y no pierdas las esperanzas.

—Ahora no, ya sé que mi buen amigo Pablo me dará ánimo.

—Hasta pronto.

Número 1 ¿Por qué recordaba siempre Ana a Pablo?

Número 2 Según lo que dice Ana, ¿cómo es su vida ahora?

 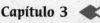

Número 3 ¿Qué noticias tiene Pablo para Ana?

Número 4 ¿Qué recuerda Pablo de Ana?

Selección número 2

La selección que vas a escuchar trata de los recuerdos de un joven, Santiago, y de lo que pasó un día cuando fue con sus amigos al campo.

Un día cuando mis compañeros de secundaria y yo fuimos a la sierra, ocurrió un incidente que ninguno de nosotros ha podido olvidar. A todos nos gustaba disfrutar del aire fresco, del arroyo y de los animales que habitaban en la sierra. Por eso, los fines de semana nos reuníamos e íbamos a nuestra querida sierra. Siempre llevábamos una carpa, comida, golosinas, refrescos y en las brasas asábamos alguna carne para almorzar.

Ese día un campesino había dejado heno en el campo para que el ganado tuviera qué comer. Bueno, con las risas, las bromas y los buenos amigos no les prestamos mucha atención a las brasas. De repente, los caballos se asustaron y corrieron hacia nosotros. Nos dimos cuenta de que por estar tan cerca de las brasas, el heno ardía. Tuvimos suerte de que todos actuamos un poco alocados, pero con serenidad. Recordamos que estábamos cerca del arroyo y allí fuimos a buscar agua para apagar el fuego.

Después de apagar el fuego, agotados y sudando, nos reímos mucho comentando la reacción que cada uno había tenido al ver el fuego. Y también aprendimos una buena lección.

Por otro lado, algo positivo sucedió ese día. Por primera vez, Graciela y yo nos dimos cuenta de que estábamos verdaderamente enamorados, aunque nos conocíamos desde que éramos pequeños. Desde ese día no nos hemos separado. Hace tres años que nos casamos, y de vez en cuando recordamos aquel día cuando miramos hacia el patio y allí vemos la misma carpa que usábamos cuando íbamos a la sierra, pero que ahora usan nuestros hijos para jugar.

Número 1 ¿Adónde iban Santiago y sus amigos?

Número 2 ¿Qué les ocurrió a Santiago y sus amigos un día?

Número 3 ¿Cuál fue el aspecto más positivo de ese día para Santiago?

Simulated Conversation

La conversación

Juan: Hola. Dichosos los ojos. ¿Qué hay de tu vida?

[student response]

Juan: Yo estoy trabajando en un hospital cerca de aquí.

[student response]

Juan: Me encanta mi trabajo. A propósito, tengo que regresar al hospital. ¿Qué te parece si te llamo este fin de semana?

[student response]

Juan: Muy bien. Ya lo apunté. Te llamo el sábado.

[student response]

Juan: ¡Claro! Me encantaría. Chao. Hablamos el sábado.

[student response]

Capítulo 4
Continuidad de los parques

Comprensión auditiva

Escucha las siguientes selecciones. Después de cada selección vas a escuchar varias preguntas. Escoge la mejor respuesta para cada pregunta entre las opciones impresas en tu libro.

Selección número 1
La selección que vas a escuchar trata de un nuevo libro de cuentos de misterio.

El escritor cubano Luis Ángel Casas acaba de publicar una nueva colección de cuentos, a través de los cuales nos trata de transportar a un mundo fantástico, lleno de misterio y horror. Uno de los aspectos más interesantes de esos cuentos es que el autor convierte cosas ordinarias en elementos extravagantes que causan catástrofes y que muchas veces llevan a la locura. En uno de los cuentos, "Escapado de la tumba", el personaje principal se encuentra en una pesadilla donde la realidad y la fantasía se mezclan constantemente. Este joven sueña repetidamente que ha matado a alguien y que la justicia lo persigue. Aunque al principio es sólo un sueño, eventualmente el sueño se convierte en realidad. Más tarde el hombre a quien supuestamente ha asesinado se escapa de la tumba. Lo demás no es justo decirlo, pues si Ud. se entusiasma al leer el libro, no se lo queremos echar a perder. La crítica ha sido un poco negativa, ya que señala que, aunque estos cuentos tienen valor, no logran totalmente su propósito debido a que son demasiado cortos. Dicen los críticos que los personajes y la acción no están suficientemente desarrollados.

Número 1 ¿Qué trata de hacer el escritor en sus cuentos?

Número 2 ¿Qué le sucede al personaje principal de uno de los cuentos?

Número 3 ¿Por qué no ha sido positiva la crítica?

Selección número 2
La selección que vas a escuchar trata de *BEM*, una revista de ciencia ficción publicada en España.

Con un cohete que simboliza una mirada positiva al futuro, así como un estilo sencillo de presentar las cosas, la revista *BEM* lanzó a la calle su primer número en 1990. Con unas ocho páginas que ni siquiera estaban grapadas, el recibimiento por parte de los lectores les dio ánimo a un grupo de aficionados al género fantástico y de ciencia ficción a continuar con su meta de publicar una revista de calidad para sus lectores. Su propósito es llenar el vacío que existe en España en el campo de este tipo de literatura ya que hay muy pocas revistas que se dedican a este género.

Hoy día se han publicado más de 60 números y la cantidad de suscriptores aumenta constantemente. *BEM* se ha convertido en una de las mejores revistas de ciencia ficción en toda la historia del género en España debido al apoyo indiscutible de sus lectores.

La revista ha ganado diversos premios por ser considerada durante varios años la mejor revista no comercial. Sus cuentos y artículos han recibido el reconocimiento de organizaciones, tales como la Asociación Española de Fantasía y Ciencia Ficción, lo que contribuye a que atraiga a los mejores escritores españoles y de todo el mundo de este género.

Es interesante notar que ninguna de las personas involucradas en la producción de la revista recibe un sueldo. El equipo entero de producción hace el trabajo por su interés en el tema de la literatura fantástica y de ciencia ficción. En fin, la revista no se publica para ganar dinero. El dinero que se gana por medio de ventas, suscripciones y publicidad se reinvierte en la producción de la revista. *BEM* acepta artículos, cuentos, reseñas de libros, etc., de sus lectores. Si su material se publica, el lector no recibe pago, pero sí un aumento en el número de revistas que recibirá con su suscripción.

Número 1 ¿Por qué parece haber tenido éxito la revista *BEM?*

Número 2 ¿Cuál es uno de los aspectos interesantes de la revista?

Número 3 ¿Qué reciben los autores cuando su material es publicado en *BEM?*

Capítulo 5
Cajas de cartón

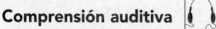

Comprensión auditiva

Escucha las siguientes selecciones. Después de cada selección vas a escuchar varias preguntas. Escoge la mejor respuesta para cada pregunta entre las opciones impresas en tu libro.

Selección número 1

Ahora vas a escuchar una selección sobre la situación de los niños en muchas partes del mundo.

Todos los niños deben tener la posibilidad de crecer saludables en un ambiente seguro, con el apoyo de sus familias y otras personas a cargo de su bienestar. El darles una educación es sin duda uno de los aspectos más importantes para prepararlos a que lleven una vida responsable y para que no sean una carga para la sociedad en que viven. Sin embargo, estudios recientes han indicado que la situación de la población infantil del mundo es alarmante. Algunos resultados de esos estudios indican que unos cien millones de niños viven en las calles y, por consiguiente, no tienen acceso a la educación. Otros ciento cincuenta y cinco millones de niños menores de cinco años viven en una pobreza absoluta. Cada día cuarenta mil niños mueren de desnutrición y de otras enfermedades, incluyendo el SIDA, por falta de agua limpia, de higiene o a causa de las drogas. Irónicamente, el resolver estos problemas sería relativamente barato. Las vacunas, es decir, las inyecciones que inmunizan para prevenir muchas de las graves enfermedades que causan la mortalidad infantil, cuestan menos de un dólar y medio cada una (un tratamiento de antibióticos cuesta un dólar), e incluso la desnutrición podría ser reducida de forma drástica a un costo inferior a los diez dólares por niño por año. Pero además de dinero se necesita voluntad. Si los países no se comprometen a luchar contra estos males de una manera sistemática y constante, el problema no mejorará y la lucha nunca se podrá ganar.

Número 1 Según la selección, ¿cuál es la situación de unos cien millones de niños del mundo?

Número 2 ¿Qué es lo irónico acerca de la situación que se describe en esta selección?

Número 3 Además del dinero, ¿qué se necesita para mejorar la situación?

Selección número 2

Vas a escuchar una selección sobre la autoestima en los niños.

Uno de los problemas que los niños pueden enfrentar después de los primeros años en la escuela es el problema de la falta de autoestima. La autoestima es la confianza en las habilidades propias. Muchos estudios han demostrado que generalmente los niños se sienten seguros de sí mismos más o menos hasta los nueve años. Desafortunadamente, en el período entre la escuela primaria y la escuela secundaria, muchos niños y niñas empiezan a perder su autoestima. Este cambio es más agudo en las niñas que en los niños, y el resultado es que muchas veces las niñas se vuelven inseguras, y esto puede afectar su vida futura. Durante mucho tiempo se pensó que los amigos de los niños y sus compañeros de clase eran los que más influían en el desarrollo de la autoestima. Sin embargo, estudios recientes indican que son los padres los que tienen más influencia en el desarrollo de la autoestima. Es muy importante que los padres y los otros adultos con quienes los niños tengan contacto los hagan sentirse orgullosos de su trabajo alabándolos, felicitándolos y diciéndoles que son competentes y apreciados. Aunque los niños no sean competentes en todas las actividades, el alabarlos en aquéllas donde demuestren interés y habilidad, los ayudará a sentirse más exitosos y seguros en sus aspiraciones.

Número 1 ¿Cuándo empiezan a perder la autoestima los niños?

Número 2 ¿Quiénes tienen más influencia en la autoestima de los niños?

Número 3 ¿Qué es importante en el desarrollo de los niños?

Simulated Conversation

La conversación

El señor Cartas: Buenos días. Soy el señor Cartas. ¿Y tú? ¿Cómo te llamas?

[student response]

El señor Cartas: Mucho gusto. ¿Cuánto hace que vives aquí?

[student response]

El señor Cartas: No te preocupes. Sé que te acostrumbrarás.

[student response]

El señor Cartas: Pronto tendrás muchos amigos.

[student response]

El señor Cartas: Aquí tienes los libros que estamos usando. Tendrás que llevarlos a casa.

[student response]

El señor Cartas: Bueno, vamos al salón para presentarte a la clase.

[student response]

El señor Cartas: Verás lo bien que te reciben.

Capítulo 6
Jacinto Contreras recibe su paga extraordinaria

Comprensión auditiva

Escucha las siguientes selecciones. Después de cada selección vas a escuchar varias preguntas. Escoge la mejor respuesta para cada pregunta entre las opciones impresas en tu libro.

Selección número 1
La selección que vas a escuchar trata de una celebración.

¡Qué temporada más bonita! La ciudad resplandece con luces. Se ve la alegría en las caras de los niños que anticipan ansiosamente la llegada del día especial. Por todas partes se oye música de fiesta. Las tiendas y los edificios están adornados, contribuyendo al ambiente de alegría. Pero, a pesar de toda esta alegría, hay que recordar que también hay tristeza. Mucha gente no podrá divertirse: los desempleados, los enfermos, los huérfanos, los pobres. Hay gente sin familia, sin amigos.

Al mismo tiempo, lo que satisface más que nada, lo que alegra mucho, es la bondad, la generosidad que se muestra en las acciones de mucha gente. Los que pueden regalan a los desafortunados, dan de comer a los que tienen hambre, visitan a los ancianos, recuerdan—y ésta es la palabra clave—recuerdan a los otros. Ellos son los representantes verdaderos del significado de la temporada. Cuando cada persona deje de pensar en sí misma y comience a pensar en los demás, bueno, entonces el mundo llegará a ser un lugar mejor para todos.

Número 1 ¿Qué celebración se describe en la selección?

Número 2 Según la selección, ¿qué satisface más que nada?

Número 3 ¿Quiénes son los verdaderos representantes de la temporada?

Selección número 2
Ahora vas a escuchar una conversación entre Jorge y Alicia acerca de la familia Canseco.

—¿Conoces a la familia Canseco? ¿Los que viven en la esquina? Se han vuelto muy famosos en sólo veinticuatro horas.

—¿Sí? ¿Y cómo fue eso? Vi a mucha gente frente a su casa y hasta había cámaras de televisión.

—Se acaban de sacar el premio gordo de la lotería. Nadie sabía quiénes habían sido los ganadores hasta hoy.

—Oye, ¿pero no fue anunciado hace más de un mes?

—Sí, pero ellos no le dijeron nada a nadie. Aparentemente querían consultar con un abogado. Además no querían que todo el mundo se les apareciera en la puerta de su casa a pedirles dinero.

—¡Ay, ahora me acuerdo! Creo que oí algo sobre ellos en las noticias de esta mañana. Pero, no dijeron lo que iban a hacer con tanto dinero.

—No, lo dijeron más tarde. Piensan vender su apartamento y comprar una casa en el Uruguay. Lo harán en cuestión de unas semanas. No quieren ver a nadie, es como si quisieran desaparecer.

—Eso no me parece bien. ¿No tienen buenos amigos o familiares aquí?

—Sí, pero dicen que se pondrán en contacto con ellos en el futuro, pero que por ahora quieren tranquilidad y tiempo para planear lo que van a hacer.

—Hasta cierto punto, comprendo. Pero, no muestran ser muy amables ni cariñosos con la gente que conocen. Creen que todos son sus enemigos y que les van a pedir dinero. Su actitud es incomprensible.

—Bueno, una vez más este incidente comprueba lo que todos dicen. Que el dinero echa a perder hasta a las personas más humildes.

—No creo que siempre sea así. Todo depende de cómo eran antes. Y si ellos actúan así ahora, es porque siempre han sido antipáticos.

—Bueno, espero que un día no necesiten a sus amigos. El dinero no es todo en la vida y nunca puede reemplazar a un buen amigo.

Número 1 ¿Qué hizo la familia Canseco por más de un mes?

Número 2 ¿Qué temían los Canseco?

Número 3 Según Alicia, ¿qué planes tiene la familia?

Número 4 ¿Qué opina Jorge de los Canseco?

Número 5 ¿Qué parece ser importante para Alicia?

Simulated Conversation

(a) El mensaje

Buenas tardes. Llama la señora Pérez, secretaria de la Escuela José Martí. Tengo una buena noticia. Haga el favor de llamar a la escuela al número ocho - sesenta y seis - veinte y cuatro - sesenta.

(b) La conversación

La señora Pérez: [El teléfono suena.] Escuela José Martí. Buenas tardes. Habla la señora Pérez.

[student response]

La señora Pérez: Te llamé porque un alumno acababa de entregarme una cartera y adentro encontramos tu tarjeta de identificación.

[student response]

La señora Pérez: Me imagino lo alegre que estarás. Puedes pasar a recogerla mañana por la mañana.

[student response]

La señora Pérez: Está bien. El alumno que la encontró se llama Pedro González y está en el décimo grado.

[student response]

La señora Pérez: Me parece buena idea que le des las gracias. Y no olvides que en el futuro debes tener más cuidado.

[student response]

La señora Pérez: No hay de qué. Hasta mañana. [Cuelga el teléfono.]

Capítulo 7
Nosotros, no

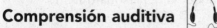

Comprensión auditiva

Escucha las siguientes selecciones. Después de cada selección vas a escuchar varias preguntas. Escoge la mejor respuesta para cada pregunta entre las opciones impresas en tu libro.

Selección número 1

A continuación vas a escuchar una selección sobre un nuevo informe de las Naciones Unidas que afecta a los habitantes de Europa y América del Norte.

Las Naciones Unidas advirtieron que, por primera vez en la historia, el número de ancianos comenzará a superar al de los niños en Europa y América del Norte. Esta situación traerá grandes problemas financieros que durarán hasta más allá del siglo XXI. Según el informe, la cantidad de personas ancianas en estas dos regiones se duplicó en los últimos 40 años, de unos 90 millones en 1950 a 185 millones en la actualidad; y para el año 2025 esta cifra aumentará a más de 310 millones de ancianos. Existirán problemas financieros si estos países se comprometen a mantener los niveles de atención de la salud y previsión social que tienen actualmente. Los servicios que estos países proveen hoy en día fueron implementados sin tener en cuenta la información que se ha obtenido a través de este estudio. Si no hay cambios en los sistemas sociales y económicos, la calidad de vida y casi todos los otros aspectos sociales se verán gravemente afectados.

Número 1 ¿Qué tipo de problemas causará la situación que se discute en esta selección?

Número 2 Según la información, ¿qué sabemos sobre el número de ancianos?

Número 3 ¿Cuántos ancianos habrá para el año 2025?

Número 4 ¿Qué deben hacer estos países para evitar el problema?

Selección número 2

Graciela y Rosa hablan sobre su amiga Caridad y sobre los problemas médicos que ella ha tenido últimamente.

—¿Qué le pasa a Caridad? Hacía tiempo que no la veía y casi ni la reconocí. ¡Cómo ha cambiado!

—Claro. Si hubieras tenido tantas operaciones como ella, nadie te reconocería tampoco.

—¿Cómo? ¿Qué tipo de operaciones?

—Ella siempre ha sido muy vanidosa y para mantenerse joven, primero se hizo cirugía plástica en el cuello. Luego, decidió arreglarse la nariz porque la encontraba demasiado larga.

—Ay, ¡qué horror!, Rosa.

—Después de la operación tuvo complicaciones. Casi se asfixió porque se le infectó la herida. Además, pensaba que el seguro médico la iba a ayudar con los gastos, pero después de una lucha legal de casi ocho meses, no recibió nada. Ahora le debe mucho al abogado y su cara no ha mejorado mucho.

—Oye, Rosa, ¿crees que todo eso vale la pena? Es triste que una persona trate de cambiar el curso de la naturaleza sólo por verse bien.

—Uno de sus vecinos dice que aparentemente hizo todo esto porque su esposo es más joven que ella y quería lucir bien a su lado.

—Eso me enfada. Parece mentira que todavía haya mujeres que no se defiendan y no se acepten tal y como son. Afortunadamente no creo que eso pase muy a menudo, pero pasa. Todas debemos ayudarnos para mantener nuestra autoestima. A estas alturas, las mujeres hemos adelantado mucho y no hay razón de cambiar por los hombres.

—Cuidado, Graciela. No le podemos echar la culpa a su esposo. Ella hizo lo que hizo por su cuenta y no porque él se lo pidió.

—Quizás tengas razón, Rosa. Aunque yo estoy segura de que él tuvo algo que ver con esto. Conozco muy bien a los hombres.

Número 1 ¿Por qué no reconoció Graciela a su amiga Caridad?

Número 2 ¿Qué complicaciones tuvo Caridad?

Número 3 ¿Qué dijo uno de los vecinos de Caridad?

Número 4 ¿Con quién parece estar enfadada Graciela?

Número 5 ¿Cuál es la actitud de Graciela al final del diálogo?

Número 6 Al final, ¿a quién defiende Rosa?

Capítulo 8
No oyes ladrar los perros

Comprensión auditiva

Escucha las siguientes selecciones. Después de cada selección vas a escuchar varias preguntas. Escoge la mejor respuesta para cada pregunta entre las opciones impresas en tu libro.

Selección número 1
Escucha la siguiente selección sobre un artículo en el cual se habla de la relación entre dos hermanas.

Hace unos meses en un artículo de la revista *Ser padres,* la escritora Josie Mejía comentó en detalle su relación con su hermana. A pesar de que ella casi siempre decía que ambas tenían poco en común, no se dio cuenta de la unión que existía entre las dos hasta el día de la boda de su hermana. Fue entonces que descubrió que el matrimonio de su hermana representaba que nunca más estarían juntas y que su vida como había sido hasta ese día cambiaría para siempre. Durante los años que siguieron al matrimonio las hermanas se distanciaron mucho más. Luego, al enfermarse su madre, ellas se vieron de nuevo unidas y el apoyo mutuo que se dieron a causa de los problemas que trajo la mala salud de su madre les hizo aprender lo que es una hermana en realidad. Aquellas diferencias que la autora encontraba cuando eran pequeñas no eran de importancia alguna, lo importante era "una unión secreta imposible de compartir con nadie más". No ha sido sino hasta ahora que la señora Mejía se ha dado cuenta de que, en realidad, ella y su hermana tienen mucho más en común que diferencias y las dos celebran la hermandad y la amistad que existe entre ambas.

Número 1 ¿Cuál es el tema de esta selección?

Número 2 ¿Qué descubrió la escritora el día de la boda de su hermana?

Número 3 ¿De qué se ha dado cuenta la señora Mejía?

Selección número 2
Escucha la siguiente selección sobre el líder campesino Emiliano Zapata.

Hace ya más de ochenta y un años que el dirigente revolucionario Emiliano Zapata fue asesinado en el estado de Morelos, México. Zapata nació en 1879 y, ya a los dieciocho años, este hijo de padres campesinos participó en una protesta para defender los intereses de los campesinos que habían perdido sus tierras. En 1909, después de negociar sin resultado alguno con los avariciosos dueños de tierras, Zapata y un grupo de campesinos ocuparon sus tierras y las distribuyeron entre los que, según ellos, verdaderamente las necesitaban.

Durante la Revolución Mexicana, Zapata se convirtió en uno de sus máximos líderes, llevando siempre al frente los problemas del campesino mexicano. Aunque algunos critican los métodos que utilizó Zapata para luchar contra las injusticias, ya que no siempre fueron dignos de admiración, no hay duda de que los mexicanos siempre lo reconocerán como un gran líder por haber dedicado su vida para darle voz al campesino explotado.

En abril de cada año, desde las calles de la capital hasta los más remotos pueblos del territorio mexicano, las organizaciones laborales recuerdan la memoria de Zapata quien fue traicionado por el ejército federal en 1919. Irónicamente, todavía hoy miles de personas se unen a las marchas y continúan exigiendo asistencia para las comunidades campesinas, así como la tierra que les pertenece. Aunque han pasado más de cien años desde que Zapata comenzó a luchar por los derechos de los campesinos y la reforma agraria, la lucha continúa. Este hecho se ha podido ver recientemente en el estado de Chiapas donde todavía se trata de terminar por siempre la marginación y la injusticia a la que se ve sometida la comunidad campesina e indígena de México.

Número 1 ¿Qué hicieron Zapata y un grupo de campesinos en 1909?

Número 2 ¿Por qué critican a Zapata algunas personas?

Número 3 ¿Qué ironía menciona la selección?

Simulated Conversation

La conversación

Luis: No sé qué hacer. Mis padres siempre están regañándome.

[student response]

Luis: Es que todo lo que hago les parece mal.

[student response]

Luis: No creo que funcione.

[student response]

Luis: Muy bien. Haré lo que sugieres.

[student response]

Luis: Muchas gracias por tu ayuda.

[student response]

Luis: No dejaré de llamarte pero no olvides que puedes llamarme cuando quieras.

[student response]

Luis: Hasta pronto.

Capítulo 9
El árbol de oro

Comprensión auditiva 🎧

Escucha las siguientes selecciones. Después de cada selección vas a escuchar varias preguntas. Escoge la mejor respuesta para cada pregunta entre las opciones impresas en tu libro.

Selección número 1

Escucha esta selección sobre los cuentos de hadas o, como se los llama en inglés, *fairy tales*.

Los cuentos de hadas, o sea los cuentos como "Hansel y Gretel", "El mago de Oz" o "Blancanieves", se han convertido en un tema muy controvertido dentro del área de la educación infantil. Los expertos en esta área han sostenido siempre que estos cuentos ayudan a que los niños empiecen a desarrollar mecanismos de defensa para situaciones que más tarde van a enfrentar en su vida. Sin duda alguna, estos cuentos también los ayudan a asegurarse de que los problemas y las situaciones difíciles puedan ser resueltos y puedan terminar felizmente.

Al mismo tiempo, es importante que los padres observen detalladamente a sus hijos y decidan si ellos deben oír o leer estos cuentos. Los niños más sensibles tendrán problemas con algunos de los temas como la tristeza, la crueldad y los incidentes peligrosos. Los niños deben saber la diferencia entre la fantasía y la realidad, y los padres deben leer estos libros de antemano y estar preparados para hablar con sus hijos sobre lo que sucede en ellos. Es importante aclararles a los niños las dudas que tengan, explicarles los estereotipos, y asegurarse de que ellos entiendan que estos libros fueron escritos muchos años atrás y que las ideas han cambiado desde entonces. Lo importante es que exista un diálogo con los hijos y que se comparta con ellos un material de lectura que sea variado y que ofrezca un balance entre la fantasía y la realidad.

Número 1 ¿Cómo pueden ser beneficiosos los cuentos de hadas para los niños?

Número 2 ¿Qué deben hacer los padres antes de leer estos libros a los niños?

Número 3 ¿Qué explicación les podemos dar a los niños sobre los estereotipos que aparecen en los cuentos?

Número 4 ¿Qué sugerencia se le da a los padres?

Selección número 2

Escucha la siguiente conversación entre David y Miguelina sobre los regalos que David le hace a su profesora.

—Oye, David, ¿qué llevas ahí?

—Es un regalo que le compré a la profesora de arte. Siempre me gusta traerle algo cuando voy de viaje.

—Eres muy amable, pero... ¿no le trajiste otro regalo hace menos de una semana?

—Sí, es verdad pero entonces era su cumpleaños. ¿Por qué te importa tanto mi amabilidad?

—En mi opinión no me parece buena idea. Tal parece que estás tratando de que la profesora te preste más atención a ti que a los otros estudiantes. Ya he visto que en la clase siempre estás de acuerdo con lo que dice ella y hasta te pones en contra de tus amigos.

—No seas envidiosa, Miguelina. La clase de arte es mi clase favorita y la señora Cepeda es una profesora magnífica.

—De acuerdo. Pero no sé si te estás dando cuenta de que muchos de tus amigos ni te hablan. No te confían nada.

—Bueno, soy muy generoso y estás confundiendo mis intenciones. No me importa lo que digan. Yo no voy a cambiar y dejar de ser como soy.

—Si quieres no me hagas caso, pero cuando te quedes sin amigos espero que puedas salir a divertirte con la profesora.

Número 1 ¿De qué se queja Miguelina?

Número 2 Según Miguelina, ¿qué quiere David?

Número 3 ¿Cómo reaccionan los amigos de David?

Número 4 ¿Qué decide David al final?

Simulated Conversation

La conversación

El profesor: Buenos tardes. ¿Deseas algo?

[student response]

El profesor: Es que ya hace dos semanas que anuncié la fecha del examen.

[student response]

El profesor: Comprendo pero si pospongo el examen nos atrasaremos mucho.

[student response]

El profesor: La verdad es que podríamos seguir con el próximo capítulo. ¿Has consultado a tus compañeros de clase?

[student response]

El profesor: Muy bien. Si es así, podemos posponer el examen hasta la semana que viene.

[student response]

El profesor: Anunciaré el día del examen en clase.

[student response]

El profesor: Buenas tardes y espero que esto no vuelva a suceder.

Capítulo 10
Jaque mate en dos jugadas

Comprensión auditiva

Escucha las siguientes selecciones. Después de cada selección vas a escuchar varias preguntas. Escoge la mejor respuesta para cada pregunta entre las opciones impresas en tu libro.

Selección número 1

Ahora vas a escuchar un diálogo entre Pablo y Marta acerca de una película que acaban de ver.

—Pablo, ¿viste la película que te recomendé?

—Por supuesto. Anoche la vi con mi esposa y los niños. ¡Qué final!

—El director es famoso por lo inesperado... la sorpresa.

—Bueno, yo no supe hasta el final que el mayordomo había envenenado al inspector.

—¡Oye, no! Él murió de un tiro. Por eso fue que la policía quería saber quién era el dueño del revólver.

—Lo siento Marta, pero te has equivocado. Cuando ellos regresaron de las carreras de caballos, el mayordomo puso unas gotas de veneno en la limonada y eso fue lo que lo mató.

—Pero, ¿no recuerdas que cuando terminó de beber fue a su cuarto y se oyeron unos disparos?

—Sí, pero eran los sobrinos que estaban cazando en el bosque.

—Bueno, parece que yo confundí todo. Quizás me haya quedado dormida.

—No seas sarcástica. Para mí todo estuvo muy claro.

—En ese caso, el director ha demostrado lo bueno que es. Tendremos que ver la película de nuevo y ver quién tiene razón.

Número 1 ¿Con quién vio Pablo la película?

Número 2 Según Pablo, ¿cómo murió el inspector?

Número 3 ¿Qué oyeron cuando el inspector fue al cuarto?

Número 4 Según Marta, ¿por qué no sabe ella lo que pasó?

Número 5 ¿Qué sugiere Marta al final del diálogo?

Selección número 2

Escucha la siguiente selección sobre Adolfo Bioy Casares, un escritor muy conocido dentro del campo de la literatura fantástica, y su relación con el gran escritor Jorge Luis Borges.

Bioy Casares es reconocido hoy día como uno de los exponentes más hábiles de la literatura fantástica. Quizás lo más interesante sobre su carrera literaria es su íntima relación con el gran maestro Jorge Luis Borges. En 1932 conoció a Borges, y desde entonces surgió una gran amistad entre ellos. Bioy Casares y Borges se reunían regularmente, compartían diferentes ideas que tenían para cuentos, y juntos empezaban a escribir. Firmaban sus inolvidables narraciones con el seudónimo Bastos Domeneq. Pero lo más admirable de esta colaboración es que entre ellos nunca surgió ningún tipo de envidia o competencia. Ambos se tenían gran respeto y siempre mantuvieron que aprendieron el uno del otro.

Bioy Casares realizó su primera creación literaria cuando tenía once años para impresionar a una chica de quien estaba enamorado. Desde ese momento en adelante continuó creando cuentos y novelas donde los personajes se movían en mundo fantástico o policial. Sus personajes son hombres y mujeres ordinarios que, aunque viven en un mundo real, tienen que enfrentarse a acontecimientos fantásticos o inexplicables. En todas sus narraciones, Bioy Casares hace que el lector participe en los misterios de su obra, hace que piense y que llegue a sus propias conclusiones sobre lo que lee.

Es importante notar que una de sus obras más originales, *La invención de Morel,* la escribió cuando tenía solamente veintiséis años. La originalidad de la obra proviene del hecho de que en ella podemos apreciar una visión futurística que va más allá de la realidad virtual, ya que en ella encontramos algunos inventos y descubrimientos recientes que no existían cuando el autor la escribió.

Aunque a Bioy Casares le hubiera gustado haber recibido el Premio Nobel, nunca lo obtuvo. En 1990 recibió el Premio Miguel Cervantes de Literatura, considerado por muchos como el Premio Nobel de la literatura escrita en español. Murió en 1999. En una entrevista hace algunos años, el autor afirmó que si hubiera podido firmar un contrato para poder vivir cien años más, lo habría firmado sin estudiar detalladamente las condiciones para poder hacerlo.

Número 1 ¿Cómo era la relación entre Bioy Casares y Jorge Luis Borges?

Número 2 ¿Con qué propósito escribió Bioy Casares su primera obra?

Número 3 ¿Por qué es muy original la obra *La invención de Morel?*

Número 4 ¿Qué le hubiera gustado a Bioy Casares?

Capítulo 11
La viuda de Montiel

Comprensión auditiva

Escucha las siguientes selecciones. Después de cada selección vas a escuchar varias preguntas. Escoge la mejor respuesta para cada pregunta entre las opciones impresas en tu libro.

Selección número 1
Ahora vas a escuchar una selección sobre la situación económica de Latinoamérica.

Durante la década de los años ochenta la economía latinoamericana recibió un gran golpe debido a su deuda externa. En la década siguiente la crisis se fue superando; poco a poco los precios se fueron estabilizando y tanto la actividad económica como la inversión extranjera vieron un aumento. Aunque las estadísticas ofrecen indicios claros de una recuperación, muchos aún se preocupan de que este desarrollo no se pueda mantener por mucho tiempo. Para lograr el continuo desarrollo, los diferentes gobiernos latinoamericanos han estado estableciendo medidas de inversión y ahorro. Aunque la inversión extranjera continúa creciendo, el ahorro interno juega un papel importantísimo, ya que en el pasado la falta de ahorros ha contribuido a la deuda externa y al fracaso de la economía de muchos de los países en esta región. Sin duda alguna, los errores del pasado han enseñado una buena lección que permitirá que el desarrollo económico no sea algo temporario, sino un crecimiento que dure mucho tiempo.

Número 1 Según la selección, ¿cuál era la situación económica de Latinoamérica en la década de los años noventa?

Número 2 ¿Por qué están preocupadas muchas personas?

Número 3 Según la selección, ¿qué aspecto juega un papel importantísimo en la economía?

Número 4 ¿Cuál ha sido una buena lección para los países latinoamericanos?

Selección número 2
Escucha la siguiente selección sobre la película *El coronel no tiene quien le escriba*, basada en la novela de Gabriel García Márquez.

Aunque muchos consideran imposible recrear para el cine el ambiente típico macondiano que García Márquez creó en muchos de sus cuentos y novelas, Arturo Ripstein, celebrado director mexicano, se propuso en 1998 rodar una película basada en la novela *El coronel no tiene quien le escriba* de Gabriel García Márquez. Según el director, él quería rodar esta película desde que tenía unos veinte años, cuando le pidió a García Márquez por primera vez hacer una película de su novela. Pero García Márquez, quien según algunos, escribió once veces la novela, lo hizo esperar hasta que el director aprendiera lo suficiente para rodar la película. Según el director, en 1995 García Márquez le dijo "...bueno, como ya aprendiste, ya puedes rodar *El coronel*..."

Ripstein escogió un pequeño pueblo de Veracruz, México, porque ésa era su manera de hacer la novela suya, y para darle a su película su sello personal. Este pueblo había sido su universo, un ambiente conocido, el mundo de su abuela, de su familia, de su infancia, y le ofrecía el ambiente propicio para la película.

La novela *El coronel no tiene quien le escriba* narra la historia de un coronel, víctima de una burocracia que lo obliga a vivir una vida angustiosa y llena de miseria, mientras espera la pensión de guerra prometida por el gobierno muchos años atrás y que nunca le llega. Todos los viernes el coronel va al muelle del pueblo a esperar la lancha que trae la correspondencia. Pero esta ceremonia, viernes tras viernes, enfatiza la frustración y casi desesperación que enfrentan el coronel y su esposa, porque viernes tras viernes el cartero le informa que no hay carta para él. La única esperanza que le queda al matrimonio es un gallo, símbolo de sus ideales y de la ilusión de que, por medio del gallo, algún día su situación económica mejore. *El coronel no tiene quien le escriba* es también una historia de amor entre el coronel y su esposa, un amor que ha sobrevivido el paso de los años y las dificultades de su situación. Al mismo tiempo, la historia también refleja la represiva situación política del país. El único hijo del coronel ha sido asesinado por conspirar contra el gobierno.

Según el director Ripstein, "*El coronel no tiene quien le escriba* es una historia que se cuenta sola. Tiene la naturalidad, la simplicidad y la elegancia de la perfección". La tan esperada producción de una de las obras considerada clásica dentro de la literatura latinoamericana vio la luz en el reconocido Festival de Cannes en 1999.

Número 1 ¿Quién es Arturo Ripstein?

Número 2 ¿Por qué no permitió García Márquez que hicieran una película antes?

Número 3 ¿Por qué escogió un pueblo cerca de Veracruz el director?

Número 4 ¿Por qué llevan una vida miserable el coronel y su esposa?

Número 5 ¿Qué espera todos los viernes el coronel?

Número 6 ¿Qué le sucedió al hijo del coronel?

Capítulo 12
Cartas de amor traicionado

Comprensión auditiva 🎧

Escucha las siguientes selecciones. Después de cada selección vas a escuchar varias preguntas. Escoge la mejor respuesta para cada pregunta entre las opciones impresas en tu libro.

Selección número 1
La selección que vas a escuchar trata de un interesante festival de teatro.

Recientemente el Instituto Internacional de Teatro organizó en Santiago de Chile el Festival de Teatro de las Naciones. Unas 40 compañías de 31 países participaron en un extenso programa de conferencias, debates, talleres y, por supuesto, presentaciones teatrales. Entre las presentaciones que merecen ser mencionadas está la que aportó Grecia: un oratorio titulado *Canto general,* basado en un famoso poema del escritor chileno Pablo Neruda. Es interesante el hecho de que esta obra debía haber sido presentada en Chile en 1973, pero debido al golpe militar la presentación no se pudo llevar a cabo. Ahora que el ambiente democrático prevalece en Chile, finalmente se ha podido disfrutar de la obra. España estuvo presente con la obra *La noche mágica*, basada en la música de marchas religiosas. Fue presentada al aire libre, con fuegos artificiales y una música que hizo a los espectadores bailar como en un alegre carnaval en el parque Almagro. Sin duda alguna, este evento, que duró unos doce días, quedará en el recuerdo de los chilenos por mucho tiempo. Las naciones representadas se vieron unidas en un ambiente de hermandad a través del teatro.

Número 1 ¿En qué se basa el oratorio *Canto general?*

Número 2 ¿Por qué no se pudo presentar la obra en 1973?

Número 3 ¿En qué está basada la obra *La noche mágica?*

Número 4 ¿Dónde fue presentada la obra *La noche mágica?*

Número 5 ¿Cuánto tiempo duró el festival de teatro?

Selección número 2
Escucha la siguiente selección sobre la escritora Isabel Allende y dos de sus novelas más importantes: *La casa de los espíritus* y *Paula*.

La chilena Isabel Allende es considerada una de las escritoras más importantes de Latinoamérica de las últimas décadas. Allende escribió su primera novela, *La casa de los espíritus*, en 1982. Esta novela, que en gran parte es autobiográfica, la puso en el ámbito de las escritoras más importantes de su generación, no sólo en Latinoamérica sino también en todo el mundo. *La casa de los espíritus* relata la saga de una familia en una época turbulenta, causada por cambios políticos que tienen lugar en el país. La autora no dice específicamente donde transcurre la novela. Se puede situar en casi cualquier país de Latinoamérica. Pero, la coincidencia de que al final de la novela se produce un golpe de estado, hace que el lector la sitúe en Chile. La novela está contada a través de personajes femeninos, personajes fuertes, determinados y muy similares a las mujeres que fueron parte de la vida de Allende mientras ella crecía. La tradición del realismo mágico, que con tanta habilidad maneja García Márquez en sus obras, está presente en el ambiente donde transcurre la acción.

Después de *La casa de los espíritus,* Allende escribió otras novelas y libros de cuentos que fueron muy bien recibidos por la crítica. Hablemos específicamente de *Paula,* una novela que tuvo mucha importancia para la escritora. En 1991 su hija Paula ingresó en una clínica de Madrid y unos días más tarde entró en coma. Un año después murió, cuando tenía sólo 28 años de edad. Según Allende, decidió escribir *Paula* para no enloquecer. Esta novela empieza como una carta donde la autora narra la historia de su familia, con la intención de que su hija la lea el día que despierte. A través de la novela podemos apreciar el sufrimiento de Isabel Allende durante la enfermedad de su hija, su esperanza de que un día llegue a despertar, y la resignación a su muerte. Allende considera *Paula* el libro más importante e inolvidable que ha escrito y que escribirá. Aunque la novela parezca ser triste, no lo es completamente. En ella no sólo documenta la enfermedad y la muerte de Paula, sino que también enfatiza los momentos felices que pasaron juntas. A Allende este libro le sirvió como una cura o catarsis ante la trágica muerte de su querida Paula.

Número 1 ¿Por qué piensan los lectores que la novela *La casa de los espíritus* tiene lugar en Chile?

Número 2 ¿Quién narra la novela *La casa de los espíritus*?

Número 3 ¿Cuándo escribió Isabel Allende la novela *Paula*?

Número 4 ¿Qué piensa Allende de la novela *Paula*?

Simulated Conversation

(a) El mensaje

Hola, es Josefina. No dejes de llamarme. Me siento muy triste.

(b) La conversación

Josefina: [El teléfono suena.] ¿Bueno?

[student response]

Josefina: Cuando te llamé acababa de ver a mi novio jugando fútbol con sus amigos.

[student response]

Josefina: Es un mentiroso. Me dijo que no podíamos salir porque tenía mucha tarea.

[student response]

Josefina: No creo que sea buena idea.

[student response]

Josefina: Está bien. Haré lo que sugieres.

[student response]

Josefina: Gracias por tu ayuda. Te llamo luego. [Cuelga el teléfono.]

Capítulo 13
Emma Zunz

Comprensión auditiva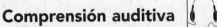

Escucha las siguientes selecciones. Después de cada selección vas a escuchar varias preguntas. Escoge la mejor respuesta para cada pregunta entre las opciones impresas en tu libro.

Selección número 1

Ahora vas a escuchar un cuento corto sobre un hombre que vivía solo y su experiencia con un ladrón.

En un pequeño pueblo de Nicaragua, Roberto, un viejo hombre de negocios, se recostó en su silla favorita en un cuarto de su casa. Unos minutos más tarde vio la sombra de un hombre que trataba de abrir la caja fuerte. En esa caja fuerte era donde Roberto tenía guardados todos sus ahorros. De repente miró los retratos que colgaban de la pared y recordó los días felices con su familia. Se mordió los labios para no decir nada, pues no quería que el ladrón lo descubriera. Después de unos minutos no pudo resistir más y suspiró profundamente. Al oírlo, el ladrón se volvió. Roberto vio la navaja que el ladrón llevaba en la mano y comenzó a sollozar. Pensó de nuevo en los retratos y empezó a hablar en voz alta sobre su vida, las dificultades que había tenido, la muerte de su esposa y la soledad que sintió cuando sus hijos lo habían abandonado. Al ladrón, que no era un hombre sin sentimientos, le empezaron a correr lágrimas por las mejillas. Sintió compasión por Roberto y decidió olvidarse de la caja fuerte. Lanzó un suspiro y salió por la misma puerta por donde había entrado.

Número 1 ¿Dónde tiene lugar este cuento?

Número 2 ¿Qué había en la caja fuerte?

Número 3 ¿Qué hizo el ladrón mientras Roberto le hablaba?

Número 4 ¿Qué hizo el ladrón al final?

Selección número 2

Escucha la siguiente conversación entre Adelaida y Gerardo sobre una obra de teatro que él acaba de ver.

—Adelaida, ¿viste la obra de teatro que se estrenó la semana pasada?

—No, no la he visto Gerardo. ¿De qué trata?

—Es estupenda. Tiene lugar en un barco donde se ha cometido un crimen. El drama empieza cuando los obreros del puerto deciden no trabajar hasta que se resuelva la muerte de uno de los trabajadores que murió debido a las malas condiciones de trabajo.

—Ay, no parece tan interesante. Parece que sólo se trata de los problemas laborales de los trabajadores.

—Eso pensé yo también. Pero, la cosa se pone buena cuando una pasajera encuentra una pequeña caja en el escritorio de su camarote. Llama por teléfono a los oficiales del barco para que vayan a buscarla. La pasajera va al cuarto de baño a maquillarse y cuando sale del baño, se han robado la cajita.

—¡Uy!, ¿y qué pasa después?

—No te quiero decir mucho porque si la vas a ver y sabes el final, no será tan interesante.

—Tienes que decirme más.

—Bueno, encuentran un revólver con las huellas digitales del criminal, una mujer que se quiere vengar de su esposo. En fin, tremendo drama. Y en medio de todo esto, sospechan de la pobre pasajera. Y su vida está en peligro.

—¿Y encuentran al criminal?

—Sí, por supuesto. Un pasajero o pasajera (no te voy a decir si es hombre o mujer) confiesa su culpa.

—¡Qué malo eres, Gerardo! Ahora sí que tengo ganas de ver la obra. Oye, ¿quieres verla de nuevo? Yo te invito.

—Mmm…, sería una buena idea. Aunque sé lo que pasa al final me gustaría verla de nuevo.

—Fenomenal. ¿Qué día prefieres ir?

—El jueves por la noche sería ideal. Termino en la universidad a eso de las cuatro.

—¿Por qué no nos reunimos en el Café Cervantes a las cinco? Así podemos comer algo ligero antes de ir al teatro y después podemos cenar.

—Buena idea. ¿Tú vas a sacar las entradas?

—Sí, esta misma tarde las compro.

—Oye, ya se me hace tarde. Tengo una cita con el profesor Machado.

—Bueno, hasta luego, Gerardo. Hablemos más tarde.

—Hasta luego, Adelaida.

Número 1 ¿Cómo empieza la obra de teatro que describe Gerardo?

Número 2 ¿Qué pasó con la pequeña caja que encontró la pasajera?

Número 3 ¿Qué <u>NO</u> quiere hacer Gerardo?

Número 4 ¿Qué decide hacer Gerardo?

Número 5 ¿Por qué tiene que irse Gerardo?

Simulated Conversation

(a) El mensaje

Hola, es Antonio. Llámame en cuanto puedas. Estoy furioso.

(b) La conversación

Antonio: [El teléfono suena.] ¿Aló?

[student response]

Antonio: Acabo de oír que andan diciendo que tú y yo copiamos las respuestas del examen de historia.

[student response]

Antonio: Yo tampoco lo creo. Debe ser porque sacamos la mejor nota de la clase.

[student response]

Antonio: En realidad no creo que nadie crea el chisme. Pero me molesta.

[student response]

Antonio: Tienes razón. Tú y yo sabemos lo mucho que estudiamos. Sacamos la nota que merecíamos por nuestro esfuerzo.

[student response]

Antonio: Bueno. Está bien. Lo mejor es no hacerle caso a los chismes.

[student response]

Antonio: Chao. Hasta pronto. [Cuelga el teléfono.]

Teatro
Capítulo 27
El delantal blanco

Comprensión auditiva

Escucha las siguientes selecciones. Después de cada selección vas a escuchar varias preguntas. Escoge la mejor respuesta para cada pregunta entre las opciones impresas en tu libro.

Selección número 1

Vas a escuchar una selección sobre las experiencias de los niños.

Por muchos años, los expertos han pasado por alto el efecto que el estilo de vida moderna tiene en los niños. Hoy día se empiezan a publicar resultados de estudios que indican claramente que los niños, tanto como los adultos, tienen presiones y ansiedades que les trae la sociedad moderna. Pero los niños están en desventaja, ya que su falta de experiencia no les permite usarla para resolver la ansiedad que puedan sentir, como lo hacen los adultos. Cuando la ansiedad se vuelve demasiado intensa, el niño puede mostrar síntomas muy visibles, como dolores de cabeza, trastornos digestivos, pesadillas y hasta pueden llorar explosivamente. Pero muchas veces los síntomas no son tan obvios, y los adultos no se dan cuenta o no quieren admitir que la ansiedad es su causa. Es importante notar que hasta bebés recién nacidos están expuestos a la ansiedad. Esta condición puede ser causada por cambios en la forma en que son alimentados, o vestidos, entre otras cosas. Cuando los padres trabajan fuera de la casa, esta situación contribuye a que el bebé se sienta incómodo en los brazos de personas desconocidas, por ejemplo. Es importante que los padres estén al tanto de las posibles tensiones que puedan causar ansiedad en sus hijos y evitar los cambios constantes, especialmente los cambios bruscos.

Número 1 ¿A qué no se le ha prestado mucha atención por mucho tiempo?

Número 2 Según la narración, ¿cuál es una de las desventajas que tienen los niños?

Número 3 Según la narración, ¿qué causa trastornos en los bebés?

Número 4 ¿Qué deben evitar los padres?

Selección número 2

La selección que vas a escuchar trata de un nuevo fenómeno en las universidades estadounidenses, específicamente en las universidades que son exclusivamente para mujeres.

Las universidades exclusivamente para mujeres han tenido un renacimiento en los últimos años en los Estados Unidos, en parte a causa de la polémica sobre el acoso sexual y la persistencia de la discriminación por sexo. Según un estudio publicado por el diario *The New York Times,* el número de matrículas en esas instituciones ha aumentado en un 14 por ciento desde 1991 y ha aumentado de 82.500 estudiantes en 1981 a alrededor de 98.000.

Muchas de las mujeres que eligen estudiar en una universidad exclusivamente para estudiantes del sexo femenino consideran que en los centros mixtos no recibirán la misma atención de los profesores, que según ellas dan mayor importancia a la formación de los hombres. El resultado de esa teoría es que las mujeres que salen de una universidad mixta están menos preparadas que sus compañeros del sexo masculino y, consecuentemente, tienen menos oportunidades en el mercado del trabajo. Las que apoyan las universidades para mujeres citan como ejemplo los casos de las mujeres que recientemente han sido elegidas como senadoras en el Senado de los Estados Unidos, como la primera dama, Hillary Rodham Clinton, quienes están llevando la voz femenina al lugar donde nacen las leyes que las afectan. Muchas de ellas se graduaron de este tipo de universidades.

El problema ahora es la enorme cantidad de solicitudes de matrícula que inunda las universidades para mujeres. Hoy día, el trabajo de los que están encargados de las oficinas de admisión se hace cada vez más difícil, debido a la feroz competencia para adquirir matrícula en estas universidades.

Número 1 ¿Qué piensan muchas mujeres acerca de las universidades mixtas?

Número 2 ¿Qué considera más importante el profesorado de las universidades con estudiantes de ambos sexos?

Número 3 ¿Qué se ha visto últimamente en el Senado de los Estados Unidos?

Número 4 ¿Qué problemas tienen ahora las universidades para mujeres?

Selección número 3
Vas a escuchar una conversación entre Luz y un amigo.

—¿Por qué andas tan enojada, Luz?

—Estoy muy triste con Juan. ¿Sabes lo que hizo?

—No, debe ser algo muy serio. Ayer Uds. estaban muy contentos.

—Pues, hoy es su cumpleaños y le envié una tarjeta por correo. Cuando le pregunté si la había recibido me dijo que no estaba seguro.

—¿Cómo que no estaba seguro?

—Es que recogió el correo y pensó que eran anuncios de publicidad y lo echó todo a la basura.

—Ése es un error muy común. Ya sabes que la mayoría de las cartas que recibimos son de publicidad.

—Tienes razón, no debo ser tan incomprensiva. Después de todo, es su cumpleaños.

—Pues, vamos a la tienda y compremos otra tarjeta. Más bien dos, tú compras una y yo otra.

—De acuerdo. Se pondrá muy contento.

Número 1 ¿Qué le pasa a Luz?

Número 2 ¿Qué hizo Juan con la tarjeta?

Número 3 ¿Por qué perdona Luz a Juan?

 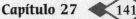

Selección número 4

Escucha la siguiente conversación entre Abelardo y Eva sobre un nuevo chico en la escuela.

—Abelardo, ¿conoces a ese chico que va allí?

—Sí, lo conocí ayer. Es nuevo en la escuela.

—Me parece muy extraño. Ya hace más de un mes que empezaron las clases y todavía no lo he visto con nadie.

—Pues mira, es muy chistoso. Tiene una personalidad fenomenal.

—Y... ¿cómo fue que lo conociste?

—Como tú, me extrañaba que no tuviera amigos, así que decidí averiguar por qué no hablaba con nadie. Lo vi en la cafetería y me senté en la misma mesa. Después de un rato, empezamos a conocernos mejor y lo pasamos muy bien.

—Eres muy valiente. Yo nunca tomaría la iniciativa de hablar con alguien que no conozco. ¡Quién sabe! ¿Y si no le gusto? Me sentiría como una tonta.

—Yo pensaba lo mismo pero ahora me siento más cómodo y no me importa si le gusto o no. Lo importante es ampliar el círculo de amigos y darles la bienvenida a los nuevos estudiantes.

—Tienes razón. Estoy segura de que he perdido la oportunidad de conocer a personas muy interesantes por no ser más amistosa.

—Has expresado muy claramente mi nueva actitud. Así que anda y salúdalo. Estoy seguro de que se van a llevar muy bien.

—¡Adelante! Estoy nerviosa, pero tengo que aprender a ser más sociable. Ya te contaré mañana.

—Hasta mañana y que lo pases bien.

Número 1 ¿Por qué le parece extraño el chico a Eva?

Número 2 ¿Cuándo conoció mejor Abelardo al chico?

Número 3 ¿Cuál es la nueva actitud de Abelardo?

Número 4 ¿Qué hace Eva al final?

Poesía
Capítulo 14
Rima LIII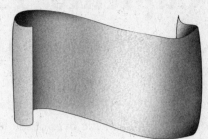

Volverán las oscuras golondrinas
en tu balcón sus nidos a colgar,
y otra vez con el ala a sus cristales,
    jugando llamarán;

    pero aquéllas que el vuelo refrenaban
tu hermosura y mi dicha a contemplar;
aquéllas que aprendieron nuestros nombres,
    ésas… ¡no volverán!

    Volverán las tupidas madreselvas
de tu jardín las tapias a escalar,
y otra vez a la tarde, aun más hermosas,
    sus flores se abrirán;

    pero aquellas cuajadas de rocío,
cuyas gotas mirábamos temblar
y caer, como lágrimas del día…
    ésas… ¡no volverán!

    Volverán del amor en tus oídos
las palabras ardientes a sonar;
tu corazón de su profundo sueño
    tal vez despertará;

    pero mudo y absorto y de rodillas,
como se adora a Dios ante su altar,
como yo te he querido… desengáñate:
    ¡así no te querrán!

Capítulo 15
Me gustas cuando callas

Me gustas cuando callas porque estás como ausente,
y me oyes desde lejos, y mi voz no te toca.
Parece que los ojos se te hubieran volado
y parece que un beso te cerrara la boca.

Como todas las cosas están llenas de mi alma
emerges de las cosas, llena del alma mía.
Mariposa de sueño, te pareces a mi alma,
y te pareces a la palabra melancolía.

Me gustas cuando callas y estás como distante.
Y estás como quejándote, mariposa en arrullo.
Y me oyes desde lejos, y mi voz no te alcanza:
déjame que me calle con el silencio tuyo.

Déjame que te hable también con tu silencio
claro como una lámpara, simple como un anillo.
Eres como la noche, callada y constelada.
Tu silencio es de estrella, tan lejano y sencillo.

Me gustas cuando callas porque estás como ausente.
Distante y dolorosa como si hubieras muerto.
Una palabra entonces, una sonrisa bastan.
Y estoy alegre, alegre de que no sea cierto.

Script

Capítulo 17
Proverbios y cantares, XXIX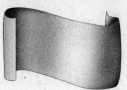

Caminante, son tus huellas
el camino y nada más;
caminante, no hay camino:
se hace camino al andar.
Al andar se hace camino,
y al volver la vista atrás
se ve la senda que nunca
se ha de volver a pisar.
Caminante no hay camino,
sino estelas en la mar.

Capítulo 18
Despedida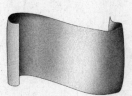

Si muero,
dejad el balcón abierto.

El niño come naranjas.
(Desde mi balcón lo veo.)

El segador siega el trigo.
(Desde mi balcón lo siento.)

¡Si muero,
dejad el balcón abierto!

 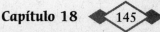

Capítulo 19
Canción de jinete

Córdoba
Lejana y sola.

Jaca negra, luna grande,
y aceitunas en mi alforja.
Aunque sepa los caminos
yo nunca llegaré a Córdoba.

Por el llano, por el viento,
jaca negra, luna roja.
La muerte me está mirando
desde las torres de Córdoba.

¡Ay qué camino tan largo!
¡Ay mi jaca valerosa!
¡Ay que la muerte me espera,
antes de llegar a Córdoba!

Córdoba.
Lejana y sola.

Capítulo 20
Selecciones de *Versos sencillos*

Selección de *Versos sencillos*, XXXIX

Cultivo una rosa blanca,
En julio como en enero,
Para el amigo sincero
Que me da su mano franca

Y para el cruel que me arranca
El corazón con que vivo,
Cardo ni oruga cultivo;
Cultivo la rosa blanca.

Selección de *Versos sencillos*, XLIV

Tiene el leopardo un abrigo
En su monte seco y pardo:
Yo tengo más que el leopardo
Porque tengo un buen amigo.

Duerme, como en un juguete,
La mushma en su cojinete
De arce del Japón yo digo:
"No hay cojín como un amigo."

Tiene el conde su abolengo:
Tiene la aurora el mendigo:
Tiene ala el ave: ¡yo tengo
Allá en México un amigo!

Tiene el señor presidente
Un jardín con una fuente,
Y un tesoro en oro y trigo:
Tengo más, tengo un amigo.

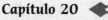

Capítulo 21
Canción de otoño en primavera

Juventud, divino tesoro
¡ya te vas para no volver!
Cuando quiero llorar, no lloro...
y a veces lloro sin querer...

Plural ha sido la celeste
historia de mi corazón.
Era una dulce niña, en este
mundo de duelo y aflicción.

Miraba como el alba pura;
sonreía como una flor.
Era su cabellera obscura
hecha de noche y de dolor.

Yo era tímido como un niño.
Ella, naturalmente fue,
para mi amor hecho de armiño,
Herodías y Salomé...

Juventud, divino tesoro,
¡ya te vas para no volver!
Cuando quiero llorar, no lloro,
y a veces lloro sin querer.

La otra fue más sensitiva,
y más consoladora y más
halagadora y expresiva,
cual no pensé encontrar jamás.

Pues a su continua ternura
una pasión violenta unía.
En un peplo de gasa pura
una bacante se envolvía...

En sus brazos tomó mi ensueño
y lo arrulló como a un bebé...
Y lo mató, triste y pequeño,
falto de luz, falto de fe.

Juventud, divino tesoro,
¡te fuiste para no volver!
Cuando quiero llorar, no lloro,
y a veces lloro sin querer...

Otra juzgó que era mi boca
el estuche de su pasión
y que me roería, loca,
con sus dientes el corazón,

poniendo en un amor de exceso
la mira de su voluntad,
mientras eran abrazo y beso
síntesis de la eternidad;

y de nuestra carne ligera
imaginar siempre un Edén,
sin pensar que la Primavera
y la carne acaban también...

Juventud, divino tesoro,
¡ya te vas para no volver!
Cuando quiero llorar, no lloro,
¡y a veces lloro sin querer!

¡Y las demás!, en tantos climas,
en tantas tierras, siempre son,
si no pretextos de mis rimas,
fantasmas de mi corazón.

En vano busqué a la princesa
que estaba triste de esperar.
La vida es dura. Amarga y pesa.
¡Ya no hay princesa que cantar!

 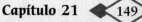

Mas a pesar del tiempo terco,
mi sed de amor no tiene fin;
con el cabello gris me acerco
a los rosales del jardín...

Juventud, divino tesoro,
¡ya te vas para no volver!...
Cuando quiero llorar, no lloro,
y a veces lloro sin querer...

¡Mas es mía el Alba de oro!

Part A
Formal Writing

Formal Writing No. 1

Fuente No. 3

El uso regular de ordenadores favorece unos mejores resultados escolares

París - Los estudiantes adolescentes que hacen un uso regular de ordenadores, en su casa o en el colegio, **tienen mejores resultados escolares en matemáticas,** según un <u>estudio divulgado por la OCDE,</u> que subraya las **diferencias de acceso a las tecnologías** de la información en unos y otros países.

La mayoría de los alumnos que utilizan un ordenador desde hace varios años tienen resultados superiores a la media en matemáticas, mientras que los que carecen de acceso a computadoras o las utilizan desde hace poco **"tienen tendencia a estar retrasados respecto al nivel de su nivel de estudios"**, afirma la Organización para la Cooperación y el Desarrollo Económico (OCDE).

Los autores del informe vinculan los "mediocres" resultados de los estudiantes —de entre 15 y 16 años— que sólo pueden utilizar un ordenador desde hace poco en parte a su situación familiar, ya que en la mayoría de los casos, son de origen social desfavorecido.

Descontando el impacto de los factores socioeconómicos, **"el efecto positivo del uso regular de un ordenador es evidente"** como ha quedado demostrado en particular en las encuestas realizadas en Alemania, Australia, Bélgica, Corea del Sur, Estados Unidos y Suiza.

No es sólo para juegos

El conocido como "Club de los países desarrollados" explica que muchos de los alumnos que tienen ordenador en su domicilio no lo utilizan únicamente para jugar, y así la mitad de los interrogados aseguraban **recurrir con frecuencia al tratamiento de textos y a Internet como instrumento de búsqueda.**

Cuenta que **las chicas dominan menos que los chicos** la ejecución de las funciones informáticas, en particular las más complejas como la programación o las presentaciones multimedia.

De los 40 países analizados —los 30 miembros de la OCDE y una decena en Desarrollo como Brasil, Indonesia, Rusia o Uruguay—, los que disponen de más ordenadores por alumno en la escuela son Liechtenstein, Estados Unidos, Australia, Corea del Sur, Hungría, Nueva Zelanda, Reino Unido, Hong Kong, Austria o Canadá.

Mientras en todos esos estados hay al menos tres computadoras por cada 10 alumnos, en Túnez, Brasil, Rusia, Serbia, Turquía, Indonesia, Uruguay o Tailandia disponen de menos de cinco ordenadores por cada 100 estudiantes.

Formal Writing No. 2

Fuente No. 3

El altruismo en niños y chimpancés

Tan temprano como a los 18 meses, los bebés ya demuestran una conducta altruista, lo que según un grupo de científicos alemanes, sugiere que los seres humanos tienen una tendencia natural a ayudar a los demás.

En una serie de experimentos publicados por la revista *Science,* niños menores de dos años ayudaron a personas desconocidas a completar tareas como apilar libros.

Los chimpancés hicieron lo mismo, lo cual provee la primera evidencia directa de altruismo en primates no humanos.

El altruismo pudo haber evolucionado desde hace seis millones de años en un ancestro común de chimpancés y humanos, señala el estudio.

Recompensas

Científicos han debatido mucho en torno a qué provoca que las personas "demuestren la bondad de sus corazones" al ayudar a gente desconocida sin importar la carencia de beneficios para ellas mismas.

La sociedad humana depende de que la gente esté dispuesta a colaborar con otros —como por ejemplo, donar a organizaciones de caridad— y muchos científicos sostienen que el altruismo es una función humana que se encuentra en nuestro cerebro.

"Se ha dicho que los chimpancés actúan principalmente para su propio beneficio, pero en nuestro experimento no hubo recompensas y aún así ellos ayudaron", señaló Felix Warneken, un psicólogo del Instituto de Antropología Evolutiva Max Planck, ubicado en Leipzig, Alemania.

"Sorprendente"

El doctor Warneken y su colega, el profesor Michael Tomasello, querían ver si los niños que aún no habían aprendido destrezas sociales estaban dispuestos a ayudar a personas que no eran de su entorno.

Los científicos llevaron a cabo tareas sencillas como dejar caer ganchos mientras se guindaban ropas o desapilar libros.

Casi todos en un grupo de 24 bebés de 18 meses ayudaron a recoger los ganchos o los libros, la mayoría lo hizo en los primeros 10 segundos del experimento.

Sin embargo, sólo lo hicieron si ellos creían que el investigador necesitaba el objeto para completar la tarea porque si los ganchos o los libros se dejaban caer deliberadamente, los niños no los recogían.

"Los resultados fueron sorprendentes porque estos niños son tan jóvenes, aún llevan pañales y apenas pueden hablar, pero ya muestran una conducta tendiente a ayudar", indicó Warneken.

Los científicos investigaron tareas más complejas como retirar un objeto de una caja con tapa.

Cuando accidentalmente dejaron caer una cucharilla adentro de la caja, y pretendieron que no sabían sobre la tapa, los niños ayudaron a retirarla.

No lo hicieron cuando pensaban que la cucharilla había sido arrojada deliberadamente.

Las tareas fueron repetidas con tres chimpancés que habían sido criados en cautiverio.

Los chimpancés no ayudaron en tareas más complejas como el experimento con la caja, pero sí ayudaron al humano que los cuidaba en tareas simples como alcanzar un objeto.

"Tanto los niños como los chimpancés están dispuestos a ayudar, pero parecen diferenciarse en su habilidad para interpretar las necesidades de ayuda de los demás en situaciones distintas", concluyeron los científicos.

Estudio en Uganda

Más evidencia sobre la habilidad de los chimpancés para cooperar, fue revelada en otro estudio publicado en la misma edición de la revista *Science*.

Alicia Melis del Santuario para Chimpancés de la isla Ngamba en Uganda, encontró que los chimpancés reconocieron cuándo era necesario colaborar y seleccionaron el mejor compañero de equipo para trabajar.

Los chimpancés tuvieron que cooperar para alcanzar una bandeja de comida halando para ello, dos cuerdas al mismo tiempo.

"Nunca habíamos visto este nivel de entendimiento en tareas de cooperación en otros animales, a excepción de humanos", aseguró.

Sin embargo, Melis expresó que aún no hay evidencia de que los chimpancés se comuniquen entre sí en torno a metas comunes, como lo hacen los niños desde una edad temprana.

Formal Writing No. 3

Fuente No. 3

Una campaña para luchar contra los prejuicios
La Fundación Secretariado General Gitano puso en marcha en el año 2004 una campaña para modificar la imagen social negativa que sufre esta población en la sociedad española. Bajo el lema "Conócelos antes de juzgarlos" se realizaron anuncios publicitarios, cuñas de radio, carteles y otra serie de iniciativas. Los resultados fueron tan buenos que han decidido reanudarla con una segunda fase que se centra en los prejuicios que tenemos y que nos llevan a discriminar a esta comunidad.

¿Por qué se produce la discriminación en nuestra sociedad? ¿Qué motivos existen para que un grupo social se enfrente diariamente a la marginación por parte de varios sectores de la población? No es un problema que aparezca de un día para otro. Al contrario, es una suma de situaciones que se van acumulando a lo largo del tiempo. En nuestro país existe un caso evidente: la población gitana que se conoce en inglés como *gypsies*. Llevan con nosotros desde hace más de mil años, pero sólo desde la aprobación de la Constitución Española son considerados como sujetos con plenos derechos. Y esto en el campo de la ley, porque en la sociedad todavía tienen que enfrentarse a múltiples casos de discriminación.

Con el objetivo de modificar esa percepción negativa que todavía existe en nuestro país, la Fundación Secretariado Gitano puso en marcha en 2004 la campaña de sensibilización social "Conócelos antes de juzgarlos". El éxito fue tal, que el pasado mes de noviembre pusieron en marcha una segunda fase. "En nuestra sociedad existe una percepción de los gitanos que no se ajusta a la realidad", asegura Benjamín Cabaleiro, coordinador de la campaña. "La población gitana no es sucia, ni vaga, ni delincuente, como muchos piensan." La Fundación había desarrollado muchas acciones para mejorar la percepción, pero necesitaban una iniciativa que llegara a más amplios sectores de la sociedad. "Queríamos trabajar en el campo de los estereotipos y los prejuicios", afirma Benjamín. Y por eso encargaron a una firma publicitaria una campaña de gran calado.

Tras las dos fases de la compaña, la Fundación está muy satisfecha con los resultados. Según un estudio que encargaron a una consultora, el grado de recuerdo en la población española es de un 15%, una cifra muy elevada. "Un 13,2% de los encuestados manifestaron que había cambiado un poco o mucho su percepción hacia la comunidad gitana", apunta Benjamín.

IMAGEN SOCIAL. En encuestas e investigaciones los gitanos aparecen como el grupo social más rechazado. En las mismas, queda patente un profundo desconocimiento sobre su realidad actual. La mayoría de los prejuicios y esteriotipos sobre esta población se arrastran desde épocas preconstitucionales y se han mantenido, a pesar del avance que la situación de los gitanos ha experimentado en las últimas décadas.

ESTUDIO. Un estudio realizado por la consultora Salvetti & Llombart revela que los estereotipos provienen en mayor medida de la imagen transmitida por los medios de comunicación y por las informaciones indirectas, que de las experiencias o relaciones directas con las personas gitanas.

SABER MÁS. Si quieres saber más acerca del desarrollo de la campaña o de las actividades que lleva a cabo la Fundación Secretariado Gitano puedes entrar en su página web: www.gitanos.org.

Los estereotipos se convierten en prejuicios

Susana Jiménez es una joven gitana que trabaja muy activamente en la Fundación Secretariado Gitano. Colaboró en la campaña de 2004 y tras comprobar los beneficios de una iniciativa así, decidió implicarse en la segunda fase. La primera parte estaba basada en los estereotipos y en las generalizaciones que hace la sociedad respecto a la población gitana. "Hicimos anuncios publicitarios, cuñas de radio, carteles, talleres y otra serie de actividades para dar a conocer esta realidad", asegura. Eran imágenes muy impactantes que pretendían invitar a la siguiente reflexión: ¿Tiene sentido juzgar a todo un colectivo por las acciones de unos pocos? Uno de los carteles, por ejemplo, reflejaba la imagen de un cielo despejado con una pequeña nube y este mensaje: Está nublado. A continuación, en la parte inferior del cartel decía lo siguiente: Así vemos a la comunidad gitana. Conócelos antes de juzgarlos.

En la segunda fase, la Fundación Secretariado Gitano ha querido centrarse en el tema de los prejuicios. El lema de la campaña es "Tus prejuicios son las voces de otros". "Cuando se interiorizan los estereotipos se convierten en prejuicios y la consecuencia directa es la discriminación", asegura Benjamín Cabaleiro.

Un intercambio cultural

Una de las actividades en las que participa la Fundación Secretariado Gitano, en este caso junto con la Asociación Iliber de Granada, es un intercambio cultural promovido por la Unión Europea. El programa se llama "Herencia, cultura y vida" y el pasado año reunió a jóvenes gitanos y no gitanos de cuatro países distintos: Irlanda, República Checa, Hungría y España. El objetivo era dar a conocer los elementos de la cultura gitana y la similitud que existe en las poblaciones de los distintos países. Los participantes tenían entre 18 y 25 años y durante el intercambio, que tuvo lugar en Strnadovský Mlýn (República Checa), desarrollaron un programa que comprendía talleres de teatro, danza, música y cultura. Según Carmen Ramos, responsable de la Asociación Iliber, la experiencia ha resultado muy positiva para todos. "Nosotros hemos participado en diferentes intercambios y nos parece una buena forma de dar a conocer nuestra cultura a jóvenes de distintos países", asegura.

Formal Writing No. 4

Fuente No. 3

Sólo para mujeres

En un centro cultural ubicado en el sur de Quito un grupo de mujeres conversa animadamente mientras toma el desayuno: té o café, pan con jamón y un plato de maíz. Algunas parecen muy tranquilas, otras tienen en el semblante una expresión nerviosa.

Es la primera clase del taller de la Escuela de Formación de Líderes Indígenas Mujeres Dolores Cacuango, un espacio en donde se dan cita mujeres indígenas de todo el país, todas ellas con un mismo objetivo en mente: aprender a ser buenas dirigentes y trasladar sus conocimientos a su comunidad.

Para venir a la escuela, "algunas tienen que caminar durante horas hasta llegar a una carretera para tomar un bus, otras tienen que hacer gran parte del trayecto en canoa", me cuenta Victoria Carrasco, religiosa de la providencia y asesora académica y pedagógica de la institución.

Esta institución que comenzó a funcionar con regularidad en 1998, se propuso devolver la confianza en sí mismas a las mujeres indígenas, ayudarlas a recuperar su autoestima y a compartir y expresar sus conocimientos a los demás integrantes de su comunidad y otras comunidades.

Las materias que dictan los profesores son variadas, las alumnas aprenden desde ecología, historia, medicina tradicional, hasta contabilidad y cómo administrar proyectos de desarrollo.

"Las mujeres hemos venido acompañando silenciosamente a los compañeros desde hace muchos años, sin embargo hemos sido invisibles. Y por muchas razones como el estar ocupadas con los quehaceres de la casa, el trabajo en el campo y los hijos, no hemos tenido la posibilidad de ampliar nuestros conocimientos", me dice Blanca Chancoso, una de las dirigentes más radicales que tiene Ecuador, y coordinadora de la escuela.

"Las mujeres estamos muy atrasito de los hombres. Por eso vimos la necesidad de crear un espacio donde podamos también intercambiar nuestros conocimientos y participar más activamente en el proceso organizativo de los pueblos indígenas", agrega.

Mientras charlamos en el patio de la escuela, las alumnas siguen llegando. "De Saraguro hasta aquí tengo doce horas. Después del viaje me siento cansada y se me hinchan los pies", me cuenta Carmen Gualán, una de las alumnas que por nada del mundo se pierde una clase.

Machismo

Según Victoria, el problema de la discriminación de la mujer, no es un tema que atañe únicamente a las sociedades occidentales, "este fenómeno también se produce en los pueblos indios".

Como ejemplo, me cuenta la historia de dos figuras históricas de Ecuador, la de Dolores Cacuango (en cuyo honor se bautizó a la escuela) y Tránsito Amaguaña, "dos mujeres que lucharon por la educación y la tierra, pero que nunca llegaron a desempeñar roles en la dirigencia, ni en las de base, ni en las nacionales".

Por otra parte me hace notar que la CONAIE (Confederación de Nacionalidades Indígenas de Ecuador) "nunca ha sido dirigida por una mujer".

Más allá del discurso de maestras y organizadoras está el testimonio de las propias alumnas, "salir por primera vez de la casa fue muy difícil, tuve que luchar con los dirigentes, con mi esposo y a mis familiares les da mucha desconfianza cuando salgo de la casa. Los hombres piensan que ya no vamos a regresar", me confiesa Martina Guamán, de la provincia Cañar.

Lealtad, servicio y transparencia

Para el mediodía, el número de alumnas ha aumentado. En este y otros sentidos la escuela tiene una política de gran tolerancia y adaptación a la situación de las alumnas. Muchas por ejemplo, no acuden todos los días de la semana o vienen con sus hijos, que se entretienen jugando en el patio con los demás niños que acompañan a sus mamás a la escuela.

A diferencia de una escuela de un sistema de educación formal, aquí no son las alumnas las que han tomado la decisión de asistir a clases, "es la comunidad la que decide quien va a ir a la escuela, las decisiones (en las comunidades indígenas) no se toman de forma individual sino mediante el consenso", señala Victoria.

Tampoco las cualidades que desde un punto de vista occidental serían las más obvias (capacidad de expresión, liderazgo, carisma, etc.) son las que se buscan en un líder indígena.

"La lealtad a la comunidad y a la organización son clave, sobre todo en un tiempo de tanta politiquería", dice Victoria. "Otro punto es la disposición y capacidad de dar tiempo y servicio a su comunidad, así como la transparencia en el manejo de fondos. Y por último, viene la capacidad", agrega.

Sin embargo, Blanca Chancoso admite que la escuela es sólo una parte en el proceso de formación de una dirigente, "una líder no se forma aquí exclusivamente. Lo que nosotros hacemos es darle una dirección a ese liderazgo para que no sea utilizado y en cambio, pueda convertirse en una luz para la comunidad".

María Dolores

El curso tiene una duración de tres años, aunque me encontré con muchas mujeres que ya se habían graduado, pero seguían asistiendo a clases "porque tenían mucho todavía que aprender", como me dijo una de las alumnas más ancianas que por nada del mundo se pierde una clase. Ella se llama María Dolores Segovia Mendieta y tiene 77 años. Muchos la conocen como Mama Lola.

Tal vez el caso de María Dolores sea una muestra de que la escuela está logrando algunos de sus objetivos.

"Yo me creía una persona insignificante. Aquí en la escuela aprendí a valorar mi trabajo y lo que me están enseñando todos los instructores. Quiero enseñarles a los demás todo lo que yo sé, como preparar remedios, 'agüitas' y como estoy viejita, quiero empezar a pasarle mis conocimientos a mi comunidad".

Formal Writing No. 5

Fuente No. 3

Los chuchos de Alaska

Agazapados, a la orilla de la carretera, un grupo de perros arriesga la vida por un hueso, un pan o una tortilla.

En sus historias de los perros seguramente no está algún momento en el cual hayan salido a trotar por las mañanas a la par de su amo. Mucho menos que, alguna vez, su agudo olfato haya sentido la fragancia del champú o las tijeras del peluquero canino.

Por el contrario, quizá nunca han tenido un nombre y, a lo sumo, los llaman "canelo o negro" como muchos otros perros que deambulan por los sembradillos de maíz o frijol entre las montañas del occidente del país.

Cualquiera que viaje a Huehuetenango, Quetzaltenango, San Marcos o Totonicapán, por la carretera Interamericana, a la altura de la cuesta de Alaska, puede observar decenas de hambrientos canes, sentados a la orilla de la carretera, a la espera de que los pasajeros de los autobuses extraurbanos o cualquier vehículo particular lancen por las ventanillas restos de comida. Huesos, tortillas o panes pueden formar parte del manjar canino.

Sin embargo, la recompensa no siempre es disfrutar este festín, pues algunas veces, los cuerpos de muchos de ellos han quedado sin vida, bajo las llantas de los mismos vehículos que les proporcionan lo mínimo para seguir con vida.

Este drama canino no es nada nuevo, pues la "costumbre" de arrojarles comida a los hambrientos canes data de hace unos 15 años. Narciso Sirín, habitante del caserío Chanoj, Alaska, cuenta que desde comienzos de la década de 1990 los pilotos de los autobuses extraurbanos empezaron a acostumbrar a estos perros a recibir restos de comida.

"Antes eran pocos, pero ahora todos vienen, porque saben que aquí encuentran comida", indica Sirín. El sonido de las bocinas y de los motores es suficiente para que todos se apresten a coger el mejor bocado.

Se podría pensar que el estatus de estos perros es de "callejeros", pero no es del todo cierto, pues según el campesino, todos tienen propietario, pero el hambre los motiva a abandonar durante el día a sus amos. Eso sí "en la noche regresan para cuidar las casas", dice el labriego.

Esta "costumbre" les ha permitido sobrevivir a estos animales, pero no los ha alejado del todo de la muerte, pues muchas veces impulsados por el hambre, se lanzan a rescatar un hueso o tortilla a media carretera y terminan aplastados por las llantas de algún vehículo.

A raíz de esto, no es raro observar cadáveres de perros sobre el pavimento. "A veces pareciera que los choferes lo hacen por maldad, pero a saber... pobrecitos los animales", dice Victorino Siguantay, otro vecino de la comunidad.

Formal Writing No. 6

Fuente No. 3

Las posadas en México

La Navidad es la fiesta más larga de México y no se limita a la conmemoración del nacimiento de Cristo. Para los mexicanos, esta celebración inicia el 16 de diciembre con las posadas y termina el 2 de febrero con el día de la candelaria. Este largo periodo —lleno de rituales y símbolos— pasa entre peregrinaciones, representaciones teatrales, largas reuniones familiares y, claro, muchas ilusiones.

Antes de la llegada de los españoles, los aztecas festejaban en el invierno la llegada del Dios de la Guerra, Huitzilopochtli. Los misioneros (franciscanos y agustinos principalmente) sustituyeron las antiguas fiestas por la Navidad cristiana y sus particularidades españolas. Hoy día la época navideña tiene todo tipo de influencias, pero conserva su sentido de fiesta religiosa familiar. Sin duda, las posadas constituyen algunos de los momentos más coloridos de estas fiestas.

Las posadas son una representación teatral interactiva. Se organizan generalmente por grupos sociales (familias o por barrios) entre el 16 y el 24 diciembre, nueve días que significan los nueve meses del embarazo de la Virgen María. En base a la tradición bíblica que dice que María y José el carpintero tuvieron que pedir asilo antes del nacimiento de Jesús, se hace una representación al aire libre formada por dos grupos: uno dentro de una casa y otro fuera. Este último simboliza el peregrinar de José y María, que buscan un lugar para pasar la noche y piden asilo entonando villancicos (cantos populares) y llevando luces de bengala y candelas. Cuando finalmente el grupo de dentro de la casa se decide a brindar asilo, todos se reúnen cantando para continuar con una fiesta donde se rompen piñatas y comparten una cena informal.

La posada marca lo que se conoce como la temporada prenavideña. No sólo predispone los estómagos a comer más, sino pone el ambiente festivo. Esta fiesta también prepara el ambiente espiritual, el nacimiento de Jesús llega con un discurso de esperanza.

Es posible que la posada simbolice la lucha del bien contra el mal; cuando las puertas de la casa se abren para recibir a los peregrinos, se alcanza el triunfo contra el pecado. Quizá por eso después se rompen las piñatas, que son ollas de barro cubiertas con papel maché formando estrellas de siete picos que representan los siete pecados capitales. Las piñatas están rellenas de dulces que simbolizan la gracia de Dios. Romper la piñata es parte del ritual de las posadas. Se forma un círculo y cada quien intenta, con los ojos vendados, golpear con un palo la piñata hasta romperla. En ese momento todos se lanzan por los dulces. Los ojos vendados simbolizan la fe, los dulces la gracia de Dios.

La época navideña llega a su momento culminante en la Nochebuena, cuando se organiza una cena y se coloca una figura del Niño Jesús en una maqueta que reproduce el lugar de su nacimiento. Es, sin duda, el momento familiar más importante del año.

Part B
Formal Oral Presentation
Formal Oral Presentation No. 1

Informe de la radio

21 de marzo, 2006

Chicago - El que los hispanos no accedan a la educación en los Estados Unidos por falta de recursos económicos es un fallo que está afectando al país entero. Esta es la opinión de la Dra. Mildred García, presidente de Berkeley College en Nueva York y Nueva Jersey, quien por su trabajo y trayectoria conoce de cerca la problemática que enfrenta una comunidad que, por sus bajos ingresos, ve frustrado su acceso a las universidades. Situación que se agrava por la reducción de becas y apoyos económicos que anteriormente estaban destinados sólo para minorías.

Los hispanos son el grupo con menor porcentaje de graduados de las escuelas superiores y las universidades. Del total de personas que obtienen un título universitario en todo el país, sólo el 10% es latino.

Entrevistada acerca de los retos que enfrentan los hispanos al momento de conseguir ayuda financiera para pagar sus estudios, la Dra. García expresó su preocupación por las dramáticas reducciones en oportunidades de becas y de créditos para la comunidad hispana.

[Recientemente] el periódico *The New York Times* publicó en su primera plana una nota que afirma que colegios y universidades a lo largo del país están abriendo a los estudiantes blancos cientos de miles de dólares en becas y otros programas creados previamente para minorías. El problema de la carencia de recursos se acrecienta cuando además la gente no sabe que hay apoyos estatales y federales a los que puede acceder, e incluso algunas instituciones que ayudan a quienes mantienen buenas calificaciones a lo largo de su carrera.

La Dra. García dijo que "los latinos tienen miedo del costo de la educación, y hasta del formulario que tienen que llenar", y enfatiza que después de pasar la barrera económica, los estudiantes tienen que entrar en un ambiente en el que la gente crea en ellos, saber y sentir que los profesores están interesados en que terminen sus estudios, y tener la certeza de que van a tener un mejor futuro en cuanto terminen la carrera universitaria.

Cada primer miembro de una familia que se titula cambia la historia de su gente, porque sienta un precedente, es un ejemplo para los demás de que sí se pueden hacer bien las cosas y tener éxito, agrega la Dra. García y ejemplifica con su propia historia. De siete latinos que se inscribieron en su generación fue la única que terminó sus estudios. Y a partir de ese momento ella motivó a primos y sobrinos a que estudiaran una carrera universitaria.

Explica además que en Berkeley College tienen un programa de ayuda económica para alumnos sobresalientes al que llaman "Becas reto", que consiste en que la escuela duplica cualquier cantidad que el alumno reciba por parte de cualquier otra institución, o apoyo económico estatal o federal, además de las tutorías que reciben individualmente.

A la pregunta expresa de ¿qué está fallando en el caso de la comunidad hispana, que no le está permitiendo alcanzar sus metas escolares?, respondió: "Nosotros le estamos fallando a nuestro pueblo, como país, desde las escuelas elementales hasta las universidades, porque desde el momento en que un alumno entra a nuestros colegios, existe un compromiso entre ese estudiante y nosotros, y tenemos la obligación de hacer todo lo posible porque esa persona concluya sus estudios. De no ser así, nosotros tenemos que revisar en que hemos fallado".

Para finalizar, la Dra. García enfatizó en el enorme reto al que se enfrentan los maestros hispanos, quienes tienen que realizar, a la brevedad, una doble tarea que consiste en "educar a nuestra gente, y educar al mismo tiempo al pueblo americano para que se dé cuenta de la importancia de tener una minoría preparada", que impulse al país no sólo con su trabajo duro, sino con su inteligencia.

Formal Oral Presentation No. 2

Informe de la radio

Los expertos recomiendan que el volumen de los reproductores digitales no sobrepase los 100 decibeles.

Marzo 18 de 2006
Uso desmedido y a muy alto volumen de los iPods podría causar sordera.

Eso indica un estudio publicado el pasado martes y que generó preocupación entre los legisladores estadounidenses.

Más de la mitad de los adolescentes que participaron en el estudio señalaron tener problemas auditivos, principalmente después de utilizar los reproductores portátiles de música digital.

"La forma en la que la tecnología y, en este caso, el uso desmedido y a muy alto volumen de los reproductores de música afecta nuestra salud es un tema muy importante", destacó Mike Ferguson, legislador por Nueva Jersey, E.E.U.U.

"Debemos llamar a las autoridades de la salud y a los industriales a reflexionar y a tomar medidas", agregó su colega de Massachusetts, Edward Markey. Ambos se pronunciaron luego de una rueda de prensa de la asociación especializada en problemas auditivos y cognitivos, Asha, que realizó el estudio.

Más de la mitad de los jóvenes estadounidenses señalaron tener problemas auditivos que a su vez los llevan a aumentar el volumen de sus reproductores digitales, retroalimentando el problema.

La asociación destacó los riesgos de pérdida auditiva debido al uso de estas nuevas tecnologías que se convirtieron en un verdadero fenómeno social. El reproductor iPod, de Apple, se convirtió en el más popular en su género con más de 22 millones de unidades vendidas en el 2005. En el 2009, cerca de mil millones de estos aparatos deberían circular en el mundo entero, agrega el estudio. La llegada de estos aparatos que permiten horas de música ininterrumpidas (antes se debía cambiar el casete o el CD) es un factor que agrava el problema, destacaron los expertos.

Límite a los decibeles

"Cada vez más fuerte y cada vez más tiempo no es la forma en la que hay que utilizar estos aparatos", estimó Brenda Lonsbury-Martin, especialista médica en audición.

Dean Garstecki, otorrinolaringólogo en la Universidad Northwestern, llama a que los usuarios consuman estos aparatos de forma responsable, manteniendo el volumen al 60 por ciento de la escala de sonido y limitándose a una hora de escucha por día. Pero solicitó que los industriales procedan a realizar modificaciones para reducir el volumen.

En este sentido, Garstecki citó a Francia, que prohibió en el 2002 que el volumen de los reproductores digitales sobrepase los 100 decibeles.

En Estados Unidos los aparatos pueden alcanzar los 115 decibeles. Por eso, un consumidor inició una denuncia en nombre del colectivo contra Apple Computer, afirmando que su reproductor iPod puede dañar el oído. Según el demandante, 28 segundos de escucha por día al nivel máximo de 115 decibeles serían capaces de dañar de forma permanente el oído.

Según la demanda, los iPods tienen fallas, ya que los aparatos no contienen advertencias sobre los posibles daños que podrían causar.

Formal Oral Presentation No. 3

Informe de la radio

Cuando el miedo no deja vivir

Son enfermedades comunes en todos los países y causan inmenso sufrimiento.

Y sin embargo la mayoría de estos desórdenes pocas veces son diagnosticados, y mucho menos tratados.

Se trata de trastornos mentales como la ansiedad o los ataques de pánico, que según los especialistas padecen una de cuatro personas.

Para informar y concienciar a la gente sobre qué son los ataques de pánico y los trastornos de ansiedad, se está llevando a cabo en Argentina una campaña nacional.

"Los trastornos de ansiedad pueden incluir los desórdenes obsesivo-compulsivos, la fobia social y el trastorno producido por estrés postraumático y fobias", dijo a BBC Mundo el doctor José Luis Amestoy, psiquiatra de la Asociación Argentina de Trastornos de Ansiedad (AATA).

"La idea de la campaña es ayudar a los pacientes a identificar los síntomas de estos desórdenes desde sus inicios, para que los tratamientos puedan ser más eficaces y menos extendidos", afirma.

Miedo excesivo

La preocupación y la ansiedad son parte normal de nuestra vida diaria.

Nos preocupamos en el trabajo, la escuela, los resultados que obtendremos en alguna competición o cualquier otro evento.

El problema es cuando la ansiedad o la preocupación se convierte en algo más que "mariposas en el estómago".

La ansiedad excesiva es un trastorno mental que puede causar inmenso sufrimiento y que conduce a una pobre calidad de vida de quien lo padece.

La gente que sufre estas enfermedades a menudo se aísla socialmente, y empeora su calidad de vida y aumenta los riesgos de mortalidad.

El problema, dicen los especialistas, es que la ansiedad a menudo puede ser muy difícil de diagnosticar, ya que en ocasiones puede carecer de síntomas obvios.

"Cuando las preocupaciones persistentes y no reales se convierten en una forma habitual de enfrentar situaciones de la vida diaria, entonces la persona está sufriendo una ansiedad patológica", dice el doctor Amestoy.

"Esta ansiedad patológica es la que persiste durante días o meses y a veces sin motivo aparente", afirma el experto.

Por lo general la persona se da cuenta que padece este trastorno por varias manifestaciones físicas y mentales.

Estos síntomas pueden ser palpitaciones, taquicardia, hormigueos, atragantamientos por sensación de ahogo o falta de aire, mareos y malestar estomacal. Pero también pueden incluir, en el caso del ataque de pánico, una sensación de muerte inminente o miedo de volverse loco.

Ayuda

Según la Organización Mundial de la Salud, unos 450 millones de personas padecen algún tipo de trastorno mental en algún momento de su vida.

Hasta ahora no se ha logrado identificar la causa de la ansiedad, pero los expertos sugieren que puede ser desencadenada por diversos factores biológicos, la historia familiar o alguna experiencia negativa.

La gente, sin embargo, tiende a descartar los síntomas y a acostumbrarse a ellos, como si fueran parte normal de la vida.

"Generalmente la persona acude al médico cuando comienza a padecer alguno de los síntomas físicos como palpitaciones o taquicardia", señala el doctor Amestoy.

"Pero antes ya hubo un proceso de ansiedad que pasó sin ser identificado", afirma.

Mejor antes que después

El psiquiatra subraya la importancia de buscar ayuda médica lo más pronto posible.

Indica que con campañas, como la que se realiza actualmente en Argentina, podrán ayudar a la gente a identificar los trastornos de ansiedad desde sus primeras etapas.

"Yo he atendido a gente que no sale de su casa desde hace cuatro años", señala José Luis Amestoy.

"Porque la gente se aísla socialmente, no se da cuenta de lo que está padeciendo o minimiza los síntomas que está teniendo y paulatinamente se va recluyendo, perdiendo calidad de vida y termina no saliendo de su casa", agrega.

Pero afortunadamente, señala el psiquiatra, existen una variedad de terapéuticas que han demostrado tener mucho éxito para tratar la ansiedad.

Éstas pueden incluir desde técnicas de relajación, ejercicio físico, hasta la llamada Terapia Cognitiva Conductual, o incluso medicamentos específicos contra la ansiedad.

"Lo importante", señala el especialista "es que la gente sepa de qué se tratan estos trastornos como la ansiedad y los ataques de pánico".

"Así podrá buscar ayudar lo más pronto posible para dejar de sufrir de esa manera", concluye el psiquiatra.

Formal Oral Presentation No. 4

Informe de la radio

Se resiste a morir

El paisaje de Santa Cruz Chinautla está escondido en algunas casas y locales, con todo y sol, luna, flores, vendedores y pájaros.

La luna y el sol se besan apasionadamente, para siempre o hasta que se quiebre el colgante de barro que se confunde entre otros tantos adornos, ollas, frutas, iglesias, ovejas, vírgenes de todas advocaciones. Es la venta de cerámica de Alejandra Raxón, quien se dedica a elaborar figuras desde hace 50 años. "Mi abuelita me enseño y poco a poco fui haciendo otros diseños", dice. Hace años compartía el local con una cooperativa de artesanos que hoy ya no existe. Ella, sin embargo, no quiere que la tradición se pierda. "Desde la tormenta Stan se ausentaron los visitantes, como si creyeran que el pueblo ya no existe, pero aquí estamos y seguimos trabajando la cerámica."

Entre cerros

Por un momento pareciera que Santa Cruz Chinautla está condenada a desaparecer. Como si hubieran conspirado los constantes hundimientos de tierra en el pueblo y la carretera, la migración de sus habitantes a la cercana capital y la pestilente corriente del río Chinautla. Sin embargo, este pueblo está vivo y luchando por mantener su ubicación.

"Quienes más daño han hecho son los areneros, que siguen extrayendo material del río, lo cual provoca los hundimientos de terreno", explica Olga Morales, quien desde hace 15 años se dedica a comercializar cerámica de varios artesanos locales y que ahora sueña con poder exportarla a Estados Unidos y a Europa. "La gente aquí hace maravillas con la cerámica, que parece fácil pero es un proceso muy lento y difícil", agrega.

Tal dificultad, es observable en algunas de las piezas que exhiben las tiendas de Raxón y Morales: en cada una de las esculturas es posible, incluso, distinguir diversos estilos creativos.

Por estos días, los estantes están siendo abandonados por los ángeles, sagradas familias, reyes magos, pastores y ovejas, para dar paso a la nueva temporada, que Olga Morales define como: "La del cariño", pues crece la demanda de objetos decorativos para obsequiar. "La gente busca fruteros (con frutas finamente modeladas en barro), jarrones, fuentes, vajillas, candeleros y hasta chimeneas", cuenta.

Antes de llegar al centro del pueblo ya es posible encontrar los letreros de venta de cerámica. Al caminar por las callejuelas polvorientas se llega a negocios como el de Efraín Martínez, quien fabrica sus propias piezas, pero también comercializa las de otros creadores. "Muchos fabricantes sólo le trabajan a las ventas del Mercado Central, sin embargo algunos nos mantenemos todavía aquí, esperando al visitante nacional o extranjero."

"Los días en que vienen más compradores son el sábado y el domingo", expone Olga Morales mientras termina de empacar la mercancía navideña que no vendió.

"Nosotras queremos que la gente sepa que la artesanía de Chinautla ha cambiado. Aquí ya no sólo hacemos tinajas y ollas, sino cualquier pieza que nos pidan, al gusto", concluye Raxón, quien luce el traje típico que la identifica como integrante de la etnia poqomam.

Formal Oral Presentation No. 5

Informe de la radio

Buenas noticias en una vieja ciudad

Es un caluroso sábado por la tarde en la pequeña Plazuela Machado, en el corazón del barrio histórico de Mazatlán. Las calles y las veredas cercanas están cubiertas de mesas de cafés a los que los residentes y los turistas acuden a cenar. A pocos pasos, en la plaza, coronada por un mirador de brillante color verde, las familias se pasean o se sientan en los nuevos bancos debajo de los árboles, admirando la nueva iluminación de los edificios. Después de muchas décadas de descuido, la antigua Mazatlán está resurgiendo, gracias a un ambicioso programa de revitalización.

Mazatlán, con una población de alrededor do 400.000 habitantes, fue fundada a principios del siglo XVI, y el descubrimiento de ricos depósitos de oro y plata en las minas cercanas la convirtieron en uno de los puertos más activos de México. Pero la ciudad antigua que los visitantes ven hoy data de la época posterior a la independencia mexicana en 1821, cuando se establecierron en la zona inmigrantes de ascendencia alemana, española, vasca, norteamericana y asiática. Durante las décadas siguientes, las conexiones marítimas y ferroviarias convirtieron a Mazatlán en un centro comercial internacional y, durante unos quince años, en la capital del estado de Sinaloa.

La época de auge continuó hasta el siguiente siglo, y en 1926, con la construcción del hotel Belmar en el boulevard Olas Altas, en el principal balneario del noroeste de México. Su fama como meca del deporte de la pesca se extendió en los años cuarenta, y en 1944 el hotel Freeman llevó a la ciudad el primer edificio de varios pisos y el primer elevador. Pero con el desarrollo del turismo, el centro histórico dejó de interesar, y los residentes más jóvenes se trasladaron a los suburbios. Peor aún, docenas de antiguos edificios fueron demolidos y reemplazados por simétricas edificaciones modernas. El golpe de gracia se produjo a fines de los años setenta con el surgimiento de la Zona Dorada, un complejo de hoteles, restaurantes, negocios y otras instalaciones orientadas al turismo, que hicieron desaparecer el atractivo de la antigua Mazatlán para muchos visitantes.

A fines de los años ochenta comenzó la transformación cuando se restauró el antiguo teatro Ángela Peralta, junto a la Plazuela Machado. El deteriorado edificio (rebautizado en 1943 en honor de la famosa "ruiseñor mexicana" que sucumbió de fiebre amarilla antes de su debut en el teatro en 1883), fue objeto de una espectacular renovación y ha vuelto a reinar como importante atracción cultural. Un edificio cercano, el antiguo hotel Iturbide, también ha sido rehabilitado y actualmente alberga la Escuela Municipal de Arte. "El teatro y la escuela son las bases de nuestros esfuerzos de restauración, y eso debemos agradecérselo a un grupo de antiguos residentes visionarios", señala Alfredo Gómez Rubio, propietario del conocido restaurante Pedro & Lola en la Plazuela Machado.

Él y otros residentes fundaron el Proyecto Centro Histórico (PCH) un año después de que el presidente Vicente Fox confiriera en 2001 la categoría de zona histórica a 180 cuadras y 479 edificios del centro histórico. La asociación está organizada siguiendo el ejemplo del Main Street Project de los Estados Unidos, que respalda la revitalización de los centros de ciudades mediante organizaciones de base popular. "Realizamos una encuesta entre los habitantes, con el fin de identificar los principales problemas de la zona y procuramos resolverlos con la ayuda de voluntarios", dice Alejandra Rico González, la joven directora del proyecto. Realizaron campañas contra los grafitti, de reforestación y de limpieza de calles, talleres de concienciación, un programa de pintura de fachadas de edificios y una página Web, pasando luego a otras mejoras de más largo alcance que comprenderán edificios para estacionamiento y un paseo peatonal.

Una donación de 300.000 dólares de la Autoridad Portuaria contribuyó a ampliar y embellecer el Boulevard Olas Altas, que conecta a la antigua Mazatlán con la Zona Dorada. El popular paseo muestra actualmente un diseño ondulante de colores azul y anaranjado y una piscina junto al mar conocida como Carpa Olivera. Pero quizá lo que más atraiga a los residentes y los turistas sea la artística iluminación de los edificios del siglo XIX, que los lleva durante la noche a pasear y cenar. "Main Street nos advirtió que no esperáramos resultados demasiado pronto", agrega Rico González, "pero ya está ocurriendo: el centro histórico está recobrando la vida". Los interesados pueden visitar el sitio en Internet, www.centrohistoricomazatlan.com.

Answer Key for
Abriendo paso: Lectura

Mary A. Mosley

Cuentos

Capítulo 1

El décimo

Antes de leer

pp. 1–2 A–B
Las respuestas variarán.

pp. 2–3 C. El día que papá se sacó un premio
Las respuestas variarán, pero pueden incluir:

1. El padre guardaba los billetes que compraba debajo de una mascota que tenía en el armario.

2. Una noche después de cenar sonó el timbre.

3. La familia se asustó porque había varias personas gritando y llamando a la puerta.

4. El padre no podía hallar el billete.

5. El padre decidió donar el dinero a una institución de beneficencia.

6. El chico está triste.

7. El chico quería quedarse por lo menos con la mitad del dinero.

p. 3 D. La generosidad
Las respuestas variarán.

p. 4 E. Una selección
Las respuestas variarán pero pueden incluir:

- la situación económica de la muchacha: "muy mal vestida, y en cuyo rostro se veía pintada el hambre"

- el lugar: "a la puerta de un café"

- el tiempo: "me subía el cuello a fin de protegerme del frío de diciembre".

- la lotería: "me vendió el décimo de billete de lotería". "El número es el 1.620".

Comprensión

p. 8 A. ¿Cierta o falsa?

1. Falsa: El narrador compra un décimo de lotería.

2. Falsa: El narrador mete el décimo en el bolsillo de su sobretodo.

3. Cierta

4. Cierta

5. Cierta

6. Falsa: El narrador pierde el billete.

7. Cierta

8. Falsa: La chica va a visitar al narrador.

9. Falsa: El narrador le dice la verdad a la chica.

10. Falsa: A la chica no le importa.

11. Cierta

12. Cierta

p. 8 B. Comprensión general

Las respuestas variarán pero pueden incluir:

1. Cree que la chica está bromeando cuando dice que él tiene suerte y que va a ganar.

2. Porque cree que es posible que el criado le haya robado el billete o que lo haya perdido.

3. El narrador se desespera, pero la muchacha lo acepta como la voluntad de la Virgen. El narrador no esperaba tal reacción de la muchacha porque ella era pobre y le había vendido el billete ganador.

4. El cambio al tiempo presente nos indica que el narrador está muy preocupado. El autor hace este cambio para indicarles a los lectores que el narrador está muy agitado y desesperado.

p. 9 C. De la misma familia

Las respuestas variarán pero pueden incluir:

vestida: vestido, vestir, desvestirse, etc.

pintada: pintar, pintura, pintor, etc.

protegerme: protegido, protección, protector, etc.

alegría: alegre, alegrar, etc.

mintiendo (mentir): mentira, mentiroso, etc.

vivos: vivir, vida, vivienda, etc.

desconfianza: confianza, confiar, etc.

riqueza: rico, enriquecerse, etc.

felicidad: feliz, felicitar, etc.

p. 9 D. En contexto

1. f	2. a	3. h	4. i	5. b
6. j	7. e	8. d	9. g	10. c

pp. 10–11 E. Al punto

1. b	2. d	3. b	4. a	5. c
6. a	7. b	8. c	9. d	

pp. 11–12 F–H
Las respuestas variarán.

Un paso más

pp. 13–14 A–F. Para conversar
Las respuestas variarán.

pp. 15–16 A–D. Para escribir
Las respuestas variarán.

p. 17 Informal Writing
Las respuestas variarán.

pp. 18–19 Comprensión auditiva
Selección número 1
   1. c   2. d   3. a   4. c

Selección número 2
   1. b   2. a   3. b   4. d   5. a

Capítulo 2
Rosa

> **Note:** The Answer Key provides answers for all of the activities that have only one correct answer. It also provides possible answers for many of the open-ended activities. These answers represent <u>suggested</u> responses to the questions and you should not expect that every student will be capable of responding with the same degree of accuracy and / or completeness.

Antes de leer

pp. 20–21 A–D
Las respuestas variarán.

p. 22 E. Una selección

1. a. Cierta

   b. Falsa: Rosa se siente indignada.

   c. Cierta

   d. Falsa: Rosa está indignada, pero los otros personajes están resignados.

   e. Cierta

   f. Falsa: Rosa no está contenta y no quiere aceptar la orden.

   g. Cierta

2. Las respuestas variarán pero pueden incluir:
   El cuento tiene lugar en la oficina de una compañía; Betty le pregunta a Rosa dónde le gustaría trabajar en el futuro.

3. Las respuestas variarán pero pueden incluir:
   La compañía va a trasladar a una empleada a otro lugar. Ella no quiere ir porque no quiere separarse de sus amigas.

p. 23 F. Expresiones idiomáticas

1. a	2. a	3. b	4. a	5. a
6. b	7. a			

p. 24 G. Otra selección

Las respuestas variarán pero pueden incluir:

1. Parecen estar en un cuarto grande que está lleno de máquinas.

2. Parecen estar buscando una máquina en particular.

3. Vienen a buscar una de las máquinas que ya no funciona.

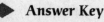

4. Las palabras que describen el tono de esta selección son "inquietante" y "misterioso". La causa es la luz y que no sabemos qué va a pasar.

5. Las respuestas variarán.

Comprensión

p. 29 A. Frases para completar

1. b   2. j   3. k   4. a   5. m

6. d   7. e   8. o   9. h   10. i

p. 30 B. Comprensión general

Las respuestas variarán pero pueden incluir:

1. Rosa habla con cierta zozobra al principio porque no sabe qué va a pasar ni adónde la van a llevar.

2. Las compañeras tratan de animar a Rosa.

3. Lo que dicen las compañeras sobre el futuro de Rosa no se cumple. El verdadero destino de Rosa es ser destruida porque ya es vieja y no funciona tan bien como las nuevas computadoras.

p. 30 C. En contexto

Las respuestas variarán pero pueden incluir:

Resignada significa que una persona ha aceptado lo que va a pasar.

Sencilla significa no muy complicada.

Sacar significa llevar a otro lugar.

Trasladarte significa llevar a otro lugar.

Recompensa significa un premio que merece una persona.

Reemplazar significa que van a poner otra cosa en su lugar.

p. 30 D. De la misma familia

Las respuestas variarán pero pueden incluir:

clara: claro, claramente, aclarar, claridad, etc.

abiertamente: abierto, abrir, entreabierto, etc.

increíble: creer, creíble, incrédulo, etc.

envidiable: envidia, envidioso, envidiar, etc.

recorrer: correr, corredor, corrida, recorrido, etc.

sorprendente: sorprender, sorpresa, sorprendido, etc.

seguras: seguro, seguridad, asegurar, inseguro, etc.

frialdad: frío, enfriar, etc.

búsqueda: buscar, busca, etc.

pp. 31–32 E. Al punto

1. b	2. d	3. b	4. a	5. a	6. c
7. c	8. d	9. c	10. a	11. b	12. d

p. 32 F. Ahora te toca a ti
Las respuestas variarán.

Un paso más

pp. 33–34 A–E. Para conversar
Las respuestas variarán.

pp. 35–36 A–G. Para escribir
Las respuestas variarán.

p. 37 Informal Writing
Las respuestas variarán.

pp. 37–38 Comprensión auditiva
Selección número 1

1. c	2. c	3. a

Selección número 2

1. b	2. a	3. c	4. a	5. c

Capítulo 3
Un oso y un amor

Antes de leer
pp. 40–42 A–D
Las respuestas variarán.

Comprensión
p. 47 A. ¿Cierta o falsa?
1. Cierta

2. Falsa: Shirley y el narrador se llevaban bien.

3. Falsa: Shirley tenía una paloma blanca.

4. Cierta

5. Falsa: Shirley hablaba español tan bien como el narrador.

6. Falsa: En Tierra Amarilla los habitantes se llevaban muy bien.

7. Falsa: El narrador y Shirley encontraron un oso que había matado una oveja.

8. Cierta

9. Falsa: El narrador se sentía dueño de sí mismo.

10. Cierta

pp. 47–48 B. La sucesión de los eventos
a. 10	b. 8	c. 2	d. 4	e. 5	f. 1
g. 11	h. 9	i. 12	j. 3	k. 6	l. 7

p. 48 C. Comprensión general
Las respuestas variarán pero pueden incluir:

1. Antes de que el narrador y Shirley se encontraran con el oso el ambiente era idílico. Los amigos se divertían. Después tenían miedo del oso.

2. El narrador y Shirley estaban enamorados. Ellos habían crecido juntos. Él le daba regalos y ellos hacían muchas cosas juntos. Cuando el narrador mata al oso, Shirley lo abraza y dice que quiere morirse de felicidad. Él le da la piel a Shirley y ella todavía la tiene después de muchos años.

3. Para el narrador la piel de oso representa su valor. Para Shirley representa el amor del narrador.

p. 48 D. De la misma familia
Las respuestas variarán pero pueden incluir:

fresco: frescura, refrescar, etc.

canción: cantar, cantante, etc.

acompañado: acompañar, compañero, etc.

crecimos (crecer): crecimiento, creciente, etc.

sentimental: sentimiento, sentir, etc.

ensangrentado: sangre, sangrar, sangriento, etc.

atada: atar, desatar, etc.

cariño: encariñar, cariñoso, etc.

p. 48 E. En contexto
Las respuestas variarán pero pueden incluir:

Un *arroyo* es un pequeño río.

La *sierra* es un grupo de montañas.

Las *vacas* son animales que dan leche.

Una *paloma* es un pájaro.

Asustarse significa tener miedo.

Huir significa salir rápidamente, escaparse.

Un *anillo* es una joya que se lleva en un dedo.

pp. 49–50 F. Al punto
1. b	2. b	3. d	4. b	5. d
6. a	7. c	8. a	9. a	10. c
11. d	12. b	13. a		

p. 50 G. Ahora te toca a ti
Las respuestas variarán.

Un paso más

pp. 51–52 A–D. Para conversar
Las respuestas variarán.

pp. 52–53 A–E. Para escribir
Las respuestas variarán.

p. 54 Otra dimensión
Las respuestas variarán.

pp. 55–56 Comprensión auditiva
Selección número 1
1. d	2. d	3. c	4. a

Selección número 2
1. b	2. c	3. a

Capítulo 4

Continuidad de los parques

Antes de leer

pp. 57–58 A–D
Las respuestas variarán.

Comprensión

p. 62 A. ¿Cierta o falsa?

1. Falsa: El hombre había empezado a leer la novela unos días antes.

2. Cierta

3. Cierta

4. Cierta

5. Falsa: Su memoria retenía sin esfuerzo los nombres y las imágenes de los protagonistas.

6. Falsa: La ilusión novelesca lo ganó casi en seguida.

7. Cierta

8. Falsa: El amante tenía la cara lastimada por el chicotazo de una rama.

9. Falsa: Él rechazaba las caricias.

10. Cierta

11. Cierta

12. Falsa: Sólo el hombre fue a la casa.

13. Cierta

14. Cierta

15. Falsa: El sillón donde el hombre estaba leyendo era de terciopelo verde.

p. 63 B. Comprensión general
Las respuestas variarán pero pueden incluir:

1. El hombre se sentó a leer la novela en el estudio que miraba hacia el parque de los robles. Estaba sentado en un sillón de terciopelo verde, de espaldas a la puerta.

2. El hombre parece convertirse en otro personaje más del cuento.

3. Fue testigo del último encuentro de los amantes en la cabaña del monte.

4. Cuando salieron de la cabaña del monte la mujer siguió por la senda que iba al norte. El amante siguió por la otra senda hacia la casa.

5. El amante llegó a la casa, entró y vio a un hombre sentado en un sillón de terciopelo verde leyendo una novela. El hombre que estaba en el sillón parecía ser el esposo de la mujer.

p. 63 C. De la misma familia

Las respuestas variarán pero pueden incluir:

dibujo: dibujar, dibujante, etc.

apoderado: poder, poderoso, apoderarse, etc.

tranquilidad: tranquilo, intranquilo, tranquilizarse, etc.

esfuerzo: fuerza, esforzar, fuerte, etc.

protegida: proteger, protección, protector, etc.

destruir: destrucción, destruidor, destructivo, etc.

p. 63 D. En contexto

Las respuestas variarán pero pueden incluir:

Un *mayordomo* es un criado que está a cargo de una casa o hacienda.

Las *intrusiones* son cosas que nos pueden distraer.

Acariciara significa tocar a alguien con amor o ternura.

Los *protagonistas* son los personajes principales de la novela.

Al alcance de significa estar cerca.

El *atardecer* significa la hora cuando se pone el sol.

Un *monte* es una montaña pequeña.

Un *puñal* es un cuchillo pequeño que cabe en el puño.

La *mejilla* es la parte de la cara debajo de los ojos.

Galopando significa ir a caballo rápidamente.

Una *escalera* es lo que usamos para subir a otro piso.

pp. 64–65 E. Al punto

1. c	2. d	3. a	4. b	5. a
6. d	7. a	8. d	9. c	10. a
11. d	12. c	13. b		

p. 66 F. Ahora te toca a ti

Las respuestas variarán.

Un paso más

pp. 66–67 A–D. Para conversar
Las respuestas variarán.

pp. 67–68 A–E. Para escribir
Las respuestas variarán.

pp. 68–69 Otra dimensión
Las respuestas variarán.

pp. 69–70 Comprensión auditiva
Selección número 1
1. b   2. c   3. c

Selección número 2
1. c   2. b   3. d

Capítulo 4   177

Capítulo 5
Cajas de cartón

Antes de leer

pp. 71–72 A–C

Las respuestas variarán.

p. 72 D. Una selección

Las respuestas variarán, pero pueden incluir:

1. La familia del narrador llegó a un campo de trabajo cerca de Fresno. Fresno se encuentra en California.

2. Buscaban trabajo.

3. La madre se sentiría triste.

4. La madre se sentía contenta después de hablar con el señor Sullivan.

5. El señor Sullivan le ofreció trabajo y un lugar donde vivir.

6. La casa del señor Sullivan tiene una cerca, rosales y luz eléctrica, mientras el narrador y su familia van a vivir en un garaje viejo gastado por los años, sin ventanas, con agujeros en el techo y el piso de tierra.

p. 73 E. El título

Las respuestas variarán.

Comprensión

p. 81 A. ¿Cierta o falsa?

1. Cierta

2. Falsa: El narrador no podía dormir porque la idea de mudarse otra vez lo entristecía.

3. Falsa: El padre del narrador compró un coche usado.

4. Cierta

5. Cierta

6. Falsa: En Fresno la familia encuentra trabajo con el señor Sullivan.

7. Falsa: El garaje donde vivía la familia era muy viejo y no muy cómodo.

8. Cierta

9. Cierta

10. Cierta

11. Falsa: El primer día de escuela el narrador estaba muy nervioso y asustado.

12. Cierta

13. Falsa: El narrador quería aprender a tocar la trompeta.

14. Falsa: Al final del cuento el narrador y su familia van a trasladarse a otro lugar.

pp. 81–82 B. Comprensión general
Las respuestas variarán pero pueden incluir:

1. Los miembros de la familia del narrador trabajan en los campos. El trabajo es muy duro.

2. Esta familia lleva una vida dura. Trabajan desde el amanecer hasta el atardecer para poder comer. Hasta los niños tienen que trabajar y no pueden ir a la escuela todo el año escolar.

3. El día que iba a ir a la escuela el narrador estaba contento, pero en la escuela se sintió incómodo.

4. El narrador tenía miedo, estaba nervioso y avergonzado porque no podía leer tan bien como los otros estudiantes. Hacía mucho tiempo que no oía hablar en inglés y casi no podía responder. Pero el maestro era amable y trataba de ayudarle.

p. 82 C. De la misma familia
Las respuestas variarán pero pueden incluir:

entristeció (entristecer): triste, tristeza, etc.

camino: caminar, caminante, etc.

empacado: empacar, empacador, paquete, etc.

cansancio: cansado, cansar, descansar, etc.

nos alejábamos (alejarse): lejos, lejano, etc.

pensamiento: pensar, pensador, pensativo, etc.

indeciso: decidir, decisión, indecisión, etc.

escritorio: escribir, escritor, escrito, etc.

p. 82 D. En contexto
Las respuestas variarán pero pueden incluir:

Mudarnos significa trasladarnos a otro lugar.

Una *choza* es una casa pequeña y no muy cómoda.

Un *colchón* es algo sobre lo que se puede dormir.

Una *cerca* es una construcción que se pone alrededor de un jardín, de un campo o de una casa.

Escondernos significa ponernos donde no nos pueden ver.

Una *manguera* es lo que se usa para echar agua a las plantas.

p. 82 E. Al punto

1. a	2. d	3. b	4. c	5. a	6. c
7. b	8. a	9. d	10. a	11. c	12. a
13. c	14. d	15. b	16. b	17. a	18. c
19. a	20. d	21. c			

p. 86 F–G
Las respuestas variarán.

Un paso más

pp. 87–89 A–F. Para conversar
Las respuestas variarán.

pp. 89–91 A–F. Para escribir
Las respuestas variarán.

pp. 91–92 Otra dimensión
Las respuestas variarán.

pp. 92–93 Comprensión auditiva
Selección número 1

1. c	2. b	3. c

Selección número 2

1. c	2. a	3. c

Capítulo 6
Jacinto Contreras recibe su paga extraordinaria

Antes de leer

p. 94 A. Para discutir en clase

Las respuestas variarán. La lista de palabras puede incluir:

árbol de Navidad	la Navidad
bailar	pescado
calcetines	regalos
cocina	zapatillas
estufa	

p. 95 B–C

Las respuestas variarán.

pp. 95–97 D. Una selección

1.

1. h	2. e	3. j	4. d	5. f
6. a.	7. g	8. c	9. b	10. i

2. Las respuestas variarán, pero pueden incluir:

a.

Regalo	Persona para quien lo piensa comprar	Razón
medias	Benjamina	para que no tenga frío
botas	Jacintín	para que sus compañeros de colegio no le pregunten si no se moja
besugo	la familia	para comer, para celebrar
turrón	la familia	para comer, para celebrar
mazapán	la familia	para comer, para celebrar

b. Jacinto va a comprarse una camiseta de abrigo para sí mismo.

c. Jacinto parece ser una persona compasiva y generosa, porque piensa en su esposa y su hijo y quiere comprarles cosas que necesitan.

Comprensión

p. 104 A. La sucesión de los eventos

a. 1	b. 12	c. 7	d. 10	e. 9	f. 2
g. 6	h. 3	i. 4	j. 11	k. 8	l. 5

p. 104 B. Comprensión general
Las respuestas variarán pero pueden incluir:

1. Quiere comprarle regalos y comida especial a su familia.

2. Jacinto y Benjamina se quieren mucho.

3. Antes de regresar a su casa Jacinto toma un vermú y come gambas a la plancha con un amigo.

4. En el metro alguien le robó a Jacinto Contreras la paga extraordinaria.

p. 105 C. De la misma familia
Las respuestas variarán pero pueden incluir:

alegría: alegre, alegrar(se), etc.

hacendosa: hacer, quehaceres, etc.

abrigo: abrigar, desabrigado, etc.

zapatillas: zapatos, zapatería, etc.

festejarse: fiesta, festejo, festival, etc.

sonrió (sonreír): sonrisa, reír, sonriente, etc.

llavín: llave, llavero, etc.

sentimental: sentimiento, sentir, etc.

poderosos: poder, apoderarse, etc.

regalado: regalo, regalar, etc.

p. 105 D. En contexto
Las respuestas variarán pero pueden incluir:

Hacendosa significa que trabaja mucho.

Festejarse significa celebrar.

Gastador es una persona a quien le gusta gastar.

Al fiado significa comprar algo y pagar más tarde.

Palideció significa que la piel perdió su color.

Una *cartera* es una cosa en la que se lleva dinero.

pp. 105–106 E. Al punto

1. b   2. a   3. b   4. b   5. a

6. c   7. d   8. d   9. b   10. d

p. 106 F. Ahora te toca a ti
Las respuestas variarán.

Un paso más

Para conversar
p. 107 A. Aquí tienes las respuestas
Las preguntas variarán pero pueden incluir:

1. ¿Qué son gambas?

2. ¿Qué es besugo?

3. ¿Qué son turrón y mazapán?

4. ¿Quién es Jenaro Viejo Totana?

5. ¿Qué es el metro?

6. ¿Quién es Teresita?

7. ¿Qué son zapatillas?

8. ¿Qué significa *al fiado?*

pp. 108–109 B–F
Las respuestas variarán.

p. 109 G. Una comparación
Las respuestas variarán pero pueden incluir:

Semejanzas	Diferencias
Los protagonistas de los dos cuentos pierden algo de valor.	Alguien le roba el dinero a Jacinto Contreras. El narrador de "El décimo" pierde el billete de lotería.
Jacinto Contreras y la chica que vende el billete de lotería son pobres y necesitan el dinero.	Jacinto Contreras es pobre. El narrador de "El décimo" no es pobre.
La acción de los dos cuentos tiene lugar en diciembre cuando hace frío.	Cuando no encuentra el billete el narrador de "El décimo" se enoja con el criado; cuando no encuentra el dinero Jacinto Contreras empieza a llorar.
Jacinto Contreras pierde el dinero del bolsillo y el narrador de "El décimo" pierde el billete de lotería del bolsillo.	"El décimo" tiene un final feliz porque la chica se casa con el narrador y son muy felices. Al final de este cuento Jacinto Contreras todavía es pobre y parece que nunca va a cambiar.

pp. 109–110 A–D. Para escribir
Las respuestas variarán.

p. 111 Otra dimensión
Las respuestas variarán.

p. 112 Comprensión auditiva
Selección número 1
    1. d   **2.** a   **3.** b

Selección número 2
    1. c   **2.** a   **3.** a   **4.** a   **5.** b

Capítulo 7
Nosotros, no

Antes de leer

pp. 114–115 A. Para discutir en clase
Las respuestas variarán. La lista de palabras puede incluir:

deprimido	peluca
divertirse	satisfecho
espejo	televisión
inútil	volver al pasado

1. El hombre se siente triste porque ya no es joven y cree que los jóvenes se divierten más que él. Está en casa el viernes a las ocho de la noche. Ese día a esa hora la gente generalmente sale a divertirse.

2. En la televisión ve a gente que se divierte y probablemente él quiere divertirse también.

3. El hombre quiere cambiar de apariencia.

4. Al final se da cuenta de que no puede volver a ser joven. Probablemente se siente triste.

5. La moraleja es que no se puede volver al pasado y que se debe estar satisfecho con la edad que uno tiene.

p. 116 B–D
Las respuestas variarán.

p. 117 E. Una selección
Las respuestas variarán pero pueden incluir:

1. La palabra *milagro* le da un tono religioso.

2. La palabra *finalmente* nos indica que hacía muchos años que trataban de hacer esto.

3. La frase sugiere que el (la) narrador(a) ya no se alegra. Probablemente es viejo(a).

4. El título del cuento indica que hay algunas personas que no van a ser inmortales.

5–6. Las respuestas variarán.

Comprensión

p. 121 A. ¿Cierta o falsa?

1. Cierta

2. Falsa: Para no morir era necesario recibir una inyección antes de cumplir veinte años.

3. Cierta

4. Cierta

5. Cierta

6. Falsa: Los jóvenes que recibían la inyección no tendrían la oportunidad de encontrarse con Dios.

7. Cierta

8. Cierta

p. 121 B. Comprensión general
Las respuestas variarán pero pueden incluir:

1. El descubrimiento era una inyección que daba la inmortalidad. Garantizaba que ningún cuerpo humano se descompondría nunca.

2. La única manera en que una persona podría morir sería un accidente.

3. Según la segunda noticia los mayores de veinte años no beneficiarían del descubrimiento.

4. La reacción inicial de los que no serían incluidos fue que ellos serían marginados. Cambiaron de opinión cuando el primer muchacho se suicidó. Decidieron que la inmortalidad no era algo tan bueno como habían pensado.

p. 122 C. De la misma familia
Las respuestas variarán pero pueden incluir:

predicho (predecir): decir, predicción, etc.

inmortalidad: mortal, inmortal, etc.

garantizaba (garantizar): garantía, garantizador, etc.

crecimiento: crecer, creciente, etc.

mundial: mundo, mundano, etc.

lejanas: lejos, alejarse, etc.

terrestres: tierra, terreno, etc.

despedida: despedir(se), despido, etc.

habitantes: habitar, habitación, etc.

monstruosa: monstruo, monstruosidad, etc.

certeza: cierto, certidumbre, etc.

dolorosa: dolor, doler, adolorido, etc.

verdoso: verde

horrenda: horror, horrorizar, horroroso, etc.

p. 122 D. En contexto

1. g	2. h	3. c	4. b
5. a	6. e	7. f	8. d

pp. 123–124 E. Al punto

1. a	2. b	3. b	4. c	5. b	6. b
7. d	8. a	9. c	10. a	11. c	12. c
13. a	14. a				

p. 125 F. Ahora te toca a ti
Las respuestas variarán.

Un paso más

pp. 126–129 A–E. Para conversar
Las respuestas variarán.

pp. 129–130 A–E. Para escribir
Las respuestas variarán.

p. 131 Otra dimensión
Las respuestas variarán.

pp. 132–133 Comprensión auditiva
Selección número 1

1. b	2. d	3. d	4. a

Selección número 2

1. a	2. a	3. a	4. a	5. c	6. a

Capítulo 8
No oyes ladrar los perros

Antes de leer

pp. 134–135 A–C
Las respuestas variarán.

p. 135 D. Los movimientos físicos
1.

    1. d   **2.** c   **3.** a   **4.** b

2. Las respuestas variarán pero pueden incluir:

    1. El hombre tiembla porque...

    2. El hombre se endereza porque...

    3. El hombre aplasta a algo porque...

    4. El hombre tropieza con una piedra porque...

    5. El hombre trata de balancearse porque...

    6. El hombre se tambalea porque...

    7. El hombre dobla las piernas porque...

    8. El hombre se estira porque...

    9. El hombre se agarra al edificio porque...

    10. El hombre se trepa al árbol porque...

p. 136 E. Una selección
Las respuestas variarán pero pueden incluir:

1. El padre dice que todos los esfuerzos que hace son por la madre de Ignacio, no por su hijo.

2. El tono de la selección es triste. El padre le habla al hijo como si le echara la culpa de muchas dificultades. Sí, parece enojado.

3. Usa la forma usted al hablar con el hijo para enfatizar lo que dice.

4. Ha tenido una pelea; ha sufrido un accidente.

5. Las respuestas variarán.

Comprensión

p. 142 A. ¿Cierta o falsa?

1. Cierta

2. Falsa: Tonaya estaba detrás del monte.

3. Falsa: El padre no quería sentarse porque no iba a poder levantar el cuerpo de su hijo.

4. Cierta

5. Cierta

6. Falsa: A medida que andaban el hijo hablaba menos.

7. Falsa: El padre tenía mucha dificultad mientras caminaba.

8. Cierta

9. Falsa: El padre no dejó a Ignacio en el camino.

10. Falsa: El cuento tiene lugar por la noche.

11. Cierta

12. Falsa: El padre creía que su hijo volvería a sus malos pasos.

13. Cierta

14. Falsa: La madre tuvo esperanzas de que el hijo la ayudara cuando creciera.

15. Cierta

16. Falsa: Al final del cuento el padre oyó los perros ladrar por todas partes.

pp. 142–143 B. Comprensión general

Las respuestas variarán pero pueden incluir:

1. Porque cuando oigan ladrar los perros estarán en Tonaya.

2. El padre estaba muy cansado.

3. La memoria de su esposa le da ánimo al padre.

4. El padre no quiere al hijo porque éste ha cometido crímenes; parece que no le gusta el hijo.

5. Ignacio se murió al final del cuento, pero no está claro.

6. Las respuestas variarán.

p. 143 C. De la misma familia

Las respuestas variarán pero pueden incluir:

temblaba (temblar): temblor, temblador, temblante, etc.

morderse: mordido, mordedor, mordiente, etc.

oscurecía (oscurecer): oscuro, oscuridad, etc.

camino: caminar, caminante, encaminarse, etc.

 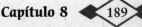

vergüenzas: avergonzar, sinvergüenza, vergonzoso, etc.

brillar: brillo, brillante, etc.

esperanza: esperar, esperanzado, etc.

p. 143 D. En contexto
Las respuestas variarán pero pueden incluir:

La *sombra* significa lo contrario de la luz.

Tambaleante significa que se mueve de un lado a otro.

Oscurecía significa que la luz desaparecía.

Tropezar significa chocar con algo y estar en peligro de caerse.

El *sudor* es el líquido que el cuerpo produce al hacer ejercicio o cuando uno tiene calor.

Las *heridas* significa lesiones o lastimaduras.

El *robo* significa apropiarse de algo ajeno.

Los *tejados* son techos de edificios o casas.

pp. 143–145 E. Al punto
1. c	2. a	3. b	4. b	5. a
6. c	7. c	8. c	9. d	10. b
11. c	12. a	13. a	14. b	

p. 145 F. Ahora te toca a ti
Las respuestas variarán.

Un paso más

pp. 146–147 A–G. Para conversar
Las respuestas variarán.

pp. 148–149 A–H. Para escribir
Las respuestas variarán.

pp. 149–150 Otra dimensión
Las respuestas variarán.

pp. 150–151 Comprensión auditiva
Selección número 1
1. c	2. b	3. b

Selección número 2
1. c	2. d	3. a

Capítulo 9

El árbol de oro

Antes de leer

pp. 152–153 A. Para discutir en clase

Las respuestas variarán pero pueden incluir:

1. El chico está en una torre.

2. Hay cajas y libros en el cuarto donde está.

3. Está encima de una caja para mirar por una rendija en la pared.

4. Mira el paisaje por una rendija en la pared.

5. Hay charcos en la tierra, unos árboles y un cementerio en la distancia. El campo da una impresión de tristeza.

6. El árbol tiene rayas alrededor para indicar que brilla. Hay pájaros en el árbol que brillan también.

7. Las respuestas variarán.

p. 153 B. Fascinación

Las respuestas variarán.

p. 153 C. Una selección

Las respuestas variarán pero pueden incluir:

1. Los aspectos que describen el ambiente son el otoño, el tiempo frío, los suelos embarrados, el tejado pajizo y requemado por el sol y las nieves. La autora trata de crear una sensación de desolación.

2.

    1. c   2. e   3. b   4. a   5. f

pp. 154–155 D. Una conversación

1. a. Falsa: Ivo veía un árbol con ramas, tronco y hojas de oro.

    b. Cierta

    c. Cierta

    d. Falsa: No le importaba nada lo que pensaba la narradora.

    e. Cierta

    f. Cierta

    g. Falsa: Mateo Heredia no tenía la llave para entrar a la torrecita.

    h. Cierta

Las respuestas a las otras preguntas variarán pero pueden incluir:

2. Porque era todo de oro y resplandecía tanto que tenía que cerrar los ojos.

3. La narradora no creyó a Ivo cuando describió el árbol.

4. Las respuestas variarán.

5. Las respuestas variarán.

Comprensión

p. 161 A. La sucesión de los eventos

a. 6	b. 10	c. 3	d. 9	e. 8	f. 4
g. 2	h. 1	i. 11	j. 7	k. 5	

p. 161 B. Comprensión general
Las respuestas variarán.

p. 162 C. Definiciones

1. d	2. e	3. g	4. h	5. a
6. i	7. j	8. c	9. f	10. b

p. 162 D. Antónimos

1. g	2. a	3. c	4. h
5. f	6. e	7. d	8. b

p. 163 E. Sinónimos

vuelta: regreso

acudí (acudir): vine

alargada: extendida

gruesa: gorda

tarea: quehacer

p. 163 F. Expresiones

1. a las afueras

2. tenía por costumbre

3. sin embargo

4. hacerle caso

5. por lo menos

6. por fin

7. dio con

pp. 163–166 G. Al punto

1. b	2. a	3. c	4. b	5. b	6. a
7. a	8. d	9. b	10. b	11. a	12. c
13. c	14. a	15. b	16. b	17. c	

p. 166 H. Ahora te toca a ti
Las respuestas variarán.

Un paso más

pp. 167–169 A–F. Para conversar
Las respuestas variarán.

p. 169 Para escribir
A. Un resumen
Las respuestas variarán. La lista de palabras puede incluir:

el árbol de oro	morir
aves	paisaje
brillar	ramas
fantasía	rendija
llave	torrecita

pp. 169–170 B–G
Las respuestas variarán.

p. 171 Otra dimensión
Las respuestas variarán.

pp. 172–173 Comprensión auditiva
Selección número 1

1. b	2. a	3. a	4. a

Selección número 2

1. a	2. b	3. b	4. d

Capítulo 9   193

Capítulo 10
Jaque mate en dos jugadas

Antes de leer

pp. 174–175 A. Para discutir en clase
Las respuestas variarán pero pueden incluir:

1. Juegan al ajedrez. Las respuestas a las otras preguntas variarán.

2. Las respuestas variarán.

3. El título del cuento es el final de un partido de ajedrez. Un "jaque mate" ocurre cuando uno de los jugadores va a capturar el rey del otro jugador y el otro no puede evitarlo.

p. 175 B. Los problemas de la familia de hoy
Las respuestas variarán.

p. 175 C. Cognados

agente de policía	revólver
asesinar	salvajes
condenado	veneno
gruñe	

pp. 175–176 D. En contexto

la puerta entornada	*the door ajar*	un revólver	*a revolver*
mayordomo	*overseer*	tiros	*shots*
lágrimas	*tears*	salvajes	*savages*
lo odiaba	*hated him*	puntería	*aim*
asesinarlo	*to murder him*	la pólvora	*gunpowder*
envenenarlo	*to poison him*	condenado	*condemned*
el veneno	*poison*	un agente de policía	*a police officer*
huellas	*tracks*	su jefe	*his boss*
sangre	*blood*		

pp. 176–177 E. El comportamiento de un criminal
Las respuestas variarán.

p. 177 F. Unas citas

Las respuestas variarán pero pueden incluir:

1. Era una casa seca, sin amor. El narrador quiere comunicar que sólo importaba el dinero, que no había sentimientos en esa casa.

2. Los sobrinos llevaban una vida mala. Eran tiranizados. Cuando crecieron era peor.

Comprensión

p. 186 A. ¿Cierta o falsa?

1. Falsa: Claudio se sintió contento, liberado.

2. Falsa: Al tío no le gustaba Matilde.

3. Cierta

4. Falsa: Guillermo odiaba al tío.

5. Falsa: Claudio convenció a Guillermo de que dejara al tío en paz la noche del crimen.

6. Cierta

7. Cierta

8. Cierta

9. Falsa: Claudio guardó el frasquito de veneno en su bolsillo.

10. Cierta

11. Falsa: Cuando regresó a casa lo estaba esperando un agente de policía.

12. Cierta

13. Falsa: Claudio confesó que él era culpable.

14. Falsa: El inspector le pidió a Claudio el revólver.

pp. 186–187 B. Comprensión general

Las respuestas variarán pero pueden incluir:

1 a. El tío abusaba de los sobrinos y cuando crecieron fue peor.

   b. Al tío sólo le importaba el dinero.

   c. El tío no quería que Guillermo se casara con su novia.

   d. El tío era testarudo y arbitrario.

   e. El tío obligaba a Claudio a jugar al ajedrez. Prolongaba los partidos para que Claudio no fuera al club y gozaba de su infortunio.

   f. El tío quería que Claudio se doctorara en bioquímica y éste no lo hizo.

   g. Parece que Guillermo tenía más razones para cometer el crimen, pero Claudio lo hizo. Claudio lo envenenó, pero el agente de policía le preguntó dónde estaba el revólver.

  2–3. Las respuestas variarán.

p. 187 C. En contexto
Las respuestas variarán pero pueden incluir:

A las veintidós significa a las diez de la noche.

Alargaba significa hacer más larga una cosa.

Un *callejón* es una calle estrecha.

El *condenado* es una persona que recibe un castigo.

Enloquece significa volverse loco.

El *malestar* significa molestia, sensación de enfermedad.

Un *paredón* es una pared.

Se alejó significa se fue, irse lejos.

Adueñado significa tomar posesión de algo.

Despachó significa despedir o deshacerse de alguien.

Las *manías* significa obsesiones / caprichos ridículos.

p. 187 D. De la misma familia
Las respuestas variarán pero pueden incluir:

envené (envenenar): veneno, venenoso, etc.

liberado (liberar): libre, libertad, etc.

se enamoró (enamorarse): amor, enamorado, etc.

saboreando (saborear): sabor, saboreador, etc.

Me clavó (clavar): clavo

alarmante: alarmar, alarmado, etc.

flaquearon (flaquear): flaco, enflaquecer, etc.

puntería: apuntar

pp. 187–188 E. Prefijos
1. descansar   *to rest*

   descuidar   *to neglect*

   desdecirme   *to retract*

2. imperturbable   *unperturbed*

   implacable   *implacable, relentless*

   imposible   *impossible*

   impotencia   *impotence*

   inconveniente   *inconvenient*

   infortunio   *misfortune*

   insignificante   *insignificant*

interminable   *interminable*

intolerable   *intolerable*

inútil   *useless*

La regla para el uso del prefijo *in-* o *im-* es que se usa *im-* antes de una palabra que empieza con la letra *p*, y se usa *in-* an*tes de una palabra que empieza con cualquier otra letra.

La forma positiva de estas palabras es:

perturbable	fortunio
placable	significante
posible	terminable
potencia	tolerable
conveniente	útil

3. rebuscar   *to look everywhere for*

   resecar   *to get very dry*

4. El prefijo *mal-* significa "bad" o "wrong".

pp. 188–190 F. Al punto

1. b	2. c	3. a	4. c	5. d	6. b
7. c	8. c	9. b	10. d	11. a	12. a
13. c	14. b	15. c	16. a		

p. 191 G. Ahora te toca a ti
Las respuestas variarán.

Un paso más

pp. 192–194 A–G. Para conversar
Las respuestas variarán.

pp. 194–195 A–F. Para escribir
Las respuestas variarán.

p. 196 Otra dimensión
Las respuestas variarán.

pp. 197–198 Comprensión auditiva
Selección número 1

1. c	2. b	3. b	4. d	5. b

Selección número 2

1. a	2. d	3. a	4. b

 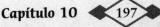

Capítulo 11
La viuda de Montiel

Antes de leer

p. 199 A. Para discutir en clase
Las respuestas variarán. La lista de palabras puede incluir:

ataúd	luto
enlutado	muerto
funerales	rezar

pp. 200–201 B–E
Las respuestas variarán.

p. 201 F. Una selección
Las respuestas variarán pero pueden incluir:

1. Es irónico que el cadáver nunca hubiera parecido tan vivo y que tuviera un crucifijo entre las manos en vez de una fusta.

2. José Montiel era una persona muy poderosa y muy cruel.

Comprensión

p. 209 A. ¿Cierta o falsa?
1. Cierta

2. Falsa: Sólo asistieron sus copartidarios y las congregaciones religiosas.

3. Cierta

4. Cierta

5. Falsa: Las cosas no marchaban bien.

6. Falsa: José Montiel se enriqueció en menos de un año.

7. Falsa: La viuda de Montiel odiaba al alcalde.

8. Cierta

9. Cierta

10. Falsa: Al final del cuento parece que la viuda de Montiel se muere o está a punto de morirse.

p. 209 B. Comprensión general

Las respuestas variarán pero pueden incluir:

1. José Montiel se hizo una de las personas más poderosas del pueblo colaborando con el alcalde. Mataron a los pobres y tomaron las posesiones de los ricos.

2. José Montiel trataba mal a su esposa. Después de su muerte ella empieza a morderse las uñas, sólo se alimenta de su resentimiento y se consume en la desesperación.

3. Una vez que José Montiel murió, los habitantes del pueblo tomaron represalias. Se comportaron de esa manera porque hacía mucho tiempo que sufrían sus abusos.

4. Los hijos hicieron bien en no ir al funeral de su padre porque los habitantes los podrían haber matado.

5. a. José Montiel nunca pareció tan vivo como cuando estaba muerto.

   b. José Montiel siempre asistía a misa aunque mataba a muchas personas.

   c. En lugar de una fusta en la mano el cadáver tiene un crucifijo.

   d. José Montiel murió de muerte natural después de matar a mucha gente.

   e. La viuda había pasado cinco años rogando a Dios que se acabaran los tiros y dos agentes de policía pasan toda una mañana disparando a la caja fuerte porque ella no sabe la combinación para abrirla.

   f. Como si toda la mala suerte que tiene no fuera bastante, la viuda le dice al señor Carmichael que no entre a la casa con un paraguas abierto porque trae mala suerte.

   g. José Montiel planificaba las muertes mientras su esposa se compadecía de los muertos.

   h. Las hijas dicen que es imposible vivir en un país tan salvaje donde asesinan a la gente por cuestiones políticas.

p. 210 C. Antónimos

vivo: muerto

de pie: sentado

feliz: triste

enriquecido: empobrecido

atardecer: amanecer

p. 210 D. Sinónimos

lanzó (lanzar): echó, tiró

retratos: fotos

había perdido (perder) el juicio: se había vuelto loco, había enloquecido

no me friegues (fregar): no me molestes

p. 210 E. Definiciones

1. e	**2.** c	**3.** g	**4.** f	**5.** b
6. a	**7.** d			

pp. 210–211 F. En contexto

Las respuestas variarán pero pueden incluir:

El *semblante* es la cara de una persona, el estado de ánimo que se le ve en la cara a una persona.

Acribillaran significa abrieron muchos agujeros.

Los *formularios* son planillas o papeles para llenar.

Recostó significa apoyó, inclinó.

Rogando significa pidiendo que algo ocurra.

Hinchados significa más grande que lo normal.

Engordó significa se puso más pesado.

Salvaje significa no civilizado.

pp. 211–213 G. Al punto

1. c	**2.** c	**3.** b	**4.** d	**5.** a	**6.** a
7. d	**8.** b	**9.** c	**10.** b	**11.** c	**12.** b
13. a	**14.** c	**15.** a	**16.** b		

p. 213 H. Ahora te toca a ti

Las respuestas variarán.

Un paso más

Para conversar
p. 214 A. Reflexiones

Las respuestas variarán pero pueden incluir:

1. La respuesta variará.

2. Montiel era el único hombre que sus padres permitieron que ella viera a menos de diez metros de distancia. La respuesta variará.

3. El error que cometió Dios al crear el mundo fue descansar el último día. Por eso no terminó la creación y hay tantas cosas mal hechas en el mundo. La respuesta variará.

4. Les aconsejaba a sus hijos que se quedaran en Europa para siempre y que no se preocuparan por ella. La respuesta variará.

5. Al final del cuento la viuda parece morir. Lo sabemos porque la Mamá Grande aparece y predice su muerte.

pp. 214–215 B–H
Las respuestas variarán.

Para escribir
p. 215 A. Un resumen
Las respuestas variarán. La lista de palabras puede incluir:

asesinar	hijos
corrupto	horroroso
enriquecerse	morir
entierro	poderoso

pp. 215–216 B–E
Las respuestas variarán.

p. 217 Otra dimensión
Las respuestas variarán.

pp. 218–219 Comprensión auditiva
Selección número 1
  1. b   2. d   3. b   4. a

Selección número 2
  1. b   2. a   3. a   4. c   5. b   6. d

 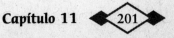

Capítulo 12
Cartas de amor traicionado

Antes de leer

pp. 220–221 A–C
Las respuestas variarán.

p. 222 D. Una selección
Las respuestas variarán pero pueden incluir:

1. Sí, el autor de las cartas es una persona educada porque en algunas de ellas habla de poetas muertos y de los pensamientos que escribieron.

2. Analía sospechaba de todo lo que tenía que ver con su tío.

3. Analía empezó a leer las cartas porque estaba aburrida en el colegio y las cartas representaban la única posibilidad de usar su imaginación.

4. Las cartas le eran útiles para burlar la censura de la Madre Superiora.

5. Cuando creció la intimidad entre Analía y el autor de las cartas, se pusieron de acuerdo en un código secreto con el cual empezaron a hablar de amor.

p. 223 E. Otra selección
Las respuestas variarán pero pueden incluir:

1. Analía tenía el alma definitivamente entregada al autor de las cartas.

2. Ya descarta sus sospechas del tío y está avergonzada de su propia mezquindad al creer que la relación es un plan de su tío para que sus bienes pasen a manos de su hijo.

3. Al final de la selección nos enteramos de que Analía está desilusionada con Luis.

p. 223 F. Predicciones
Las respuestas variarán.

Comprensión

p. 234 A. ¿Cierta o falsa?
1. Cierta

2. Cierta

3. Falsa: La primera vez que el tío fue a visitar a Analía ambos habían cambiado mucho y no se reconocieron.

4. Cierta

5. Cierta

6. Cierta

7. Falsa: Estaba segura que era un hombre feo, tal vez enfermo, contrahecho.

8. Cierta

9. Cierta

10. Falsa: Analía detestaba a Luis.

11. Falsa: Cuando nació el hijo, la relación entre Analía y Luis se empeoró.

12. Cierta

13. Falsa: Luis murió cuando se cayó de un caballo.

14. Cierta

15. Cierta

p. 235 B. Comprensión general

Las respuestas variarán pero pueden incluir:

1. Analía conoció a su futuro esposo por las cartas que ella creyó que él le escribía cuando ella estaba en el colegio. Cuando ella cumplió dieciocho años él fue a visitarla.

2. Analía y Luis no se querían y después del nacimiento de su hijo su relación empeoró.

3. La boleta de notas del hijo contiene una carta escrita por el maestro y Analía reconoce la caligrafía.

4. Analía fue a visitar al maestro al final del cuento para verificar que él era el hombre que le había escrito las cartas de amor. Lo reconoce inmediatamente porque lo ha visto en sus sueños.

p. 235 C. De la misma familia

Las respuestas variarán pero pueden incluir:

sospechaba (sospechar): sospecha, sospechoso, etc.

confianza: confiar, confiado, desconfiar, etc.

se reconocieron (reconocer): conocer, conocido, etc.

sentimentales: sentimientos, sentir, etc.

escritura: escribir, escritorio, etc.

enterrarlo: tierra, entierro, etc.

p. 235 D. Antónimos

1. c	2. d	3. l	4. g	5. k
6. e	7. h	8. a	9. j	10. b

 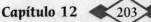

p. 236 E. En contexto

Las respuestas variarán pero pueden incluir:

Las *almohadas* son algo sobre lo que se pone la cabeza al dormir.

Mojada significa no seca.

El *sudor* es el líquido que produce el cuerpo al hacer ejercicio o cuando uno tiene calor.

Temblando significa moviéndose con sacudidas rápidas.

El *luto* es el período que sigue a la muerte de una persona.

Una *viuda* es la esposa de un hombre que se murió.

Quemar significa destruir algo con fuego.

Las *muletas* son aparatos que se usan para ayudarle a una persona a caminar.

p. 236 F. Al punto

1. a	2. d	3. c	4. b	5. c	6. b
7. d	8. a	9. c	10. c	11. b	12. c
13. b	14. a	15. a	16. d	17. b	18. a
19. c	20. b	21. d	22. b	23. c	

p. 239 G. Ahora te toca a ti

Las respuestas variarán.

Un paso más

pp. 240–241 A–E. Para conversar

Las respuestas variarán.

p. 242 A–E. Para escribir

Las respuestas variarán.

p. 243 Otra dimensión

Las respuestas variarán.

pp. 244–245 Comprensión auditiva

Selección número 1

1. b	2. d	3. d	4. b	5. c

Selección número 2

1. b	2. c	3. a	4. b

Capítulo 13
Emma Zunz

Antes de leer

p. 246 A. Para discutir en clase
La lista de palabras puede incluir:

beneficios	huelga
dueño	letreros
empleado	quejas
fábrica	sueldo

Las respuestas variarán pero pueden incluir:

1. Estos personajes están en una fábrica. Las descripciones variarán.

2. Hay un hombre viejo que parece ser el dueño de la fábrica y una mujer más joven que parece ser una empleada. Las respuestas a las otras preguntas variarán.

3. Afuera hay una huelga. Las respuestas variarán.

p. 247 B–C
Las respuestas variarán.

pp. 247–248 D. Una selección
Las respuestas variarán pero pueden incluir:

1. Después de recibir la carta Emma tuvo una sensación de malestar en el vientre y en las rodillas.

2. Emma pensó que la muerte de su padre era lo único que había sucedido en el mundo, y seguiría sucediendo sin fin.

3. El padre de Emma había robado dinero.

4. Según el padre de Emma, Aarón Loewenthal había sido el verdadero ladrón.

5. Las únicas personas que sabían la verdad eran Emma, su padre y Loewenthal.

Comprensión

p. 255 A. ¿Cierta o falsa?
1. Falsa: Emma Zunz recibió una carta de un compañero de pensión de su padre en Brasil.

2. Cierta

3. Falsa: Emma pensó que la muerte de su padre era lo único que había sucedido en el mundo.

4. Cierta

5. Falsa: A Emma los hombres le inspiraban un terror casi patológico.

6. Cierta

7. Cierta

8. Cierta

9. Falsa: Loewenthal era avaro.

10. Falsa: Las cosas no ocurrieron como había previsto Emma.

11. Falsa: Emma le disparó a Loewenthal tres veces.

12. Cierta

pp. 255–256 B. La sucesión de los eventos

a. 11	b. 13	c. 4	d. 14	e. 1
f. 15	g. 6	h. 3	i. 7	j. 9
k. 12	l. 2	m. 10	n. 8	o. 5

p. 256 C. Comprensión general
Las respuestas variarán pero pueden incluir:

1. Emma leyó en el periódico que un vapor extranjero estaría en puerto esa noche, llamó a Loewenthal para decirle que quería hablar con él sobre la huelga sin que los otros lo supieran y rompió la carta del amigo de su padre.

2. Emma pensaba vengarse matando a Loewenthal.

3. Emma trató de explicarle a Loewenthal por qué lo iba a matar pero es posible que él no la hubiera podido escuchar antes de morir.

4. Sí, el final es irónico, porque la historia no era verdadera pero todo el mundo la creyó.

p. 256 D. De la misma familia
Las respuestas variarán pero pueden incluir:

creciente: crecer, crecido, crecimiento, etc.

cajero: caja, cajón, etc.

sentimiento: sentir, sentido, etc.

festejar: fiesta, festival, etc.

oscurecer: oscuro, oscuridad, etc.

hambrientos: hambre, hambruna, etc.

encadenaban (encadenar): cadena

sombrío: sombra, sombreado, etc.

ladridos: ladrar

p. 257 E. Sinónimos

1. a   2. e   3. g   4. d

5. f   6. h   7. c   8. b

p. 257 F. Antónimos

1. d   2. c   3. f   4. a   5. e   6. b

p. 257 G. En contexto

Las respuestas variarán pero pueden incluir:

Fechada significa que un documento tiene una fecha específica.

Del corriente significa del mes en el que estamos.

Acto continuo significa que una acción ocurre inmediatamente después de otra.

Creciente significa cada vez más grande.

De vuelta significa al regresar.

Peligró significa que corrió un gran riesgo.

Un *asiento delantero* es un lugar para sentarse que está al frente de un vehículo.

pp. 258–260 H. Al punto

1. a   2. c   3. b   4. a   5. d   6. d

7. c   8. c   9. d   10. b   11. a   12. d

13. a   14. b   15. a   16. b   17. d   18. a

p. 260 I. Ahora te toca a ti

Las respuestas variarán.

Un paso más

pp. 261–262 A–G. Para conversar

Las respuestas variarán.

pp. 263–264 A–F. Para escribir

Las respuestas variarán.

p. 265 Otra dimensión

Las respuestas variarán.

pp. 266–267 Comprensión auditiva

Selección número 1

1. d   2. b   3. a   4. c

Selección número 2

1. d   2. b   3. a   4. b   5. b

Poesía
Capítulo 14
Rima LIII

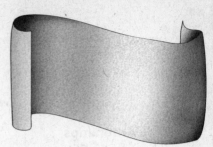

Antes de leer

p. 270 A

Las respuestas variarán pero pueden incluir:

Aves	**Flores**	**Edificios**	**Agua**
el ala	las flores	el balcón	las gotas
las golondrinas	el jardín	las tapias	el rocío
los nidos	las madreselvas		
el vuelo			

p. 270 B

Las respuestas variarán.

p. 270 C

1. Las oscuras golondrinas volverán a colgar sus nidos en tu balcón,...

2. Las tupidas madreselvas volverán a escalar las tapias de tu jardín...

3. Las palabras ardientes del amor volverán a sonar en tus oídos;...

Comprensión

p. 273

1. Las respuestas variarán pero pueden incluir:

	¿Qué harán?	¿Cuáles no volverán?
las golondrinas	volverán a colgar sus nidos en el balcón; con el ala a sus cristales jugando llamarán	aquéllas que refrenaban el vuelo a contemplar la hermosura de la mujer y la dicha del poeta; aquéllas que aprendieron los nombres del poeta y de su novia
las tupidas madreselvas	volverán a escalar las tapias del jardín y sus flores se abrirán	aquellas cuajadas de rocío
las palabras ardientes del amor	volverán a sonar en sus oídos	
su corazón	tal vez despertará de su profundo sueño	
otras personas	no la querrán como el poeta	

2. La persona a quien le habla el poeta oirá las palabras ardientes del amor; tal vez su corazón despertará.

3. El poeta ha querido a su amada mudo y absorto y de rodillas, como se adora a Dios ante su altar.

4. Al final del poema el poeta parece decir que nadie querrá a su amada como él la ha querido. Las respuestas a las otras preguntas variarán.

Un paso más

p. 274 A–B
Las respuestas variarán.

Capítulo 15

Me gustas cuando callas

Antes de leer

p. 276 A–C

Las respuestas variarán.

Comprensión

p. 278

Las respuestas variarán pero pueden incluir:

1. El poeta le habla a su novia. Parece que el poeta tiene una relación íntima con ella.

2. La voz del poeta no alcanza a la persona con quien habla porque está demasiado lejos de ella. El poeta decide callarse con el silencio de ella.

3. El poeta compara el silencio a la luz de una lámpara y a la simplicidad de un anillo porque éstos comunican algo sin hacer sonido.

4. Al final del poema el poeta se siente alegre porque la persona de quien habla está presente y porque está viva.

Un paso más

p. 278 A–B

Las respuestas variarán.

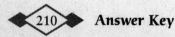

Capítulo 16
Adolescencia

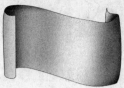

Antes de leer

p. 280 A

Las respuestas variarán.

p. 280 B

Las respuestas variarán.

1. Los sustantivos en el poema:

   aguas   muchacho

   camino   pasaje

   corriente   pie

   espejo   puente

   luz   vez

2. Los adjetivos en el poema:

   alegre   breve   otro   vencida

Comprensión

p. 282

Las respuestas variarán pero pueden incluir:

1. El autor ya no es adolescente porque dice que la adolescencia vino y se fue.

2. Sí, el poeta piensa sobre la adolescencia positivamente. Dice que vino y se fue dulcemente.

3. Nos está tratando de comunicar que esta época de la vida es muy breve—verte y ya otra vez no verte—pero que la persona cambia mucho durante estos años.

4. Los dos últimos versos de la primera estrofa significan que la adolescencia es muy breve pero también alegre.

5. La última estrofa compara la vida a un río. El muchacho está mirando su reflexión en el agua que fluye y se desvanece como la vida.

6. El autor quiere ver fluir y desvanecerse a la adolescencia en el espejo del agua.

Un paso más

p. 282 A–B

Las respuestas variarán.

Capítulo 17
Proverbios y cantares, XXIX

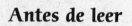

Antes de leer

p. 284 A
Las respuestas variarán.

Comprensión

p. 286
Las respuestas variarán pero pueden incluir:

1. El caminante a quien le habla el poeta es el (la) lector(a).

2. Las huellas son las cosas que el caminante ha hecho en su vida.

3. Se hace camino andando. El poeta quiere decir que cada persona tiene que crear su propia vida.

4. Cuando mira hacia atrás el caminante ve la senda que nunca va a volver a pisar.

5. En los dos últimos versos el poeta nos está tratando de comunicar que la vida es breve y efímera, como la estela de un barco en el agua.

6. Las respuestas variarán.

Un paso más

p. 286
Las respuestas variarán.

Capítulo 18
Despedida

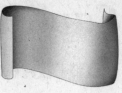

Antes de leer

p. 288 A
Las respuestas variarán.

Comprensión

p. 290
Las respuestas variarán pero pueden incluir:

1. El poeta quiere que dejen el balcón abierto para ver y oír lo que pasa afuera.

2. Desde su balcón puede ver a un niño que come naranjas y puede sentir a un segador que siega el trigo.

3. El niño puede ser el símbolo de la juventud y el segador el símbolo de la muerte.

4. Usa signos de exclamación en la última estrofa y no en la primera para que estos versos se lean con emoción.

5. Las respuestas variarán.

Un paso más

p. 290 A–B
Las respuestas variarán.

Capítulo 19

Canción de jinete

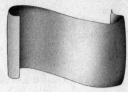

Antes de leer

p. 292 A

Las respuestas variarán.

Comprensión

p. 294

Las respuestas variarán pero pueden incluir:

1. No es la primera vez que el jinete va a Córdoba porque dice que sabe los caminos.

2. No llegará a Córdoba porque va a morir antes de llegar.

3. El poeta cambia la descripción de la luna de grande a roja porque el rojo es el color de la sangre.

4. La repetición de los dos primeros versos al final del poema refuerza el sentimiento de soledad y el presentimiento que algo malo le va a ocurrir antes de llegar a Córdoba.

5. El tono del poema es misterioso porque aunque el poeta dice que va a morir no sabemos cómo ni por qué cree eso.

Un paso más

p. 294 A–B

Las respuestas variarán.

Capítulo 20
Selecciones de *Versos sencillos*

Selección de *Versos sencillos*, XXXIX

Antes de leer

p. 296 A
Las respuestas variarán.

Comprensión

p. 298
Las respuestas variarán pero pueden incluir:

1. La rosa blanca representa su buena voluntad y la cultiva todo el año.

2. Al poeta le importa mucho "el amigo sincero".

3. El poeta tiene la misma actitud hacia "el cruel" que hacia "el amigo sincero".

Selección de *Versos sencillos*, XLIV

Comprensión

p. 300
1.

	Cosas que poseen
el leopardo	un abrigo
la mushma	un cojinete
el conde	su abolengo
el mendigo	la aurora
el ave	un ala
el señor presidente	un jardín con una fuente y un tesoro en oro y trigo

2. Algunas de estas cosas tienen valor, pero para los que las poseen tienen mucho más valor. Para el autor un amigo es más importante que todo lo demás.

3. Cada estrofa termina con la palabra "amigo". El autor hace esto para dar énfasis a esta palabra.

4. La amistad parece ser una preocupación constante del autor.

Un paso más

pp. 300–301 A–C
Las respuestas variarán.

Capítulo 21
Canción de otoño en primavera

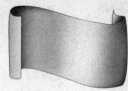

Antes de leer

p. 303 A

Las respuestas variarán pero pueden incluir:

1. En el otoño la temperatura baja y comienza a hacer frío. En la primavera el tiempo mejora y hace más calor.

2. Cuando se acerca el invierno mucha gente se siente triste. A mucha gente no le gusta el invierno porque el mal tiempo y el frío hacen la vida más dura. También mueren las flores y las hojas se caen de los árboles. El invierno provoca un sentimiento de tristeza en mucha gente.

3. Para muchas personas la primavera representa un renacimiento porque reaparecen las flores, la hierba y las hojas de los árboles. Asociamos la alegría y el amor con la primavera.

p. 303 B

Las respuestas variarán.

p. 303 C

Las respuestas variarán.

Palabras que tienen que ver con el amor:

el abrazo	la pasión
el beso	la ternura
el corazón	

p. 304 D

Temas que aparecen en el poema:

- el encuentro de un nuevo amor
- la fugacidad de la vida
- la pérdida de la juventud
- la pérdida del amor
- el querer seguir amando
- el querer volver al pasado

Comprensión

p. 308

Las respuestas variarán, pero pueden incluir:

1. El poeta era demasiado tímido y la "dulce niña" era el objeto de su amor. La idealiza comparándola con el "alba pura". Parece que la relación existe principalmente en su fantasía.

2. La persona que describe en las estrofas 6–8 es tierna y apasionada. Toma su ensueño y lo mata.

3. El poeta cambia el tiempo del verbo porque ya es viejo y su juventud quedó en el pasado.

4. En la estrofa 14 habla de "las demás" y dice que estuvieron en "tantas tierras" y "tantos climas". Son excusas para hacer versos o producto de su fantasía.

5. No, el poeta no tuvo una vida feliz porque pasó toda su vida buscando el amor ideal y nunca lo encontró. En el verso 58 nos dice que estaba triste de esperar a su princesa.

6. Las respuestas variarán.

Un paso más

p. 308 A–B

Las respuestas variarán.

Capítulo 22
Oda al tomate

Antes de leer

p. 310 A

Las respuestas variarán pero pueden incluir:

1. Una oda es un poema lírico que generalmente expresa emoción.

2–3. Las respuestas variarán.

p. 310 B

Las respuestas variarán. Una posible manera de agrupar las palabras:

Alimentos	Partes de alimentos	Preparación	Sensaciones	Acciones	Utensilios
aceite	jugo	almuerzos	aroma	asesinar	cuchillo
cebolla	mitades	cocinas	fragancia	hervir	mantequilleras
ensaladas	pulpa				saleros
olivo					vasos
papas					
perejil					
pimienta					
tomate					

p. 310 C–D

Las respuestas variarán.

Comprensión

p. 314

Las respuestas variarán pero pueden incluir:

1. Los dibujos variarán.

2. El autor quiere decir que el tomate va a dar su vida para alimentarnos a nosotros. Para asesinarlo "se hunde el cuchillo en su pulpa viviente". Dice que la pulpa es "una roja víscera" como si fuera carne.

3. El tomate y la cebolla se casan. Participarán los otros alimentos.

4. Algunas de las personificaciones:

v 14: se desata / el tomate

v 16: invade / las cocinas

v 18 entra por los almuerzos

v 19: se sienta / reposado / en los aparadores,...

v 28: Debemos, por desgracia, / asesinarlo

v 32: en su pulpa viviente, / es una roja / víscera

v 41: se casa alegremente / con la clara cebolla

v 46: aceite, / hijo / esencial del olivo

v 56: el perejil / levanta / banderines

v 61: el asado / golpea / con su aroma / en la puerta

v 83: nos entrega / el regalo / de su color fogoso...

5. Las respuestas variarán.

Un paso más

pp. 314–315 A–F

Las respuestas variarán.

De la prensa
Capítulo 23
La fiesta de San Fermín

Antes de leer
pp. 317–318 A–E
Las respuestas variarán.

Comprensión

p. 322 A. ¿Cierta o falsa?

1. Cierta

2. Falsa: La fiesta se extiende por poco más de una semana.

3. Cierta

4. Cierta

5. Falsa: En el encierro nunca faltan los heridos y hasta los muertos.

6. Cierta

7. Cierta

8. Falsa: En el último acto de la fiesta cantan "El pobre de mí".

pp. 322–323 B. Comprensión general
Las respuestas variarán pero pueden incluir:

1. Algunas actividades de los sanfermines:

    visitar los bares de Pamplona

    bailar

    coquetear

    conocer a la gente de Navarra

    comer y beber

    correr en el encierro

    asistir a las corridas

    cantar

    saltar desde la fuente de Santa Cecilia hacia abajo

    participar en el desfile

2. La celebración empezó en tiempos de San Fermín.

3. Los sanfermines se celebran en la fiesta del patrono de Pamplona. La celebración dura ocho días.

4. La celebración empieza al mediodía del 6 de julio cuando el alcalde y los consejales de Pamplona lanzan un cohete del balcón del Ayuntamiento.

5. Las bancas del parque no están libres porque mucha gente de todas partes del mundo asiste a las fiestas.

6. El encierro empieza a las ocho de la mañana. La gente corre aproximadamente 800 metros hacia la plaza San Jonnos delante de los toros.

7. El encierro se originó porque no había camiones para llevar los toros a la plaza.

8. Es extraño que la Casa de la Misericordia organice la corrida porque los toros son matados sin misericordia.

9. La Fuente de la Navarrería, en la que hay personas que saltan desde una fuente hacia la muchedumbre que está abajo, y el Estruendo de Iruña, un desfile, son dos eventos recientes.

10. La última noche de la fiesta la gente canta una canción triste.

p. 323 C. De la misma familia
Las respuestas variarán pero pueden incluir:

gritan (gritar): grito

festejan (festejar): fiesta, festival, etc.

descansan (descansar): descanso, cansar, cansado, etc.

liberadas (liberar): libre, libertad, etc.

escándalo: escandaloso, escandalizar, etc.

diaria: día

reciente: recientemente

tristeza: triste, entristecer, etc.

p. 323 D. En contexto
Las respuestas variarán pero pueden incluir:

Perseguida significa seguida por alguien o algo.

Asustados significa que tienen miedo de algo.

El *alcalde* es el jefe del gobierno de una ciudad o pueblo.

El *amanecer* es el principio del día cuando aparece el sol.

Los *heridos* son las personas a quienes los toros les hacen daño.

Los *desvelados* son las personas que no durmieron por la noche.

Un paso más

pp. 324–325 A–C. Para conversar
Las respuestas variarán.

p. 325 A. Para escribir
Un resumen
Las respuestas variarán. La lista de palabras puede incluir:

asustado	durar
cantar	encierro
celebración	festejarse
corrida de toros	herir
divertirse	peligro

pp. 325–326 B–D
Las respuestas variarán.

Capítulo 24
Fernando Botero, El espejo convexo

Antes de leer

pp. 327–328 A–C
Las respuestas variarán.

Comprensión

p. 332 A. ¿Cierta o falsa?

1. Falsa: El mundo que crea Botero es apacible, tranquilo y feliz.

2. Falsa: El tema principal de la obra de Botero es la figura humana.

3. Cierta

4. Cierta

5. Cierta

6. Falsa: Empezó a esculpir a mediados de los años setenta.

7. Cierta

8. Cierta

9. Falsa: En sus naturalezas muertas las frutas son exuberantes en sus volúmenes.

10. Cierta

p. 332 B. Comprensión general
Las respuestas variarán pero pueden incluir:

1. Botero desarrolló su estilo propio mientras estuvo en Europa. El muralista mexicano Orozco y los pintores florentinos del "quattrocento" influyeron en su estilo.

2. A Botero no le gustan los cuadros de figuras estilizadas.

3. Pinta a gente gruesa porque son metáforas de momentos eternos que inmovilizan por un instante la muerte.

4. Le gusta pintar las corridas de toros porque las imágenes y el color están allí y el pintor no tiene que inventarlos.

5. Las respuestas variarán.

 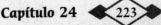

p. 333 C. De la misma familia
Las respuestas variarán pero pueden incluir:

pintura: pintar, pintor, etc.

tranquilo: tranquilizar, tranquilidad, etc.

inmovilizan (inmovilizar): móvil, inmóvil, etc.

belleza: bello, embellecer, etc.

despreocupada: preocupado, ocupado, ocupar, preocuparse, etc.

poderosas: poder, apoderarse, etc.

grabada: grabar, grabadora, etc.

recuerdo: recordar

p. 333 D. En contexto
Las respuestas variarán pero pueden incluir:

Hinchados significa que tienen el volumen aumentado.

Las *leyes* son reglas.

Un *espejo* es una superficie brillante que refleja las imágenes.

Las *arrugas* son pliegues que aparecen en la piel al envejecer.

El *paisaje* está formado por los elementos de la naturaleza característicos de un lugar.

Las *abejas* son los insectos que hacen la miel.

Los *talleres* son lugares donde los artistas trabajan.

Un paso más

p. 334 A–C. Para conversar
Las respuestas variarán.

p. 334 A. Para escribir
Un resumen
Las respuestas variarán. La lista de palabras puede incluir:

arte	estilo
belleza	forma
crear	grueso
cuerpo	influencias
escultura	pintura

pp. 334–335 B–D
Las respuestas variarán.

Capítulo 25
La Tomatina

Antes de leer
pp. 336–337 A–C
Las respuestas variarán.

Comprensión

p. 341 A. ¿Cierta o falsa?

1. Cierta

2. Falsa: El pueblo de Buñol, de sólo unos 9.000 habitantes, es mucho más pequeño que Valencia.

3. Falsa: Los participantes lanzan los tomates a cualquier cosa que se mueva.

4. Cierta

5. Falsa: La Tomatina carece de reglas y de una organización formal.

6. Falsa: El dictador Francisco Franco creyó que era un desorden excesivo y lo prohibió en los años cincuenta.

7. Falsa: La Guardia Civil ha detenido a gente en numerosas ocasiones.

8. Cierta

9. Cierta

10. Falsa: La Tomatina ha contribuido a la fama y a la economía de Buñol.

p. 341 B. Comprensión general
Las respuestas variarán pero pueden incluir:

1. La fiesta de la Tomatina consiste en lanzar tomates a cualquier cosa que se mueva.

2. Durante la época del dictador Francisco Franco la fiesta fue prohibida.

3. Algunos critican la fiesta porque se desperdicia comida mientras existe hambre en el mundo. Los buñolenses contestan que no hay que amargarse, que la vida es corta y hay que divertirse.

p. 342 C. Definiciones

1. escasez
2. una muchedumbre
3. maduros
4. los vencedores
5. lejano
6. arrestos

p. 342 D. De la misma familia

Las respuestas variarán pero pueden incluir:

guerra: guerrero

creada: creación, creador, etc.

encabezado: cabeza

risas: reírse

limpiar: limpieza, limpio, etc.

amargarse: amargo, amargor / amargura, etc.

p. 343 E. Sinónimos

1. d	2. f	3. g	4. k
5. h	6. b	7. c	8. e

Un paso más

pp. 344–345 A–D. Para conversar

Las respuestas variarán.

p. 345 A. Para escribir
Un resumen

Las respuestas variarán. La lista de palabras puede incluir:

celebrarse	mantener el orden
criticar	pueblo
guerra de comida	tomates
lanzar	tradición
limpiar	valor cultural

pp. 345–346 B–D

Las respuestas variarán.

Capítulo 26
Los indios kunas

Antes de leer

p. 347 A. La geografía de Panamá
Los mapas variarán pero deben incluir los ocho lugares mencionados.

p. 347 B. Grupos de palabras

Geografía	Tradiciones	Ocupaciones
el clima	los antepasados	los curanderos
húmedo	los aretes	hacer canastas
los lagos	las argollas	hacer canoas
los ríos	las canciones de cuna	los pescadores
seco	el carnaval	ser jefe
la selva tropical	la deidad	
	los ritos	

p. 348 C–D
Las respuestas variarán.

Comprensión

p. 354 A. ¿Cierta o falsa?
1. Cierta
2. Cierta
3. Falsa: Los kunas son personas de estatura pequeña.
4. Cierta
5. Cierta
6. Falsa: Los kunas organizan juntas en la casa de reuniones donde discuten las cosas que afectan a su comunidad.
7. Cierta
8. Falsa: La mola es un tejido o una prenda.
9. Falsa: Solamente las mujeres pueden hacer las molas.
10. Falsa: Los diseños de las molas son todos distintos y hay mucha variedad.

 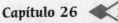

p. 354 B. Comprensión general

Las respuestas variarán pero pueden incluir:

1. Los kunas llegaron al lugar donde viven ahora porque se resistieron a la colonización de los españoles.

2. El vivir allí les permite a los kunas mantener su cultura y sus tradiciones porque están aislados.

3. Los kunas respetan la tierra porque para ellos todo lo natural representa una deidad.

4. Los matrimonios son planeados y el esposo va a vivir en casa de su esposa y trabaja para sus padres.

5. Los kunas llegaron a tener autonomía resistiendo la opresión. Luego un acuerdo les garantizó la autonomía.

6. Según tradición kuna, las molas se originaron en el siglo XIX cuando la Divina Providencia envió a Ibeorgun y a su hermana Olokikadiryai para que les enseñaran a diseñar y confeccionar las molas.

7. Sólo las mujeres las hacen; los diseños se inspiran en la flora y la fauna, en símbolos religiosos o mitológicos o en figuras geométricas; tardan hasta un mes en ser elaboradas.

8. Los kunas tienen problemas de sobrepoblación, escasez de tierra y enfermedades en las plantaciones de coco.

p. 355 C. Un resumen gráfico

Las respuestas variarán pero pueden incluir:

Los kunas

Geografía	Tradiciones	Alimentación	Ocupaciones	Problemas	Apariencia
República de Panamá	mitos y leyendas	maíz	pescadores	sobrepoblación	bajos
Kuna Yala	todo es deidad	arroz	granjeros	escasez de tierra	cuello corto
la costa y las islas cercanas	monogamia	cacao	caciques	enfermedades del coco	espaldas anchas
selva tropical	mujeres confeccionan molas	yuca	curanderos	jóvenes salen del pueblo	piernas cortas
clima variado	ritos de curación y pubertad	coco		conflictos con modernización	pies pequeños
					aretes y argollas

p. 355 D. Un resumen oral

Las respuestas variarán.

p. 355 E. De la misma familia

Las respuestas variarán pero pueden incluir:

habitan (habitar): habitante, habitación, etc.

pescadores: pescar, pescado, etc.

alimentación: alimentos, alimentar, etc.

venta: vender, vendedor, etc.

extenso: extender, extensión, etc.

canciones: canto, cantar, cantante, etc.

pp. 355–356 F. En contexto

Las respuestas variarán pero pueden incluir:

La *selva* es un terreno extenso con mucha vegetación.

La *caza* significa la búsqueda de animales para comer.

Los *aretes* son joyas que se llevan en las orejas.

Un *tronco* es la parte más gruesa de un árbol que emerge de la tierra.

Se mude quiere decir se traslade.

Los *rascacielos* son los edificios muy altos que se encuentran en grandes ciudades.

Un paso más

p. 356 A. Para conversar
Un pedido

Las respuestas variarán. Información sobre las molas puede incluir:

- vistosos diseños y colores
- diseños incluyen flora y fauna, elementos mitológicos, dibujos geométricos, objetos extranjeros
- sólo las mujeres las confeccionan
- cada uno tiene un estilo único
- tardan hasta un mes en hacerlas
- se originaron en el siglo XIX cuando la Divina Providencia mandó a dos personas para enseñarles a las kunas a hacerlas
- pueden ser vestidos, ropa, tela o tejidos
- infinita variedad
- se confeccionan con telas de hilo de Panamá y Colombia
- el precio oscila entre 5 y 100 dólares

pp. 356–357 B–C

Las respuestas variarán.

p. 357 A–C. Para escribir

Las respuestas variarán.

Teatro

Capítulo 27

El delantal blanco

Antes de leer

pp. 359–360 A–C

Las respuestas variarán.

p. 360 D. Una selección

Las respuestas variarán pero pueden incluir:

1. Según la señora, la ropa que lleva una persona cambia la manera en que esa persona mira el mundo.

2. Cuando la señora se puso el primer par de medias el mundo entero cambió. Toda la gente era diferente.

3. Las respuestas variarán.

p. 361 E. Otra selección

Las respuestas variarán.

Comprensión

p. 376 A. ¿Cierta o falsa?

1. Falsa: La señora y su hijo están en la playa con la empleada.

2. Falsa: La empleada lee una revista de historietas fotografiadas.

3. Cierta

4. Falsa: La señora cree que la vida del campo es muy agradable.

5. Falsa: La señora le dice a la empleada que entre en la carpa.

6. Cierta

7. Cierta

8. Falsa: A la señora el cambio le molesta.

9. Cierta

10. Falsa: Los jóvenes se llevan a la señora a la fuerza.

11. Falsa: El caballero distinguido le habla a la empleada.

12. Cierta

pp. 376–377 B. Comprensión general

Las respuestas variarán pero pueden incluir:

1. Parece que la señora es de la clase alta. Parece que lleva una vida aburrida.

2. La señora va a la playa en coche porque le gusta que la vean en un coche que no muchas personas tienen. Esto nos dice que la señora es muy vanidosa.

3. Al principio de la obra la señora trata a la empleada con desprecio.

4.

	Antes	Después
LA SEÑORA	cree que es especial porque todos pueden ver que tiene clase	se entera de que no es especial
	le da órdenes a la empleada	sigue las órdenes que le da la empleada
	cree que la revista de la empleada es tonta	lee la revista de la empleada
LA EMPLEADA	usa Ud. con la señora	usa tú con la señora
	trata a la señora con respeto	le da órdenes a la señora
	no presta mucha atención al niño	actúa como la madre del niño

5. El caballero distinguido cree que el comunismo ha cambiado el orden establecido de la vida pero que al final el orden se restablecerá.

6. Las respuestas variarán.

p. 377 C. De la misma familia

Las respuestas variarán pero pueden incluir:

peleador: pelear, pelea, etc.

quemarte: quemadura, quemado, etc.

industrias: industrial, industrioso, etc.

gordo: engordar, gordura, etc.

ridículo: ridiculizar, ridiculez, etc.

mandar: mandato, mandamiento, etc.

nubes: nublado, nublar, etc.

encerrada: cerrar, cerradura, encierro, etc.

tranquila: intranquila, tranquilizar, etc.

p. 377 D. En contexto

Las respuestas variarán pero pueden incluir:

La *sombra* significa falta de luz.

Una *toalla* es una tela que se usa para secarse.

Una *ola* es una onda formada por el movimiento del agua.

Secuestraron significa sacaron a una persona contra su voluntad.

Una *patada* es un golpe que se da con el pie.

Un *delantal* es una prenda que cubre la ropa para protegerla.

Las *nubes* son masas de pequeñas gotas de agua suspendidas en el aire.

La *arena* es un conjunto de partículas diminutas de piedras que generalmente se encuentran en la playa.

Las *uñas* son lo que se encuentra en la parte superior de las extremidades de los dedos.

Tuteando significa dirigirse a una persona usando tú.

Las *carcajadas* son grandes risas.

Una *mentirosa* es una persona que no dice la verdad.

Una *nuera* es la esposa de un(a) hijo(a).

pp. 378–380 E. Al punto

1. a	2. b	3. a	4. c	5. d	6. d
7. c	8. d	9. b	10. b	11. a	12. b
13. b	14. a	15. a	16. c	17. b	18. a

p. 380 F. Ahora te toca a ti

Las respuestas variarán.

pp. 381–382 A–G. Para conversar

Las respuestas variarán.

p. 382 A. Para escribir
Un resumen

Las respuestas variarán. La lista de palabras puede incluir:

actuar	playa
caballero distinguido	ponerse
cambiar	revista de historietas fotografiadas
delantal	rico
empleada	traje de baño

p. 382 B. Los personajes principales

Las respuestas variarán. Las listas de adjetivos pueden incluir:

Para describir a la señora:
desalmada
inconsiderada
odiosa
sarcástica

Para describir a la empleada:
confundida
modesta

pp. 383–384 C–I

Las respuestas variarán.

p. 385 Otra dimensión

Las respuestas variarán.

pp. 386–388 Comprensión auditiva

Selección número 1
1. a   2. d   3. a   4. c

Selección número 2
1. b   2. c   3. a   4. c

Selección número 3
1. a   2. c   3. b

Selección número 4
1. a   2. b   3. a   4. c